Widow to Widow

The Series in Death, Dying, and Bereavement
Consulting Editor
Robert A. Neimeyer

Beder — Voices of Bereavement: A Casebook for Grief Counselors
Davies — Shadows in the Sun: The Experiences of Sibling Bereavement in Childhood
Harvey — Perspectives on Loss: A Sourcebook
Klass — The Spiritual Lives of Bereaved Parents
Leenaars — Lives and Deaths: Selections from the Works of Edwin S. Shneidman
Lester — Katie's Diary: Unlocking the Mystery of a Suicide
Martin, Doka — Men Don't Cry...Women Do: Transcending Gender Stereotypes of Grief
Nord — Multiple AIDS-Related Loss: A Handbook for Understanding and Surviving a Perpetual Fall
Roos — Chronic Sorrow: A Living Loss
Rosenblatt — Parent Grief: Narratives of Loss and Relationship
Tedeschi & Calhoun — Helping Bereaved Parents: A Clinician's Guide
Silverman — Widow to Widow, Second Edition
Werth — Contemporary Perspectives on Rational Suicide

FORMERLY THE SERIES IN DEATH EDUCATION, AGING, AND HEALTH CARE
HANNELORE WASS, CONSULTING EDITOR

Bard — Medical Ethics in Practice
Benoliel — Death Education for the Health Professional
Bertman — Facing Death: Images, Insights, and Interventions
Brammer — How to Cope with Life Transitions: The Challenge of Personal Change
Cleiren — Bereavement and Adaptation: A Comparative Study of the Aftermath of Death
Corless, Pittman-Lindeman — AIDS: Principles, Practices, and Politics, Abridged Edition
Corless, Pittman-Lindeman — AIDS: Principles, Practices, and Politics, Reference Edition
Curran — Adolescent Suicidal Behavior
Davidson — The Hospice: Development and Administration. Second Edition
Davidson, Linnolla — Risk Factors in Youth Suicide
Degner, Beaton — Life-Death Decisions in Health Care
Doka — AIDS, Fear, and Society: Challenging the Dreaded Disease
Doty — Communication and Assertion Skills for Older Persons
Epting, Neimeyer — Personal Meanings of Death: Applications for Personal Construct Theory to Clinical Practice
Haber — Health Care for an Aging Society: Cost-Conscious Community Care and Self-Care Approaches
Hughes — Bereavement and Support: Healing in a Group Environment
Irish, Lundquist, Nelsen — Ethnic Variations in Dying, Death, and Grief: Diversity in Universality
Klass, Silverman, Nickman — Continuing Bonds: New Understanding of Grief
Lair — Counseling the Terminally Ill: Sharing the Journey
Leenaars, Maltsberger, Neimeyer — Treatment of Suicidal People
Leenaars, Wenckstern — Suicide Prevention in Schools
Leng — Psychological Care in Old Age
Leviton — Horrendous Death, Health, and Well-Being
Leviton — Horrendous Death and Health: Toward Action
Lindeman, Corby, Downing, Sanborn — Alzheimer's Day Care: A Basic Guide
Lund — Older Bereaved Spouses: Research with Practical Applications
Neimeyer — Death Anxiety Handbook: Research, Instrumentation, and Application
Papadatou, Papadatos — Children and Death
Prunkl, Berry — Death Week: Exploring the Dying Process
Ricker, Myers — Retirement Counseling: A Practical Guide for Action
Samarel — Caring for Life and Death
Sherron, Lumsden — Introduction to Educational Gerontology. Third Edition
Stillion — Death and Sexes: An Examination of Differential Longevity Attitudes, Behaviors, and Coping Skills
Stillion, McDowell, May — Suicide Across the Life Span — Premature Exits
Vachon — Occupational Stress in the Care of the Critically Ill, the Dying, and the Bereaved
Wass, Corr — Childhood and Death
Wass, Corr — Helping Children Cope with Death: Guidelines and Resource. Second Edition
Wass, Corr, Pacholski, Forfar — Death Education II: An Annotated Resource Guide
Wass, Neimeyer — Dying: Facing the Facts. Third Edition
Weenolsen — Transcendence of Loss over the Life Span
Werth — Rational Suicide? Implications for Mental Health Professionals

Widow to Widow

Second Edition

How the bereaved help one another

Phyllis R. Silverman, Ph.D.

Brunner-Routledge
Taylor & Francis Group

NEW YORK AND HOVE

Published in 2004 by
Brunner-Routledge
270 Madison Avenue
New York, NY 10016
www.brunner-routledge.com

Published in Great Britain by
Brunner-Routledge
27 Church Road
Hove
East Sussex BN3 2FA
www.brunner-routledge.co.uk

Copyright © 2004 by Phyllis R. Silverman
Brunner-Routledge is an imprint of the Taylor & Francis Group.

Printed in the United States of America on acid-free paper.

Cover design: Elise Weinger
Cover image © Elise Weinger

10 9 8 7 6 5 4 3 2 1

Library of Congress Cataloging-in-Publication Data

Silverman, Phyllis R.
    Widow to widow : how the bereaved help one another / by Phyllis R.
Silverman. — 2nd ed.
        p. cm. — (Series in death, dying, and bereavement)
    Includes bibliographical references and index.
    ISBN 0-415-94749-9 (pbk. : alk. paper)
    1. Widows—United States.   2. Widows—United States—Psychology.
3. Bereavement. 4. Self-help groups—United States. I. Title. II. Series.

    HQ1058.5.U5S57 2004
    306.88—dc22

2004009011

I walked a mile with Sorrow
And ne'er a word said she;
But Oh, the things I learned from her
When sorrow walked with me.

Robert Browning Hamilton

CONTENTS

Series Editor Foreword   xi

Preface   xiii

Acknowledgments   xix

Introduction   1
    A History of the Widow-to-Widow Program   1
    Primary Prevention in a Human Service Intervention   2
        Considering an Intervention for the Widowed   2
        The Search for a Strategy   3
        Where Widowed People Looked for Help   4
        The Pivotal Idea of Transition   6
            Widows Helping Widows   7
    The Intervention at Work: The Widow-to-Widow Program   8
        Choosing a Community   9
        An Advisory Board   9
        Identifying the Newly Widowed   9
        The Widow Aides   10
        Doing the Work   11
    What We Learned   11
        Widows Who Accepted Help   13
        Need To Find Understanding   14
        Help with Concrete Problems   14
        Family Issues   14
        Widows Who Refused Help   15
        The Widowed Service Line   15
        Conclusion   16
    Implications   17

Section I   Various Dimensions of Widowhood

Chapter **1**   **Theoretical Perspectives on Grief and Helping**   **25**
Death Is Not a Respecter of Age   26
What Is Grief?   27
Making Meaning in a Developmental Context   28
Is Grief a Normal Life Event or an Illness?   31
   Grief As an Illness   31
   Grief As a Life-Cycle Event   33
   Grief in a Relational Context   34
Detachment Revisited   37
The Effect of Culture and Society on Grieving   40

Chapter **2**   **Widows and Widowers: Gender Differences**   **45**
Gender in a Societal Context   45
Differences in Coping Styles   52
Differences in Outcome   53
How Do These Factors Influence Change?   55

Chapter **3**   **Grief As a Time of Loss and Change:**
The Nature of Transition   **59**
Mourning As a Time of Transition   60
Spousal Death As a Disequilibrating Event   61
My Place in the World Is Lost   63
Redefining the Self   65
Change Over Time   67
Reality vs. Disbelief: "It Didn't Really Happen, Did It?"   67
Uncertainty: What Will Happen Next?   70
Reconstruction: Building a New Life   72

Chapter **4**   **Help in a Mutual-Help Context**   **75**
The Nature of Help   75
The Widowed As Helpers   78
Helping Networks   79
Mutual Help and the Professionalization of Services   80
The Influence of Social Support on the
   Provision and Acceptance of Help   82
Mutual Help and the Bereaved   84
What Is Mutual Help?   85
Connecting Help to the Motion of Transition   87
   Affinity: "I'm a Widow, Too"   88
   Presence: Learning From Others Like Themselves   89
   Self-Generation: Changing Self and Others   90

Section II   On Helping

Chapter **5   Could This Really Be Happening to Me?**   97
Unexpected and Anticipated Deaths   99
The Silence of the Grave Becomes Real   102
Their New Status As Widowed   103
Connecting to Other Widowed People   104
Financial Concerns   106
Confronting Family Issues   108
Beginning To Grieve   109

Chapter **6   Uncertainty: What Will Happen Next?**   113
The Pain Is Still There   114
A Place for the Deceased   117
Seeing Beyond Family and Old Friends   118
Others Like Me   120
Finding New Friends   123
I'm Not the Same Me!   125

Chapter **7   Looking to the Future: The Fruits of Help**   129
Not Everyone Is Helped   133
A Revised Definition of Widowed   134
Reorganizing Their Daily Lives   136
Life Looks Different Now   139
A New Sense of Self   140
Dating and Remarriage   143
Establishing a New Relationship with
   the Deceased: Continuing Bonds   147
Helping Others   147

Chapter **8   Parenting Alone: Widowed with Dependent Children**   151
How Do I Tell My Children?   152
Attending the Funeral or Not   154
We Are All Grieving   155
The Daily Routine Changes   156
Protecting Their Children From Their Grief   159
Understanding Their Children's Grief   161
Worries About the Children   164
What Will I Do If Something Happens to You?   167
Children Help, Too   169
Problem Children, Problem Parent   170
Connecting to Their Dead Parent   172
Conclusion   172

Chapter **9**   **The Older Widowed**   **175**
Dealing with Their Grief and Changes in Their Lives   176
Many Changes Are Involved   177
A Changing Sense of Self   178
Help From Another Widow   179
Remaining Independent   180
Role of Adult Children   181
When My Children Don't Need Me   186
When You Need More Than Family   188
Children with Problems   190

Conclusion   **193**
Mutual Help Today   195
How To Find Groups   199
Using the Internet   199
Finding Local Groups   200
Finding Professional Help   200
Starting a Program   200
Taking the Initiative   201
Consider the Following in an Outreach Program   202
Role of the Professional   203
The Professional as Leader or Facilitator   203

Appendices

Appendix 1   **Research Findings**   **205**
Appendix 2   **The Widowed As Helpers**   **229**
Appendix 3   **Resources for the Widowed**   **233**

References   **239**

Index   **251**

SERIES EDITOR FOREWORD

Persons who move unwillingly into the world of widowhood in these early years of the 21st century enter a landscape that is both timeless and transformed. On the one hand, the raw pain of loss, the visceral anguish associated with the severing of a life-bond of partnership, and the disorientation, distress, and gnawing loneliness that can result are likely as prehistoric in origin as humanity itself. On the other hand, the contemporary North American widow or widower seeks reorientation, emotional support, and companionship in a social field that is remarkably modern, with burgeoning opportunities for participation in secular or faith-based self-help groups, community centers, hospice-based bereavement services, funeral home aftercare, programs for retired persons, and innumerable chat rooms and online mutual support groups available via the Internet. As a result, the ancient problems of the bereaved, perhaps exacerbated by the gradual erosion of community in much of the industrialized world, are at least partially redressed by the creative proliferation of contexts for connection with others contending with similar loss.

And, yet, as remarkable as it seems, this social system providing sustenance for the bereaved is of quite recent origin. Indeed, its first fragile shoots were nearly invisible as recently as 30 years ago. It was in this far more barren landscape that Phyllis Silverman sowed the seeds of the mutual support program known as Widow-to-Widow, drawing on concepts in public health to construct a pioneering outreach program for grieving spouses. This book chronicles that innovation and the revolutionary social movement it ultimately spawned.

Silverman's insight that bereavement was a normal life-cycle transition with a clear beginning but an indefinite ending prompted her to recognize that the great majority of widows needed neither professional treatment nor crisis intervention. Instead, they needed ongoing assistance, both practical and emotional, in coping with the stress of adapting to a life fundamentally transformed by loss. Her carefully crafted solution — recruiting bereaved peers who could draw on a rich fund of experiential knowledge to help those in similar circumstances — broke new ground by viewing the bereaved population as its own greatest resource. In recounting the experiences of the initial "aides" selected and trained for this outreach role as well as those of the women they served, Silverman both depicts the struggles faced by all those who have known the loss of a spouse and illuminates how mutual support can companion people in that struggle. Moreover, her careful attention to changing demographic, economic, and cultural trends and her blending of the "voices" of widows and widowers both past and present give the book contemporary relevance for those professionals, organizations, and volunteers undertaking the development of support services in their own settings. Her detailed descriptions of the unique challenges faced by such groups as older and younger widows or men and women who have lost a spouse provide further guidance for the useful tailoring of these services.

To me, the most important message of the book was an abstract one, only occasionally addressed specifically but whose spirit pervaded every page. That message might be summarized as the recognition that the loss of a loved one represents a form of collective vulnerability to which all humans are subject, coupled with the implication that we share a collective responsibility to legitimate, assist, and guide one another through this troubling transition. As such, Silverman's book — and the life work it represents — provides a powerful counterpoint to the over-professionalization of bereavement services and the "commodification" of care in a world that too often treats personal distress in impersonal ways. *Widow to Widow* is a clarion call to community and an inspiration to all readers, professional and lay, who seek to foster the indigenous healing that comes with strengthening the supportive links formed by helping hands.

Robert A. Neimeyer, Ph.D.
Editor, Series in Death, Dying, and Bereavement

PREFACE: WITH A LITTLE HELP FROM A FRIEND

This book is a new edition of *Widow to Widow*, which was first published in 1985. That edition, now out of print, was a report on the original widow-to-widow program, which demonstrated the value of one who has been widowed for some time reaching out to the newly widowed. In the context of a mutual-help exchange, the widowed helpers offered support, neighbor to neighbor, in the widows' own homes. They were role models who offered hope for the future and served as a source of the information needed by the newly widowed to effectively cope with their grief and adapt to the many accompanying changes in their lives.

Today, it is common practice for the widowed, both men and women, to seek out other widowed people and to join a support group. In many ways, findings from the original widow-to-widow program were instrumental in legitimizing this approach to helping the widowed and in stimulating these services. These groups can be found in local hospice programs, faith-based communities, funeral homes, and senior centers. Sometimes the widowed meet in informal groups in members' homes. The Widowed Person's Service, a national initiative reaching out to the widowed that is sponsored by the American Association of Retired Persons (AARP), is built on the widow-to-widow model. It is testimony to the current relevance of a work that was completed more than 30 years ago that a new edition of this book now seems in order.

In a vastly changing social climate that supports evidence-based practice and professionalization of care for the bereaved, the original findings of the widow-to-widow experiment have a compelling validity. It comes down on one side of a contemporary debate about the merit of the growing role of the professional helper in serving the bereaved. The findings from the original project point to the special value of personal help from a peer in a mutual- or self-help context that reflects on and can also enhance the quality of communal life.

Coincidentally, just as I finished this manuscript, an article by Jerome Groopman appeared in *The New Yorker* (January 26, 2004) titled "The Grief Industry." This article focuses on the need to depathologize grief. This is a theme that is present throughout this new edition and which points to the importance of family, partners, companions, friends, and community in helping the bereaved. Groopman questioned whether evidence exists to justify the notion that the bereaved invariably need the care of mental-health professionals. He writes of the clear value of peer counselors who have provided support, information, and basic comforts to those workers dealing with the aftermath of 9/11. As non-mental-health professionals, peer counselors did not know the language of pathology, but the help they offered enhanced the mourners' natural resiliency, helping to return control to them. The 9/11 bereaved found this effort to be more helpful than other types of help offered. Groopman quotes Steven Hyman, now provost of Harvard University and former director of the National Institutes of Mental Health, who reminded the reader of the power of their social networks in helping people create a sense of meaning and safety in their lives.

This was and remains the message of the widow-to-widow program. This message leads us to appreciate that we all need to be experts. While, fortunately, not all of us will experience a major disaster such as the destruction on 9/11, all of us will become bereaved over the normal course of living. Our expertise lies in our appreciation of what we can do for ourselves and for each other.

That I was invited to do a new edition of this book can be seen as a reflection of the times about what should be an appropriate response to grief. I join in the debate with this book on the side that recognizes the importance of social support from peers. Perhaps these issues should not be posed as a competition. It is important to recognize that everyone needs support, or what I refer to as "a little help from a friend." This book is about the role of a particular friend, one who has been down the same road before. We live in a fast-moving, ever more impersonal world. We have a continuing need for others in our lives, and both the original volume and the new edition are focused on how we can foster this special mutuality. We need professional knowledge but we need to learn how to use it in a collaborative partnership with the bereaved so control remains in their hands.

This new edition integrates what we learned from the original program with what has been learned over the years about bereavement to make whatever wisdom has been generated available to a new audience with the hope that the widowed can find the support they need when they need it. In the earlier edition, I described the history of the original program and provided some theoretical understanding of grief from what I had learned over the years from working with the widowed and other research I had done. The main text of the book consisted of stories told in the widows' own words that described how help was offered in response to to their changing needs. I have continued to use the words of the widowed themselves to illustrate my thinking throughout this new edition. I have expanded the section discussing matching the help offered with the changing needs of widowed people and have incorporated new data gathered specifically for this edition. In particular, the new edition looks at how the experiences of the widowed have changed in many ways yet still remain much the same, thus underscoring the many ways in which the experiences of the widows who participated in the original widow-to-widow project are still relevant. When updating the book, I drew on research I have done since the original edition was published that supports the findings of the original widow-to-widow program. This research has expanded my understanding of how gender, the social context, and personal cognitive and emotional developmental qualities affect how the widowed cope with the death of a spouse and find new meaning in their lives and new directions. I also have drawn on the increased understanding of the bereavement process that is now available. I include widowers in this book. I also include men and women involved in long-term committed relationships who were not married to each other but who view themselves as widowed upon the loss of their partners. I also consider same-sex couples in similar commitments who experience themselves as widowed when their partners died. Almost all of my own recent research, in preparation for this book, has been with widowed people who have been involved in widow-to-widow experiences, mutual-help organizations, or support groups. Many of these people agreed to talk with me individually so that I could learn more about their experience. Some were helpers and some were recipients. All of these people are my teachers, and it is their words that give this book meaning.

☐ What I Have Learned

The original program taught me a great deal, and this seems to be an appropriate place to pull some of it together. Perhaps the most important thing I learned is that I have to accept death as part of life. When I was first approached to do this work, I was very reluctant to accept. I closed my eyes when I passed a cemetery and could not really talk about the place of death in my life. I have now found a place for it in my life and the lives of my family. I accept my vulnerability. I have learned to grieve the death of my parents, the death of friends, and the death of a small grandchild. I have learned to never say "I understand" to a widowed person because at the end of the day I go home to my husband. I have learned that if we have not walked in their shoes we cannot understand. We can empathize and we can listen, but doing so is very different from actually experiencing the death of a spouse and finding a way to live in this world without that person. Helena Lopata, whose recent death has saddened us all and whose research with the widowed covered more than three decades, wrote about her husband's death in 1993. She wrote that only then did she realize how little she had understood about what the widowed were experiencing (Lopata, 1996a).

I have learned that in doing this work the boundaries between the personal and the professional are often blurred. I have learned that in close proximity to the bereaved our common humanity is what binds us. I have been inspired by people's resiliency and their creativity in meeting adversity and prevailing. I have learned that being widowed is an experience unto itself, with its own pain and momentum. I have learned that widowhood is a life-altering event that will be experienced by nearly every married person at some stage in our lives. Our understanding of grief needs to be expanded to include more than a view of the emotional pain associated with a death. Our view of grief has to reflect changes in the feelings, behavior, needs of the bereaved, and the very way they live their lives. I have learned that grief is not an illness or a condition from which people recover. It is an expected life-cycle transition that is a natural part of the life cycle. I learned that widowed people negotiate the meaning of their loss over their lifetime; they do not forget. They do find ways to make a different sort of connection to the deceased as one of the many important relationships in their lives. I have learned that the people I most want to help are my best teachers, and only by working together can we make a difference.

The book is divided into two sections. The first section is preceded by an introduction to provide the reader with a history of the original project. The first section then focuses on the various dimensions of widowhood and provides an overview of the grieving process as we see it today, an analysis of the role of gender in how the widowed approach their loss, a discussion on grief as a time of transition, and finally a description of what I mean by mutual help and what is involved in helping the widowed in this context. The second section focuses on what is involved in helping. The first three chapters focus on the stories of the widowed and matching the helping process to their changing needs over time. The following two chapters address the special needs of families with dependent children and the experiences of older widows and widowers. In the concluding chapter, I describe how to develop an intervention for the widowed with a focus on resources available today. The appendices present some of the data on who accepted and who refused the offer of help in the original widow-to widow project, several brief examples of the help offered in the words of the widowed helpers, and a directory of resources.

ACKNOWLEDGMENTS

In writing acknowledgments for this second edition, it seems important to include the acknowledgments from the first edition. It was these people who made it possible for me to write this book in the first place and who in many ways are part of the legacy of this work. Let me begin with what I said then:

"There are many people I want to thank for their help in making this book possible. Gerald Caplan is foremost in my mind for his excellence as a teacher who introduced me to the concepts of prevention in mental health when I was his student at the Harvard School of Public Health and for his willingness to support me in trying new ideas when I came to work for him at the Laboratory of Community Psychiatry in the Department of Psychiatry at Harvard Medical School. In addition, without the cooperation and financial support of the National Funeral Directors Association (NFDA) and the Massachusetts Funeral Directors Association (MFDA), the Widow-to-Widow program would have remained only an idea. Howard Raether, then Executive Director of the NFDA, and Sheldon Daly, then Executive Director of the MFDA, were instrumental in recruiting the cooperation of their organizations.

"The demonstration project would never have moved from the planning table to implementation without the wonderful women who came to work with me. Adele Cooperband, the late Dorothy McKenzie, Mary Pettipas, Elizabeth Wilson, and Cary Wynn were the aides who reached out to the newly widowed. The success of the program was a result of their willingness to share the pain of their own widowhood, as well as their mistakes and successes, with the women they served. Ruby Abrahams and Cecile Strugnell, my research associates, documented what we did. I am also grateful to Ruth Abrams and Faye Snyder, who managed the project when Gila and then Aaron were born."

I know that, since 1986, Howard Raether, Sheldon Daly, Adele Cooperband, and Ruth Abrams have died. May their memories be blessed by the work they have done and its continued value.

I want to thank Susan Eckrich, Director of the Widowed Person's Service and Grief and Loss Program of the American Association of Retired Persons (AARP). In the late 1990s, she thought that it was time for a new edition of the book. Robert Neimeyer, acquisitions editor for the bereavement series published by the Taylor & Francis Group, read the book and agreed with her. He encouraged me to submit a proposal, and we now see the result. I am most appreciative for the support and encouragement I received from the editorial staff at Brunner-Routledge. The AARP staff was very helpful to me when I needed information and updates on its programs.

Leah Sherman, Nancy Sherman, and Francine Fuller, who facilitate support groups in the Boston area, introduced me to widowed men and women who had been in their groups and who agreed to share their stories with me. I hope I have correctly represented what they taught me and have captured the spirit of their experience. I said I would respect their privacy. They know who they are, and I say "thank you" to them all.

I cannot list over the years all the colleagues as well as the widowed people whom I have met and who have been helpful to me as my ideas developed out of the original work. In many ways, they are referenced throughout the text. I am most grateful to them for their ideas, their reflections on their experiences, and the exchanges that took place between us. In particular, I want to thank the families who participated in the Harvard/MGH Child Bereavement Research project. They shared their stories willingly and provided invaluable insights into what it means for a child or adolescent when a parent dies.

This is a book about the value of social support from peers. We all need this kind of help at various times in our lives, and I certainly did as I began writing this new edition. I was supported by family, friends, and colleagues. I do want to thank Joan Berzoff, who, when I faltered in starting this book, reminded me of the value of mutual help and that this should be the focus of the book. She was right. I also worked closely with Carol Galigainitis, who edited a good part of the book as I wrote. She was more than an editor. She willingly shared her own experience as a young widow. She was a friend and an active provider of moral support, helping me to clarify what I wanted to say and where my ideas would lead. Her questions came not only from her own lived experience but also from her academic training. We both learned from this collaboration.

I must thank Iris Saltsburg, a dear friend and colleague, for reading a draft of the book to be sure that it was not lost in jargon and that it came together in a meaningful whole.

I have been a Scholar-in-Residence at the Brandeis University Women's Studies Research Center (WSRC) for the last few years. I am part of an unusual feminist community that has played various roles in my life as I worked on this book. In particular, members were very helpful in clarifying how the roles of women and the roles of wives have changed over the past 35 years. Thank you for your support, your concern, and your feedback about my thinking and my writing. Ashley Shaw, who graduated this year from Brandeis, worked with me for a year and a half as part of the Scholar-Student Program of the WSRC. She was challenged by the subject of my research and worked long hours in the library searching the literature and helping with the bibliography. Her facility with the Internet boggled my mind. I wish her well as she leaves the university and many thanks for the pleasure of our partnership.

In 1986, I thanked my family. Without them, I said at the time, I would have been finished in a quarter of the time, but the book would not have been as rich. Ann, Bill, Nancy, Gila, and Aaron grew up with this project, learning that there is life and there is death — thank you. Now that they have grown and I have grandchildren, I thank them for that gift as well and for their patience and interest in what I am doing. To my husband, Sam, my partner and my friend, thank you for all the discussions then and now and for all the evenings when I had no energy to cook and you took me out to eat. The role of mother and wife takes on new meaning when the children are grown. He was always there to be supportive and offer encouragement. Together, we have retired but stopping does not seem to be our style. In a book about widowhood, I have to acknowledge that I am very grateful that we still have each other and I have learned to appreciate every minute of it, even when I get impatient and disgruntled with whatever!

Introduction

☐ A History of the Widow-to-Widow Program

What does it mean to be widowed? This was a question put to me in 1965 when I was looking for interesting employment to support myself while I completed my work for my doctorate degree. I was talking with Dr. Gerald Caplan, director of the Laboratory of Community Psychiatry (LOCP) at Harvard Medical School and my instructor at the School of Public Health. His current research at the LOCP was focused on the widowed, but I had no idea how to answer any questions about widowhood. I knew, of course, that it was associated with death, but death was not something I could easily deal with. I closed my eyes when I went by cemeteries, and I was not prepared to make a connection to any related issues. Caplan was asking me to explore what services might be most helpful and relevant to people whose spouses had died. The question of what makes help pertinent to people in need was the subject of my doctoral dissertation. I was being offered work that sounded very germane to my interests and would give me the administrative support I needed to complete my dissertation. In the time before computers, this was no small matter. I could not refuse.

The research for my dissertation focused on a population of African-Americans who had dropped out of counseling and therapy. While their therapists thought that this help was necessary for their clients' well-being, these clients nonetheless did not return. My research tried to answer the question of what made this offer of help irrelevant to these clients, many of whom had made the effort to come to the agency for several meetings and then chose not to continue? What I learned from this study was that therapists come to their work with their own ideas about what is helpful and their own understanding of the critical problems people face. Little or no agreement existed between the views of therapist and their clients with regard to the nature of the problem and what to do about it. At the time, the therapists seemed unaware of this discrepancy and made no effort to develop a consensus.

1

This offer of work would provide me with an opportunity to initiate a program, and, if I allowed myself to deal with my death-avoidance behavior and learn more about widowhood, then I might be able to take a more in-depth look at what makes an offer of help relevant and timely. This is exactly what happened.

☐ Primary Prevention in a Human Service Intervention

Considering an Intervention for the Widowed

In Caplan's discussions with me, he expressed his interest in developing an intervention program for the widowed, but he was not sure what kind of help might be needed. It was also not clear what sort of program could be appropriately sponsored by the LOCP, a research and educational institution and part of a large research university. The research at the LOCP was driven by an interest in the preventive aspects of public health and how to apply this approach to mental-health issues. The work there was concerned with a number of life-cycle crises. A goal of any of the existing intervention projects sponsored by the LOCP was determining how to prevent the development of emotional problems resulting from ineffectual coping with a particular crisis. Projects focused on the birth of a premature infant and the death of a spouse (Glick *et al.*, 1974). Psychiatric wisdom at the time suggested that the death of a spouse placed the newly widowed person at risk of developing serious emotional difficulties (Parkes, 1965: Maddison & Viola, 1968; Marris, 1958). At that time, no simple measures of risk for the widowed were available, and even today little consensus has been reached with regard to what qualities in an individual make them more likely to develop emotional difficulties when they become widowed (Parkes, 1996; Stroebe & Schut, 2001b; Relf, 2003).

It is common public health practice to immunize whole populations in order to prevent any one segment of that population from becoming ill. The recent discussion on immunizing the American people against smallpox in light of the threat of terrorist attacks offers one example. The gatekeeper and provider of services, in such instances, is the healthcare system. Trying to follow a similar public health approach with the widowed, however, presented many problems. One problem was how to identify widowed people who were potentially at high risk for developing problematic behavior. Without a definitive measure of risk, we would have to reach everyone in this target population. Another problem was how to systematically identify the widowed in any given community.

Once we identified them, how would we involve them in a program? How would we know which needs of the widowed might lead to subsequent problems if they remained unmet? What would inoculation against the pain of spousal loss look like? Who would deliver the service? Should it be a new program or a modification of an existing service? How could we ensure that our program would be acceptable to the newly widowed and likely to be used by them. At the time, I did not consider an approach involving widows reaching out to other widows.

The Search for a Strategy

I began exploring the services offered by social agencies and mental-health centers with which I was familiar. As I talked with directors and selected staff, I discovered that widowed people were making little use of their services. Most practitioners I spoke with believed that the traditional counseling services they offered were a sufficient response to the needs of the individual and that the agency availability was sufficient to meet the needs of the larger population — in this instance, the widowed. They did not understand or appreciate a public health approach that focused on a total population and tried to reach everyone in that population. According to these professionals, the bereaved could not recover until they faced their anger and guilt, as well as other emotions the professional staff associated with grief. Such was the service they could offer.

Several agencies let me review client records, but very few widowed people were served by these agencies (I determined marital status from the face sheet). Often when the widowed did request help, it was not until around two years after the death. Neither the client nor the agency identified grief as the presenting problem. When children were the focus of a request for help, the parent might casually mention their spouse's death, but not necessarily connect it to the presenting problem. The intake and subsequent treatment plan rarely identified the death as being central to the problem.

As I read the agency records of treatment sessions, I sensed that many therapists were not able to deal with the widow's intense pain but were not aware of this failure; for example, when the topic of death was raised the therapists tended to change the subject. When I asked one social worker about this, she said that when she talked to a widow she thought of her own husband and how she might feel if something happened to him. She found these feelings were too overwhelming to face. Today, when it is theoretically more acceptable to seek grief counseling and therapists think of themselves as being better prepared, widowed people still describe encounters with therapists who do not understand or tolerate the experiences and pain associated with the death of a spouse. They feel that these therapists seem to be in a hurry to fix the things that the widowed have begun to understand can never be fixed.

In their study of Americans' views on mental health, Gurin and colleagues (1960) confirmed what I was learning with regard to the limited utilization of psychological therapies by this population. They found that most people went to friends, family, clergy, and physicians for help with what they characterized as their problems in living. Most of this study's respondents believed that the use of psychiatric services implied something was wrong and stigmatized those who used this help. When the bereaved failed to turn to mental-health professionals to help them manage the intense pain associated with death, it was because they felt their situations were not appropriate for clinical intervention of this sort. They did not see what could be gained.

As I gathered more information, I came to appreciate that death is not a respecter of age and that the widowed are not necessarily older people. Today, the percentage of women widowed has declined, but the rate at which women are widowed continues to be double that of men (AARP, 2003). Of all married women, 75% will be widowed at least once in their lifetimes. The median age at which a woman is widowed is 52, and every year one million women become widowed. A widowed woman is likely to live about 15 years after the death of her spouse. Men are more likely to remarry, and their earlier status as a widower is not reflected in the census data. Widowhood is the only change in status related to death that is reported in the U.S. census, and the most recent U.S. census reported 11 million widows and 2.5 million widowers in the United States. The number of widowers is low because many of them remarry.

Where Widowed People Looked for Help

Using obituary notices, I made a short list of the widowed population from a Boston neighborhood. I called them and explained that I was conducting a survey of where people might go for help if there was a death in the family. None of them mentioned the death that had recently occurred. I did learn, however, that they felt that help from friends and family would be most appropriate at such a time. They felt that psychiatric treatment was for people with psychological problems, not for those dealing with a death in the family. They did mention clergy, funeral directors, and physicians as additional resources (Silverman, 1966).

So, where *did* the bereaved go for help? In a community-wide survey, Maddison and Walker (1967) found that widowed people who turned to clergy and physicians for help were usually disappointed. The clergy's message of "It was God's will" was of little consolation to the newly bereaved. A physician's typical statement, "Time will heal," and the prescription of tranquilizers might have eased the pain in the short run but did not help over time. Those surveyed found the funeral directors to be the most helpful because they knew what to do when the death occurred. Most relevant to my work was the finding that other widowed people were the most helpful, largely because they understood what the widowed were feeling, and when they said they understood it was true. This finding was a key factor leading to the development of the original widow-to-widow program.

In time I learned that, in addition to funeral directors, clergy, family, and friends, other caregivers that widows encountered shortly after the death were Social Security employees, lawyers, and their husbands' employers. Social Security employees were only interested in the widow filling out forms to determine her benefits. If she had no dependent children at home and was not yet 62 years of age, she was not eligible for any benefits. She often needed to deal with a lawyer to probate the will and she had to negotiate with her husband's employer for back pay or death benefits. If her husband had been a veteran, she might have some additional income due her. If she had no other sources of income, she could apply, in the interim, for emergency general relief from public welfare and quickly start looking for work, sometimes for the first time in her married life. Women who are widowed today often face similar financial pressures. With the 1996 changes in the Welfare system, no emergency services are supported by funds from the federal government. Local resources vary from state to state, and in some places the widow must turn to voluntary agencies for emergency funds.

Following on Maddison and Walker's findings I began looking for places where I might find examples of the widow as helper. I found a program directed by a widow employed by Sharon Memorial Park, a local cemetery in Sharon, Massachusetts. This widow brought other widows together for an annual educational and social evening. A suburban Boston Elks Club also hosted a social club for the widowed. Parents Without Partners had several chapters in the Boston area, although most of their member were divorced.

I found other initiatives elsewhere in the United States. Two large organizations run by voluntary members were sponsored by the Catholic Archdiocese: the Post Cana Conference in Washington, D.C., and the Naim Conference in Chicago, Illinois. Each group reached out through personal contacts, church registries and bulletins, or local newspapers. For a time, the Naim Conference used its parish registry to match, by age and circumstances of death, the newly widowed with experienced members. The visit took place about a month after the death (sooner, if necessary).

These programs each had either a professional advisory board or an advisor assigned by the sponsoring church group. Invariably, however, the widowed themselves took the initiative in designing the program, making program decisions, and doing the helping. The professionals gave them moral support and legitimized the organization in the community; however, these professionals realized the limitations of their knowledge about widowhood and recognized the widowed as the experts from whom they could learn. Members of these groups had a compelling ability to help each other, as confirmed by those in the organizations with whom I spoke.

At about the same time, a physician's wife in England organized the Cruse Club for a group of widows who were her husband's patients. The club's newsletter featured widows sharing their personal stories. These widows also commented on how they benefited from the opportunity to meet others whose husbands had died. What I was hearing from these various sources was that other widows understood their pain, refrained from telling them to have a stiff upper lip, and provided role models for how to cope. They came away with hope for the future and with solid ideas about how to get there.

Was organizing a club for the widowed under my direction a potential model for an intervention with the widowed? If used without modification, however, this approach would not achieve the goal of reducing risk in the larger population of widows and widowers. We would only attract those who were interested in joining a social group.

The Pivotal Idea of Transition

When I began my work with the widowed, mutual help (or self-help) was primarily associated with such organizations as Alcoholics Anonymous and programs that parents had established for their mentally handicapped children. Recovering alcoholics helped other alcoholics, and parents helped other parents. While it was probably common practice throughout the ages for the bereaved to help each other, formal mutual-help programs for the bereaved, as we have come to know them, were rare. I visited the mutual-help organizations noted earlier and became acquainted with men and women who had been widowed for a period of two or three months to several years, sometimes longer. From them I learned how their responses to the death and their needs, both psychological and social, changed over time. These organizations were meeting these different needs in different ways over time.

At this time, researchers and clinicians talked about the crisis in the survivor's life that resulted from spousal death. I found the term *crisis* to be too time-limited a concept (Silverman, 1966; Caplan, 1974b). The widowed described their situation as ongoing and essentially irreversible. At about this time, I read articles by Tyhurst (1958) and Bowlby (1961) and found that their concepts of transition helped me understand what I was learning (Silverman, 1966). People in transition may experience a crisis in their lives that in many ways over time can be experienced as multiple crises and that they deal with these crises differently as time passes. In so doing, they move through various stages or phases that characterize their feelings and experience at the time. As a result, I hypothesized that a critical aspect of help would be to facilitate movement through the phases of this transition. From this perspective, change is inevitable and the focus of help shifts over time. I began to realize that, after the death of a spouse, the widowed survivor could not reconstitute his or her life as it was before, as the crisis model suggested.

As I came to recognize that different needs and tasks become relevant at various stages in the widow's transition, the real service gaps became clearer to me (Silverman, 1966). For example, soon after she is widowed, the surviving spouse receives a good deal of help from family and friends. Over time, as her needs change, the widow needs to have someone hear her pain and legitimize her feelings; however, family and friends have often returned to their own lives, expecting that she will have recovered from the death and be able to manage. The widow may also need help — with finances, with being a single parent, with going to work, with learning to live alone, or with managing her extreme and profound feelings. In effect, she is dealing with change and has to learn to reorder her entire life within this changed context.

I hypothesized that the widowed would appreciate extra help three to six months after the death, when their friends and family have returned to their own lives. By then, the widowed have begun to recognize the full implications of their widowhood. Only then do they realize the need to learn new skills, not only to deal with their feelings but also with the many changes in their lives resulting from the death. I concluded that widows would need a service specifically designed for them that would bring together a variety of services that changed as their needs changed and that helped them learn how to be a widow. We learn what is required to sustain a sound marriage and to be a good parent, and in the same way we need to learn how to be widowed.

Widows Helping Widows

I looked for a way to implement this finding with regard to the value of widowed persons acting as helpers. I found a model in the New Careers for the Poor program, which was very active in Washington. D.C. and New York City (Pearl & Riessman, 1965). They hired lay people to reach out to economically and socially deprived people who did not utilize available human services that the agencies thought might be helpful to them. These helpers were empathetic and interested in helping others. They lived in the same neighborhoods and had backgrounds similar to those to whom they were reaching out and therefore were welcome into residents' homes. In effect, they became a bridge between their "clients" and the community agencies and often offered direct help themselves.

When the program for the widowed was being developed, instead of choosing people because of race or economic status I wondered whether we could use marital status as our criterion for recruiting helpers. If the outreach came from a widowed person who lived in or near the target community, who had accommodated to her own loss, and who wanted to help others, would she be welcome? These people would come as friends, neighbors, and fellow sufferers so there would be no stigma or question of psychiatric deficits (Silverman, 1967, 1969a; Silverman et al., 1974). Equally important, following this model made it seem possible to reach out to every newly widowed person in a target community.

In the proposed program, women who had been widowed for about 2 years and had a base of experience to draw on would contact those whose spouses had recently died. This offer would come at a time when the widow might be most stressed and too disorganized to look for appropriate help. My colleagues in the New Careers for the Poor program suggested that these helpers should not work alone; however, if I was their supervisor, I would become their model for helping and this would be counter to our objectives and program design. These helpers needed peer support to help them develop their own expertise out of their own experience. Thus, our helpers would be other widows who were willing to use their experience to help others, who lived in or near the target community, and who would support each other in their work. My role evolved over time to that of consultant (Silverman et al., 1974; Silverman, 1978, 1982a).

☐ The Intervention at Work: The Widow-to-Widow Program

The concern of the LOCP was primarily with demonstrating the feasibility of this kind of intervention as it was now conceptualized. I was responsible for developing and implementing the idea and for the day-to-day working of the project, as well as documenting how it worked in reality, what activities were central to its achieving our goal, and the results.

Choosing a Community

My colleagues and I chose a working-class community of 250,000 people that, unlike other parts of the city of Boston, had recognized geographic boundaries and a heterogeneous racial and religious population. I was familiar with the community because I had worked there on another community project. The annual death rate in the state was 2 per 1000 per year. We expected a similar rate in this community. This would provide a sufficiently large population of bereaved (we estimated that approximately 250 people of all ages were widowed each year) to test and evaluate the feasibility of this new model of intervention in which we would reach every new widow with an unsolicited offer of help.

An Advisory Board

A community advisory board of local clergy was recruited to provide a link between the LOCP and the community. They helped to set policy, legitimize the service in the community, decide on the target population, and enlist widowed helpers by word of mouth. While initially the project aimed to reach both widows and widowers, I found it was practically impossible to recruit widowers as helpers. They were all employed and were not available to work in the daytime to handle many of the administrative aspects of the project. Because the advisory committee believed that widows reaching out to widowers would be misunderstood in this community, they advised that, until men could be found to help, the project should serve only widows. They also recommended that because the community already had a range of services for the elderly, only women whose husbands were less than 65 years of age when they died would be included in this first effort. I agreed that the aide, as she was eventually called, would be available to the newly widowed person for at least one year after the death, to visit her or talk with her on the phone as needed. Ultimately the board recruited five women who lived in or near the target community and who had roots in that community.

Identifying the Newly Widowed

The Bureau of Vital Statistics provided the project with death certificates for all men from the community who had died before age 65. Because religion is not indicated on the death certificate and both Protestant and Catholic women were served by the same funeral homes, I reached out to ask the funeral directors serving this community to help identify the religious affiliation of the deceased. The aide's first contact with the new widow was a letter written on informal note paper that listed the names of the program's community advisors. In the note, the aide explained that she was a widow and offered to visit, suggesting a time. The note provided the new widow with the aide's home telephone number so she could confirm or cancel the aide's proposed visit. The program paid for an extra telephone in the aide's home so that these calls would not interfere with her family's life.

The Widow Aides

Adele Cooperband, Dorothy MacKenzie, Mary Pettipas, Elizabeth Wilson, and Carrie Wynn served as aides for the life of the project. Each had been widowed for from two to five years. Because the project would require a sustained effort in order to determine the feasibility of the idea, the aides were paid a small salary that did not jeopardize their Social Security benefits. This salary was paid for by a grant from the National Funeral Directors Association. Four of the women had dependent children, and Adele Cooperband's children were grown. Carrie Wynn was African-American, and the others were Caucasian (Silverman, 1967, 1969b; Silverman *et al.*, 1974). Because it was important that the new widow be able to identify with the aide and be comfortable inviting her into her home, each aide reached out to people of similar background and religion. Ruby Abrahams (1972, 1976) was part of the research staff of the project (see Appendix 1) and wrote about the different helping styles the various aides developed, focusing on the degree of sharing of their own lives and the amount of reciprocity involved. (Abraham's research also included volunteers from the Widowed Service Line, described later in this chapter and in Appendix 1.) Some aides were more comfortable expanding their friendship network, while others felt they needed to limit the number of people they could involve in their lives; however, these aides for the most part, developed a balance. All of them clearly stated that they, too, were widowed and easily shared their experiences as widows with the new widows. They had the ability to listen and to share their own experiences as the situation required. They were forthright in answering the widows' questions, which were often quite direct with regard to how they managed.

These five women very quickly introduced me to the realities of widowhood. Although I was questioning the concept of crisis and was considering instead the concept of a transition, I still referred to a resolution of grief within 6 weeks (Lindemann, 1944), and as part of an orientation for the aides I prepared several talks on what we knew about grief at that time. The aides were amused by the naiveté of my presentations. They were quick to correct my misconceptions, saying that it takes at least two years to "get your head screwed on so that you can look to the future" (Silverman *et al.*, 1974). They were not comfortable with the concept of recovery, although they could not always say why. They talked about their experiences shortly after they were widowed, when they wondered what was wrong with them because they did not feel better within the socially acceptable length of time permitted for mourning. They also said that they could not reconstitute their lives as before. While people kept telling them they should be back to normal, it just was not happening. After listening to these women I decided that my job was to let them teach me. Rather than fitting the data into an existing theory, I hoped a theory would emerge from the experience of the aides and the newly widowed women they were trying to help.

Doing the Work

The original widow-to-widow outreach program was active for two and a half years (Silverman, 1970, 1972) until our funding ended. Two other demonstration programs followed, one of which was an effort to reach an elderly population. The Jewish community agency serving this community employed Adele Cooperband to reach out to Jewish women in this community whose husbands died at age 50 or older (Silverman & Cooperband, 1975). At the same time, following a model for service that was getting a good deal of attention at the time, we developed a telephone hotline for the widowed that was staffed by two of the aides and involved as volunteers several of the widows served by the widow-to-widow program. It was known as the Widowed Service Line and could be supported by our very limited remaining budget.

☐ What We Learned

Much of what we learned from this work is told in the stories that are threaded throughout the following pages in this book. The statistical and empirical findings from all three initiatives are presented in a more formal manner in Appendix 1, as well as a brief description of the research methods used to analyze the qualitative data collected. The discussion here covers the findings that seem particularly relevant for current practices that replicate the original program model and try to address the needs of the widowed.

We reached 430 widows during the life of the original widow-to-widow project; of these, 65% responded positively to the offer of assistance. Before some widows accepted the offer of help, the aide had to reach out more than once. It is important to keep in mind that this was a new idea and that people were unaccustomed to unsolicited offers of help and were not sure they could trust this person offering to help. The neighborhood was changing and was not always safe. The widows came from diverse backgrounds with a variety of life experiences. Some had serious and long-standing financial, physical, or emotional problems; were accustomed to asking for help; and had established relationships with social agencies, public welfare, or psychiatric clinics. Most, however, had never before had any contact with an agency or received assistance from anyone outside the family. Thus, this population provided an unusually broad picture of widowhood. We knew about every widow in the community. We were able to demonstrate the value of a "little help from a friend" and the kinds of assistance and support that widows need during this time.

The results show that our idea worked in practice. No standardized measures were available to tell us if the widowed were better off for our being in their lives. For those who became involved, their personal testimony told us that we had made a difference. We identified those women who had major mental illnesses and as far as we knew the only episodes of major emotional illness in this population during the time of the project occurred in those women who had prior problems of this sort. In reflecting on their experiences, the widows who became involved were grateful for the offer of help even though they may have had other sources of assistance and meaningful connections. Typically, many of these widows reflected both their family's wishes and their own values in wanting to appear independent and competent to manage on their own. Because they did not initiate a request for help, the majority who accepted did not feel they were compromising their wish to be independent in accepting this unsolicited offer of help. It seemed to give them permission to accept their pain and their need for other kinds of support. It was clear to them that they did not have to prove, to either the aide or themselves, that they could manage without help. In fact, the aides did not talk about the need to talk to someone but rather about the benefits of talking to another widow who had walked the same path.

Most women maintained active relationships with children and other nearby family and friends as well. Over time, though, the nearby (and generally once-helpful) relatives often grew unsympathetic and impatient. They wanted the widow to be done with her mourning and return to her former state of functioning. They did not understand the range of her needs and that she could not return to the way she was before the death. Consequently, widows welcomed the program's open-ended offer of help so they could become involved when they were ready to do so.

Widows Who Accepted Help

The aide was available in a flexible, informal manner over the first year of each new widow's bereavement. This allowed the widow to consider her changing needs and to decide if and when she wanted the aide's help. Those who were most likely to accept were women whose husbands had been ill for an extended period of time. Women who did not work were very receptive, as were those with dependent children at home. These single parents seemed to experience a greater urgency in their situation than did other widows. The widows who were approached became involved in the program at various times and in different ways. Many responded readily to the aide's initial offer to visit. Some would only talk to the aide on the phone, and some waited for six or eight months before accepting an invitation to a social gathering sponsored by the program. This informal gathering provided the widow with an opportunity to meet the aide in person as well as to meet other widows involved in the program. Some women initially said that they had no need for help and then called back a year later. They remembered this resource as they became aware of their changing needs.

Seventy-five percent of the older widows in the Jewish group accepted the offer of help. By this time, the original widow-to widow program was becoming known in the community. Many of these widows anticipated an offer of assistance. Similar to their younger counterparts, older widows who worked were less likely to accept the offer of help. Two-thirds of these women lived alone. Family consisted of children and siblings with whom the widow had regular contact. One widow whose sister had received help earlier in the program was in turn offered assistance by this sibling as she had been helped.

It is interesting that women who moved in with their children responded eagerly to the aides' offers. These widows felt isolated and lonely in their new neighborhoods where their only connection to the community was through their children. A widow's loneliness was exacerbated if she did not drive a car. Studies since have demonstrated that women who reject the grandmother role and who remain actively involved with peers have a better adjustment than those who do not (Arling, 1976). Several women had no family in the area. One woman, for example, had a nephew in a distant city, and she saw the aide's arrival as "a piece of heaven dropping into my living room."

Need To Find Understanding

Almost all participants accepted help because they needed to talk with someone who would understand their feelings. Although they did not always want to talk directly about these feelings, they were grateful that the aides acknowledged them and that they were typical of the experience of the newly widowed. All of these women complained of loneliness and their need for companionship. They also wanted information about how others had managed. Many women simply needed reassurance that they could weather the current crisis successfully.

Help with Concrete Problems

In this working-class community, many women had difficulty covering living expenses. Some framed this by asking for advice about or support for getting a job or going back to school. Others wanted specific advice about managing what money they had, and many needed help with benefits claims. Some widows considered moving to a safer neighborhood. This particular area was in transition and was becoming dangerous. One widow's husband was murdered in the hall of their apartment building, making the danger even more real. Others felt that their housing was inadequate, and some wanted to move to be nearer to relatives. Older women who could not drive needed transportation to get medical care; some of the younger women had to learn to drive.

Family Issues

Some women specifically mentioned difficulties with relatives or family who did not understand their current situation. Those with dependent children mentioned that they were having problems with them. Some children acted up and had problems at school; their widowed parents did not understand that their behavior could be related to their children's grief. Some women still had adult children living at home or offered shelter to sons and daughters after a marriage failed or because of other problems. For some widows this was a blessing, while for others it created additional tensions. As the aides got to know these women, they found four who had histories of alcoholism and four others with histories of schizophrenia or severe depressive illness. My job was to help the aides recognize the problem, to limit their involvement accordingly, and where possible to make appropriate referrals to community agencies, if none was already involved. In all of these situations, their husbands had been the buffer that enabled these women to function in the community.

Widows Who Refused Help

The widows who refused help could be divided into two distinct groups. Some never became involved in any way during the active period of the project, while a second group, much smaller initially, responded favorably on the telephone but subsequently refused any other contact. A year after the project ended, a research associate called these women, many of whom agreed to be interviewed. This gave us a rare opportunity to gain insight into people who usually are absent from research findings. These findings are elaborated in Appendix 1. In all, 35 women who had initially refused the offer of assistance agreed to be interviewed. These women reported that they refused because (in descending order of frequency): (1) they were too busy with work, family, or putting their husbands' affairs in order; (2) they received plenty of support from family and friends; (3) their grown children refused to allow the aides to talk with their mothers (some of these widows in the interview felt that they should have stood up to their children); and (4) they were independent and did not need support. We concluded that some widows had adequate coping styles and sufficient help so that they did not need further assistance. Often these widows were not the first to be widowed in their family or among their friends, and they benefited from the experience of others in their network.

The Widowed Service Line

During its first seven months of operation, 750 people called the Widowed Service Line. The calls fell into three main categories: the widowed who wanted to find someone to listen to their stories, the widowed who wanted to meet people, and the widowed who wanted to obtain specific practical information. Most callers complained of their loneliness and the need to meet people. Many were happy to simply find someone to listen. More than half of those who called the Widowed Service Line had heard about it from television, and one-fifth read about it in their newspapers. Some church bulletins printed announcements about the line, and a few people learned about it from a friend. As the line became better known, mental-health professionals and clergy referred widowed people when they felt unable to help. As with those who accepted help from the widow-to-widow program, the people most likely to call the service line were those living alone and those with children under the age of 16. Regardless of age, the callers living alone or with dependent children at home seemed to experience the most immediate pressures after their loss. Although most of the people who called were not working, those most likely to call for help in making new friends were employed. While a job might alleviate the immediate distress of bereavement, it is no substitute for the opportunity to talk about widowhood with another widowed person or to find the direction needed to reconstruct a social life.

The service line afforded an easy opportunity to put people in touch with each other. For example, two women called who were newly widowed and pregnant, and another young caller had delivered her baby after her husband died. With the callers' permission, the volunteers arranged for the women to meet, and they formed an informal support group. Others with less dramatic stories were introduced to each other on the telephone so that they could share their loneliness or even become friends. The line also enabled people to exchange services. Some women offered childcare, others looked for roommates, and several men offered to make house repairs in trade for a home-cooked meal. Some women wanted advice on decisions such as buying a car. Volunteers often arranged such matches.

Several people with very serious emotional problems called the line. Many were drinking excessively (evident during the first call) and were referred to AA or another program if they acknowledged their problem. One woman threatened suicide. Each time we received such a call we found that the widow or widower had an active network of helpers and/ or were involved with existing programs in the community. These callers had difficulties far beyond the capabilities of the service line.

The line also had silent consumers. We know that many more people read our advertisements than those who actually called. A widow I met socially several years later told me that she kept the phone number by her bed. She never called, but she found it comforting to know that someone was near by. This widow found solace in the mere fact that the line existed, and I assume that she was not unique.

Conclusion

This work provided new insights into the needs of the widowed and a new understanding of what it means to be bereaved. What we found challenged our understanding of bereavement as a simple time-limited process and pointed clearly to how the needs of the widowed change over time. It became apparent that change is critical to any accommodation the widowed have to make. This work also had an impact on the way services to the bereaved are provided in this country and abroad. We demonstrated the unique and affirming role another widow plays in helping the new widow discover not only how to live with and through her grief but also to deal with the changes in her life as well as in herself.

☐ **Implications**

In the late 1960s, little talk about the needs of the dying or of the bereaved could be heard. Kubler-Ross (1969) had just published her book that brought the discussion of death and dying into the open. Hospice was an idea that was developing in Great Britain but it would be another 5 years before hospice programs were developed in the United States (Connors, 1997; Corless & Nicholas, 2003) Most people died in the hospital, and no services for the family were provided afterward. Today, we are witnessing a radical change in the care of the dying (Field & Cassel, 1997; Field & Behrman, 2002), and gradually we are attending more and more to the needs of the bereaved. Hospice is now available in most communities in the United States, and by law hospices are required to follow surviving families for one year after the death of the relative served by the hospice. They also can provide links to bereavement services for other mourners in the community whom they did not serve.

In many ways, the original widow-to-widow program was the stimulus for a growing number of support programs for the widow. This program model has been replicated and adapted many times over throughout the United States, Canada, and Western Europe, as well as almost certainly in other parts of the world of which I am unaware. It would seem that it was an idea that coincided with and perhaps added some stimulus to the growing self-help movement out of which many programs for the bereaved developed (Silverman, 1978; White & Madara, 2002).

In the largest effort to date, the American Association of Retired Persons (AARP) in 1974 began the Widowed Person's Service. It modeled its program after the original widow-to-widow program and used volunteers to reach out to the newly widowed, ultimately developing a network that now includes more than 250 local chapters throughout the United States. It also sponsors an active website and chat line and reaches out to the younger widowed as well.

Vachon (1979; Vachon *et al.*, 1980) replicated this program in Toronto, Canada, in a demonstration research project with a control population which led to the community-based program Community Contact for the Widowed of Toronto, which continued for many years. Vachon's research documented the value of social support and the value of another widowed person as helper. Helen Antoniak replicated the program in the San Diego widow-to-widow program. Lund (1989), in part stimulated by the original widow-to-widow findings, examined the consequences for elderly widows and widowers of participating in social support groups either led by peers or led by professionals. His findings supported the special value of another widowed person as helper. Lieberman (1996) studied the effect on the widowed of participating in a self-help/mutual-aid organization and confirmed its positive impact on the widowed members.

Countless local groups, too numerous to begin to keep track of and too far-flung to identify, have followed the model and flourished. These ideas stimulated the imagination of the clergy and funeral directors and led to development of a workbook on how to set up local community programs (Silverman, 1976). To Live Again, a mutual help organization that started in Philadelphia, has chapters across eastern Pennsylvania and over 1000 members. Among other mutual-help groups that have sprung up or grown larger over the years is THEOS (They Help Each Other Spiritually), which was started by Bea Decker in Pittsburgh and is now a national organization. Another is the Naim Conference, which initially served the Archdiocese of Chicago in the early 1960s and now has branches in other midwestern cities. Some groups that use the name "widow-to-widow" provide either discussion groups led by a professional or are primarily social. Funeral directors across the country also have started after-care projects or stimulated others to develop mutual-help efforts for the widowed (Weeks & Johnson, 2000). Today it is accepted practice for funeral services to sponsor or collaborate with widowed programs and other mutual-help efforts for bereaved people. Other bereavement-related groups have formed to help individuals in addition to trying to bring about change related to the specific circumstances of death. Mothers Against Drunk Driving (MADD) is an example of the many groups of this type.

Still other interventions and organizations for bereaved people have arisen through professional or quasi-professional initiatives. Many professional people have been organizing and leading support groups. While most of these efforts technically should not be called mutual-help or widow-to-widow programs, they do provide mutual help opportunities for the participants. Healthcare professionals are becoming more aware of the need to involve the bereaved in directing their own care (Monroe & Oliviere, 2003).

Widowhood is probably the most researched aspect of bereavement The professional literature has grown exponentially (*e.g.*, Lopata, 1979, 1994, 1996a; Shucter, 1986; Stroebe & Stroebe, 1987; Parkes, 1996); an exhaustive list is impossible within the bounds of this book. It is interesting to see how these ideas circulate and stimulate each other. Our understanding of widowhood is supported, as well, by many books by the widowed themselves about their own experience. I mention Lynn Caine (1974) here because her memoir about her reaction to her husband's death was one of the first in my experience to gain national attention. Initially, she argued with me that the idea of the widow-to-widow program had little meaning in her urban lifestyle. Over time, her experience changed her thinking as she began to realize how important this kind of help was; even on the elevator of a Manhattan apartment building she watched neighbors talking to each other about experiences they shared, often revolving around the death of a spouse. Shernoff (1997) added to our understanding of widowhood by writing of his own experiences and those of his peers who as gay men realize that they are in fact widowed when their partner of many years dies. Silver (1995) wrote a very moving article that appeared in *Ms Magazine*; in it, Silver, as a lesbian woman, claimed the role of widow after her partner's death, thus emphasizing the importance of making the role more inclusive.

Some of the data included in this new edition are from other research done with the widowed in the years since the original widow-to-widow project (Silverman, 1987a, 1988a,b). I draw, too, on my collaboration with Scott Campbell to write a book about widowers that provided me with a deeper appreciation of what the death of their wives means to men (Campbell & Silverman, 1996). As the original widow-to widow program reached out to more and more families with dependent children, I realized that children may be more at risk than their surviving parents. In 1987, J. William Worden and I were awarded a National Institute of Mental Health (NIMH) grant to study the impact of the death of a parent on bereaved children, and I draw on data from this study, as well (Silverman & Worden, 1993; Worden, 1996; Silverman, 2000a). My work has been guided by the use of qualitative research methods that focus on the process and storylines of the people involved (Strauss, 1987; Silverman, 2001c). All of these people are my teachers, and it is their words that give this book meaning.

Various Dimensions of Widowhood

This book is about how the widowed face the silence of the grave and find a way through their grief to learn new ways of living in the world. The process of grief is examined not to find ways of controlling or eliminating it but rather so that we can begin to understand it. This understanding gives direction to our efforts and to those of the widowed themselves to create a safe environment that can provide them with the support necessary to cope effectively with their pain and the myriad changes they now face. As noted in the introduction, the goal of such support is to promote the widowed person's ability to cope with these changes and with their pain. Help involves creating learning opportunities to find new ways to meet these different needs.

It is not easy to describe this grief and what we learn from it, but we can try to do so by telling people's stories, sharing their struggles, and developing theories that help organize this information. The theories outlined in the following chapters are incomplete and imperfect. They all acknowledge the inevitability of pain following a death, not only for the surviving spouse or partner but also for the many other affected mourners. They also acknowledge the fact that the widowed are changed by this experience and suggest directions this change can take.

These chapters highlight several issues. Grief is presented as a normal life-cycle transition, and the concept of transition is used to map the changes associated with becoming a widowed person. Grief is comprised of at least two parts: the emotions (pain, sadness, and emptiness) that we typically associate with grief and the changes that occur as the widowed recognize that they no longer can live their lives as before. Invariably, one partner in a committed relationship will become widowed when the other dies. At one time, the relationship of a woman to her husband was defined by law and religion; if he died, his widow was expected to exhibit certain behaviors associated with that role. Changes in women's roles, particularly the role of wife, are especially relevant for how widows cope today. Data from the original widow-to-widow program highlight these differences. Women today have many more options. When examining the role of widow throughout history, it is clear that the role of widower also must be considered because it, too, has evolved and changed. Widowed persons often have to develop their own definitions of the new roles they assume; they change in the way they define themselves, in the way they see themselves in relationship to others, and in the way they live their daily lives. We no longer talk of getting over or recovering from grief, of putting the past behind us. The widowed make an accommodation and as part of doing so they find a new place in their lives for the deceased.

These chapters illustrate that what is lost is more than a relationship but a way of life, and they focus on the meaning that the relationship had for the widowed. Changes in the widowed are described using a developmental lens aimed at explaining how the widowed change emotionally and cognitively as a result of their new position in society. They develop a new appreciation of their ability to act on their own behalf and their new ability to be involved in more complex exchanges with others, in addition to developing new coping strategies.

Taking a developmental approach allows us to see loss as an impetus for growth (Kegan, 1982; Silverman, 2000a). In the face of disruptions precipitated by spousal death, the widowed are challenged to shift not only how they make sense of their world but also how they see themselves in that world. This model describes an increasingly complex and coherent way to understand relationships between self and other, a model that depends not on chronological age but on interpersonal dynamics. By seeing themselves as capable of relating to others in different ways with greater variety in their responses, the widowed are able to understand and respond to the death in a broader context. Characteristics of the behavior of any widowed person are discussed, as are sociocultural aspects of the experience, family issues, life-cycle issues, and ways in which meaning is constructed around issues of faith and belief.

Overall, the following chapters are designed to lead the reader to an appreciation of the unique aspects of the widowed learning from each other. The first chapter examines various theories of grief and the impact of cultural and historical factors on how it is view today. The second chapter looks at how the ways in which men and women are socialized in Western society make a difference in how they respond to their widowhood. The third chapter describes how viewing grief as a time of transition provides a map for looking at how grief changes over time for the widowed. The final chapter in this section focuses on how people cope in the context of a mutual-help experience and the help the widowed offer each other.

CHAPTER 1

Theoretical Perspectives on Grief and Helping

When he was sick, I did more and more things alone. When I took my son to college I was alone and that would have never happened before. I went for walks alone, but nevertheless he was still there to kind of do it together with. Now he's gone. I didn't think it would be so final. For the first few months, the chasm is so huge I couldn't approach it. It's not that you don't intellectually understand that he's gone, but emotionally it's just … it's just huge.

50-year-old widow six months after her husband died

'Til death do us part is a vow most couples make when the partners commit themselves to each other; thus, most marriages or committed relationships that do not end in divorce will end with the death of one of the partners. Due to the centrality of the nuclear family in contemporary society, this relationship is typically the primary source of mutuality, care, and connection. After 22 years of marriage, a middle-aged widow explained what she lost:

What did I lose? Who will I share my life with, the joys and the burdens? I lost a sense of meaning, direction, security, and purpose. Nothing can make up for the loss of the intimate connection you share with your spouse. He just knew my heart.

With this death, the surviving spouse or partner changes his or her role to that of a widowed person who has to deal with the grief that follows this loss. The view of grief that guides the work presented in this book is that it is a normal life-cycle experience — a process for which the beginning may be clear but the ending is not. Over time, the process undergoes many perturbations. We must all live with the fact that death occurs, that it is an invariable part of the life cycle. To mourn the death of someone we care about and who has played an important role in our lives is part of the human condition. Appreciating the importance of relationships throughout our lives — those we have before a death and those we develop afterwards — is central to understanding grief and why the widow-to-widow approach works. This chapter examines grief as an expected part of the life cycle within a relational and developmental context that is influenced by changing historical and cultural forces.

☐ Death Is Not a Respecter of Age

Typically, widowhood is associated with the elderly. Death rates among the young have decreased over the last century, and as people live longer death has become a less significant part of the daily life of most American families. With improved childbirth care, the death rate among young women has dropped considerably. Because of improved prevention and treatment of infectious diseases, overall death rates have fallen in most Western countries. Nevertheless, modern medicine cannot change the fact that we all will die. Ironically, despite our resistance to accepting death as a fact of life, it is ever present in our lives. In some communities, murder is a daily event. Our country engages in wars in which our soldiers are routinely killed. The AIDS epidemic touches all segments of our society, and terrorists have reached our shores. These and other types of death do not respect age, and today many elderly parents survive their adult children.

Younger women most frequently die of cancer and young men of both cancer and heart disease. In America today, the passing of a young wife or husband is often the surviving spouse's first encounter with death:

> I'm 23 years old. All my friends are dating and worried about getting married and I am already a widow with two children.

The death of a young husband, unexpected and out of turn in the life cycle, destroys this widow's expectations about the role of death in her life. We assume that older men and women have more experience with death, but the elderly may feel as unprepared as their younger counterparts, as explained by an 80-year-old widow:

I know that people in our age group expect that one of us will go first. I always thought it would be me, but not now, not today. It is interesting; it was not something we talked about, even though we knew he was so sick.

☐ What Is Grief?

The English language has three words to differentiate various aspects of the grieving process: *bereavement*, *grief*, and *mourning* (Stroebe, 2001; Bowlby, 1980). *Bereavement* refers to a specific state of being (*e.g.*, "I am bereft"). *Grief* encompasses one's reactions to a death, including feelings, visceral responses, actions, and thoughts, such as crying, pining, inability to sleep or eat, lethargy, and psychological and/or physical pain. *Mourning* is defined as the social expression or acts of grief that reflect the influence of the cultural context on individual behavior. This definition implies that, regardless of their private feelings, mourners express their public grief according to the traditions and mores of the society in which they live. Despite the subtle differences among these words, no one word, by itself, reflects the fullness of the experience of spousal death) and one aspect of a widowed person's reaction cannot be understood completely without considering the others. In this book, I will use these words interchangeably to reflect the full significance of the death, as I am writing about bereaved men and women who are grieving and mourning.

The grief that accompanies this death has at least two key components: one focusing on *emotions* and the other on *change*. The emotional reactions include sadness, general malaise, depression, despair, dejection, anxiety, guilt, and loneliness, some of which the newly widowed may never have experienced before. Widows and widowers might be agitated, fatigued, socially withdrawn, and preoccupied with thoughts and images of their dead spouses. They also may not be able to eat or sleep or may be unable to grasp that the death has really occurred. At times, they might feel out of control and overwhelmed by their grief. A middle-aged widower described his reaction to his loss:

> Grief? It's a lot of pain and it takes up a huge amount of space. I felt that I had little tolerance for things not going right. I would say thinking about her a lot and feeling the pain of her not being there. You sort of turn and say, "Well, that's where she used to be." So there's a sense of disbelief, a feeling like she is going to reappear at some point.

Following a death, the widowed person now faces many irreversible and instantaneous changes that often are accompanied by a sense of disorder and disarray. The survivor's social world, in which the deceased is no longer a living presence, is irrevocably transformed. A widow must construct another type of relationship with her dead husband, as well as a new relationship to herself and the world around her, as one widow explained:

> I used to be queen of the shopping malls. Now I feel as if my whole life is mush.

Grief is a process in constant motion. For those in mourning, change is a faithful companion as they negotiate and renegotiate the implications of their loss over time (see Chapter 3); however, more than a life has been lost. A relationship, as well as the survivor's role in that relationship, is gone, along with that person's way of relating to the world. Jacobs (1999) noted that grief is more than simply a decreasing state of emotions, but instead reflects a complex evolving process. Over time, the widowed learn that they can integrate their loss into a new world view through a process that involves learning new skills to cope with new feelings and new roles. This accommodation helps the widowed gain a sense of control and enables them, in effect, to begin the next stage of their lives. The widowed person must learn a great deal about how to live in this changed world. At various stages in the life cycle, particularly when we marry and have children, we recognize the need to learn new skills to cope with new feelings and new roles. Learning is necessary now, as well, and becomes a fundamental aspect of the grieving process.

A middle-aged woman explained two years after her husband died:

> People are different in terms of what they are looking for after the death, but all people are on some path to create a new life.

☐ Making Meaning in a Developmental Context

The path the widowed choose to take to create a new life is guided by the way they make sense of death and the void left in their lives. Humans are "meaning makers" who strive to punctuate, organize, and anticipate their engagement with the world by arranging it in themes that express their particular cultures, faith system, families, and personalities (Neimeyer, 1998, 2001). In their study of bereaved families, Kissane and his colleagues (1996) observed that meaning making involves an attempt to create order out of chaos and to gain a sense of control over the uncontrollable. In the words of a 75-year-old widower reflecting on his struggle to deal with the chaos in his life and to find new meaning:

> At times I feel like a lost ship being tossed about in a storm. After being with someone for 39 years I found it difficult to find myself again. She was my "safe haven," someone I could talk with, confide in, to love and be loved…. I know it will be a long and rough road to find out my bearing and just and true self again. But I have to do it for my peace of mind.

This quest for meaning can be looked at from a development perspective (Shapiro, 1994; Silverman, 1987a,b, 2000a). What does this actually mean? Development can be seen as an evolutionary, emotional, and cognitive process that both influences and reflects how people organize their world and make sense of it. When we talk of development in children, we often focus on the physical maturational process, but emotional and cognitive, as well as physical, changes continue from birth through adulthood. Movement is constant and inevitable. In adults, development occurs through their expanded awareness of the external world and an ability to reflect on own experiences so they develop a more complex way of relating to others in their lives (Kegan, 1982). The widowed have to find a way of seeing themselves as well as others from a different perspective. To do so, they need to do a good deal of learning as part of their grieving process.

In his examination of the grieving process, Attig (1996) asks how do we relearn the world? How do the widowed take in new information? Learning styles cannot be separated from where the widowed are developmentally, which not only impacts their learning styles and what they need from helpers but also how they see their grief and their new situation. One dimension to consider is whether the widowed are concrete thinkers or are able to think abstractly. A more concrete thinker sees things in a linear fashion and may have trouble moving outside themselves to see what needs doing. They may need more specific instructions about how to proceed. Some widowed people can never move past their own pain to look outside themselves for solutions or see what is happening within a larger context. In the words of one widow 6 years after her husband died:

> All I could think about was he died *on me*. Nobody can understand how much it hurts. The only time life was ever good was when he was alive

Someone who can think more abstractly can usually step back from the problem to consider the situation. These people have a greater ability to generalize and consider how different ideas and suggested solutions may apply to their particular situations. Forced by necessity and opportunity, most widowed people move toward a more complex view of the world. A woman in her late 60s talked about her direction of change:

> Making important decisions for myself was a new concept to me. I now voice my own opinions and I am sometimes surprised that I am doing this — right or wrong. I seem to be in a different place in how I see myself. I would have chosen to get here in a different way, but given no choice, here I am!

Another widow built on a learning style she already had in place:

> Good or bad, my style is to get mobilized. I stepped back and began to look at what being alone means. What do I want now for my life?

Defining a problem is a first step in beginning to cope and in gaining a sense of control, both of which enable widows or widowers to find new ways to see themselves in the world, prodding them toward a new way of making meaning from their situation (Silverman, 1988b, 2000a). White and Epston (1990) described this phenomenon as the ability to be both performer and audience to one's own performance.

Making meaning, then, can best be understood as both a developmental process and a relational one. Cultural traditions and attitudes also influence this process. A key example, critical to understanding the dilemma faced by many widows, is reflected in the way society has traditionally defined the role of woman and wife as subordinate to that of her spouse. In a sense, the widow knew herself through her relationship with her husband (Silverman, 1987a,b, 2000b). In this context, the widow must develop a new way of seeing herself, a new way of relating to the world to find the new voice she may need to deal with the death of her husband:

> I learned to speak out and speak up, and people listened.

In essence, "voice" is a metaphor for the person's world view, her place in it, and the influence of others, including prevailing community values and attitudes (Gilligan, 1993). We can talk of the inner voice and the voice of others as they influence the reactions of the widow or widower. Some voices are given more credence than others. For example, the widow's voice may not be heard when others dictate that she listen to the voice of an expert who knows how she "should feel" or "should grieve." Do helpers pay attention to who speaks out, who is heard, who says what he or she means, who is silent, and who is silenced but communicates nonverbally (Belenky et al., 1996)? Examples of silenced or muted voices that are not heard can be found among "widowed" people whose relationships to the deceased were not socially accepted. Couples who were not married or who were involved in a same-sex relationship (called *disenfranchised mourners* by Doka, 2002) often do not have legal standing in dealing with details of a death, and sometimes the surviving partners must mourn in private. Society does not support the way in which they have given their life meaning and direction. In the words of a woman whose partner died suddenly in an accident:

> We were together for 12 years. When she died I had no standing in the hospital to make any decisions about what to do. At the funeral the clergy acted as if I didn't exist. Fortunately my partner's family were very supportive. I was really a "widow" but at first I didn't understand that this applied to me. I'm becoming more respectful of my needs.

Identifying herself as a widow gave her life new meaning and a direction for the changes she had to make. It legitimized her feelings and provided her with a context and a community in which to deal with this experience. She was prompted to find a new way of making meaning.

☐ Is Grief a Normal Life Event or an Illness?

As we have seen, the nature of the grieving process can be understood in many ways. One is to view grief as a foreign object or disease that, with proper treatment, can be expunged or cured. Another is to see grief as an ever-changing process and as a normal life-cycle experience.

Grief As an Illness

For the most part, contemporary views of grief are framed by modern psychological theories. According to Meyer (1988), in the twentieth century we witnessed the "creation of the modern psychological individual." This author examined the qualities that define the individual in relation to the complex social changes in Western economic, cultural, and political systems that foster individualism. When we frame the needs of the dying and the bereaved in psychological terms, we focus primarily on the inner world of people, ignoring other aspects of their lives. In so doing, we often slip into viewing grief as an illness. In fact, many professionals adopt the language of medicine to describe the mourner's experience. The bereaved are told that they have a condition from which they will "recover," that their reactions are "symptoms," and that with proper "treatment" their pain can be expunged.

This view of grief permeates many layers of our society. Mental-health specialists conducting research on bereavement during the twentieth century generally understood the pain and tumult of grief to be pathological symptoms, leading to the belief that grieving "correctly" could prevent these signs of "illness." Proper treatment leading to "good grief" focused on talking out the feelings associated with the death. This focus inevitably led to a mixed message that the bereaved who did not share their feelings were grieving incorrectly, but so were the bereaved who talked too much over too long a period of time, indicating an inability to "recover."

This approach to grief is a natural corollary to our culture's interpretation of death as an affront and a medical failure (Aries, 1981; Fulton, 1965; Feifel, 1986). A 60-year-old widow talked about her husband's death:

> He had a heart condition. If the doctor knew that people rarely recover from this type of attack, he did not say so. We really believed that he would be cured. We had such faith in what the doctor could do. Then, when he died, the doctor kept saying he was sorry — sort of saying it should not have happened. I would have laughed if I hadn't been so upset. I ended up reassuring the doctor.

Recent research, however, indicates that all mourners do not share the same experiences of grief and that some people do not feel the need to express their feelings in public (Lofland, 1985; Wortman & Silver, 1989). Those widows and widowers who do not display the prescribed picture of grieving may not suffer from repressed grief but instead may reflect the widowed person's culture, ways of making meaning, and/or coping styles. Martin and Doka (2000) identify other effective styles of grieving: (1) *traditional mourning patterns*, where feelings are openly expressed, and (2) *non-traditional modes*, where people do not value talking and focus less on feelings. Their analysis considers gender differences that cannot be ignored as we consider the cultural and social contexts that influence differences in how men and women mourn — a topic that is visited over and over again throughout this book.

It is important to note that the vast majority of the widowed do not exhibit emotional problems (Stroebe *et al.*, 2000). In the original widow-to-widow program, the only widows who developed serious emotional difficulties had prior histories of psychiatric illness (Silverman et al., 1974). Raphael (2001) wrote about the prevalence of emotional problems in the bereaved:

Research and the study of bereavement phenomenology, including reactions from different kinds of deaths, have made it quite clear that for the majority of people, grief, although psychologically painful and distressing, is a normal process reflecting both the strengths and value of human attachments and the capacity to adapt to loss and adversity. (Raphael *et al.*, 2001, p. 587)

Nevertheless, the language of illness persists. Many experts conducting research on "traumatic grief" hope to demonstrate that such grief should be designated as a psychiatric syndrome in the next edition of the *Diagnostic and Statistical Manual of Mental Disorders* (DSM-V) (Jacobs, 1999; Prigerson & Jacobs, 2001). With this approach, grief is viewed as being time limited, and the goal of help is to recover the mourner's sense of psychological well-being or bring about a return to the mourner's former sense of well-being. Members of the media perpetuate this illness paradigm when they, for example, describe survivors of 9/11 as seeking "closure" and "recovery."

A continuing goal of most bereavement research is to identify specific factors in the bereaved that would increase their risk of developing serious mental-health problems. There is no agreement, however, on the definition of "good outcome" or when it is best to measure this outcome (immediately after the death, at the one- or two-year anniversary, or later). Also, a consensus has not been reached with regard to differentiating between risk factors that were present before the death as opposed to those as-yet-unidentified components of the bereavement process that increase a mourner's vulnerabilities (Lund, 1989; Osterweis *et al.*, 1984; Stroebe & Schut, 2001b). The small minority who have difficulty needs attention, but we cannot generalize from their experience to the larger bereaved population.

Grief As a Life-Cycle Event

Applying a medical model can reduce our understanding of human behavior to a simple cause-and-effect linear model, implying control where none may be possible. We must consider the implications of assuming that a normal life-cycle event is a treatable illness. Using the language of sickness and health, our society takes grief to the "doctor's office," where it can be contained and controlled and will not intrude on the greater community. A widower aptly articulates how this affected him two years after the death of his wife:

This is the same group of people that tell you to go on antidepressants and you will be all better. They don't know how to deal with pain. They are so afraid they are going to get it themselves (as if grief is contagious) so with counseling and medication and you will be all better.

A young widow responded:

That's true. I've been taking antidepressants, not so much as I was before my husband died. And if I have an extremely bad day, my own family will say, "Did you take your pills today?" They think it is a magic potion. Just drives me crazy to have to make others feel comfortable.

When professional experts handle grief, the community does not have to deal with the fullness of the mourners' pain or the myriad changes that result from a death. To confront grief is to confront our own mortality, which we seem to desperately want to avoid (Lifton, 1974). As a society, we have difficulty accepting the normal pain and suffering that accompany many life events, and our tendency to "medicalize" grief is an attempt to wrest control over the uncontrollable (Kleinman & Kleinman, 1997). Grief becomes a private experience that focuses on the personal psychological meaning of the death to the mourner. Without the rituals and communal outreach that might guide their mourning and with no encouragement to take a wider view on death as a part of life, the widowed tend to blame themselves instead of questioning the socially accepted definition of grieving.

As we observe a mourner's suffering, we should consider what is right with him or her, not what is wrong. The widow-to-widow project has helped us refocus from an attempt to prevent some as-yet-undefined negative outcome to *promoting competence*. This involves helping people to become experts in effectively managing their own grief and their own lives, with the implication that there is no one good outcome nor one way to arrive at it. With this view, it is essential to consider the many aspects of the larger social context in which the bereaved live.

Grief in a Relational Context

We are social creatures, and our relationships frame and focus who we are and who we become. Notions of society, reality, and the self are all created through an interactive social process (Charmaz, 1994). By extension, a relational paradigm of grief suggests a dynamic, interpersonal process involving the deceased, multiple mourners, those who are a part of their lives, and the cultural traditions and mores that shape people's behavior and understanding. To really understand someone's reaction to the death of a loved one, we must consider the fullness of the mourner's life before and after his or her loss.

Rarely does a single mourner exist. Grief is an interactive, collaborative process (Shapiro, 1994) that gives rise to the following questions: Who is affected by the death other than the spouse? Are there dependent children or adult children living outside the family home? Are other relatives involved? How has the family changed and what is its current state? We need to consider friends, as well (Shapiro, 1994; Silverman, 2000a): How have these people related to each other in the past? Inevitably, the death disrupts the balance of relationships as mourners deal with grief in their own ways:

> It's interesting: My husband's older sister is very supportive; his younger sister stays away. His parents are great. They were afraid that when Jim died they would lose us, too, and I had to reassure them that this would never happen. They like to talk about him and that is nice. They need to, really. His business partner is the same way. I like to visit with him because he likes to talk about Jim. My parents, on the other hand, skirt around it all the time. In some ways, this is what I would expect — that's the way they always were about dealing with feelings and difficult situations.

Dependent children needing care have a major impact on the grieving process:

> When my wife got sick, the children were 8 and 13. We tried to keep them reasonably informed. Their needs were always on our minds. And for me that continued after she died: trying to understand and be there for them. Not always easy given my condition.... I wasn't really functioning very well.

The deceased, too, has a profound influence on the mourning process:

> Boy, if I ever get angry with my husband for dying, it's for leaving me with his mother and mine. He was a great buffer and now I have to manage all their "nonsense" by myself. But it is important for my daughter's sake. She needs them and they need her, especially now.

Stroebe and Stroebe (1987) identified factors that can be considered "voices" in the widowed person's life and that affect the partner's experience of loss, including the person's relationship to the deceased, situation demands, and individual coping resources. Using different language,

Neimeyer (1998, 2001), as noted above, described the important contribution of family history and culture, as well as personal qualities of the mourner, to the way the widowed make meaning of the death. In his two-track model, Rubin (1996) emphasized the importance of this larger social context but emphasized the mourner's relationship to the deceased and the critical place of this relationship in the grieving process.

Bowlby's work in the 1940s highlighted the importance of being in connection with others and the negative psychological consequences of losing these relationships. He postulated that people (as well as all mammals) are instinctually motivated to form attachments to a nurturing maternal figure (Bowlby, 1969/1982, 1973, 1980). He defined "attachment behavior" as any form of action that helps attain or retain proximity to this differentiated and preferred individual and which leads to affectionate bonds. In Bowlby's terms, the formation of a bond is generally described as "falling in love," "maintaining" a bond, or "loving" someone, and losing a bond can be described as "grieving." Attachment is demonstrated through the need to touch or cling. Both men and women value attachments and affiliations, and no person develops and matures in isolation of others. Being involved with others is essential to our sense of well-being.

Bowlby's work has contributed greatly to our understanding of the universal need for relationships that provide love, guidance, and support and has led us to look at grief in a relational context. Bowlby also has had a major influence on how we understand grief in children. He observed the behavior of children who were separated from their parents as part of an evacuation from war-torn London. He labeled their reactions as "grief," firmly establishing that children have the capacity to mourn. Contemporary theorists have expanded Bowlby's findings to various types of attachment behaviors in children, and his research has also been used to understand the responses of children facing the death of an important nurturing adult.

As we consider Bowlby's theories and current research on bereavement, we see the importance of looking at loss within a relational context. We are interpersonal, interacting creatures, and we meet our need for others in a variety of ways. In fact, we spend much of our lives balancing the tensions between our own needs and the needs of others, and this balancing act will shift over the life cycle, depending on our stage of development and role as child, spouse, or parent in the relationship.

Weiss (1969, 2001) explored the nature and variety of human relationships and observed that people draw on a "fund of sociability" to satisfy their various needs. People, he said, require nurturance, guidance, reassurance of worth, and integration into an alliance where they feel secure and attached. Different needs may be satisfied in different relationships. Stress and tension can develop in a relationship such as a marriage when one expects all these needs to be met within that partnership. Furthermore, if most of these needs are met within one relationship, the loss of that relationship can be devastating.

Beyond sexual intimacy, marriage offers daily companionship and affection. It also provides a framework of mutual need around which partners organize their daily lives; therefore, for both men and women, marriage or a committed relationship is a universally accepted way to meet important social and emotional needs. Any one marriage may fulfill more or less of these needs, depending on the social climate; the partners' social class, religious, and ethnic backgrounds; and the expectations of each other.

Weiss (1990) noted that the presence of a wife in a man's life helps him feel emotionally complete and invulnerable to loneliness, and that most men delegate responsibility for social warmth and connection to their spouses. Women with whom I have spoken confirm this portrayal of themselves as caretakers, nurturers, and general managers of the family. When a spouse dies, the surviving partner loses a central relationship that has identified how that person has lived and related to others and the community (Yalom, 2001). The couple's definitions of the roles of wife, husband, or partner influence how the widower or widow will experience the many losses following the death. Yalom (2001) described the special meaning of the marital relationship in women's lives over time and noted that even today in many places a more traditional view prevails. Women are the caretakers, the glue that holds the family together. Regardless of how they defined themselves when they were married, the sense of loss is very real. A young widow explained:

> We planned to grow old together. Now there is no one to ask about what I did today, or to worry about if either of us is not feeling good. Who will comfort me, and who can I comfort? I didn't have to ask questions; we were just there for each other. I have to find a whole new direction.

☐ Detachment Revisited

The works of Freud (1961) have had a major impact on our perception of grief as an illness with treatable symptoms. In his early characterizations of grief, Freud believed that mourners had an obligation to "let go" of the deceased or to "decathect the object" (Silverman & Klass, 1996) so that they could redirect their emotional energy toward new relationships. This depiction of grief implied that people could have only one kind of relationship or one significant relationship at a time. It is clear from Freud's personal letters that his own experiences did not follow this trajectory of grief (Silverman & Klass, 1996); nevertheless, his description of grief and its resolution has dominated most twentieth-century Western thinking about bereavement.

In 1944, influenced by Freud, Lindemann studied people mourning those killed in a nightclub fire in Boston, and he identified the three tasks of these mourners: (1) emancipation from the bond to the deceased, (2) readjustment to the environment in which the deceased is missing, and (3) formation of new relationships. Lindemann also observed intense guilt in survivors of this fire, which killed hundreds (Lindemann, 1944). These feelings are not unlike those of Holocaust survivors, who often have difficulty reconciling their own survival with the death that surrounded them (Frankl, 1984; Valent, 2002). Today, when the bereaved do not exhibit guilt, others often label this behavior as repression or avoidance. Lindemann proposed that grief ended when the mourner severed his or her relationship to the deceased. By "letting go" of this relationship, the bereaved could adjust to an environment in which the deceased is no longer present. In taking this approach to grieving, Lindemann focused on the mourner's inner emotional life built on his or her attachment to the deceased.

Recent research has questioned the ability of mourners to "let go" and put the "past behind them" (Silverman & Silverman, 1979; Rubin, 1981; Silverman, 1986; Klass, 1988; Silverman *et al.*, 1992; Silverman & Klass, 1996; Stroebe *et al.*, 1996; Walter, 1999). Data suggest that the bereaved remain involved with the deceased, which produces a paradox: We cannot live in the past or carry on as if the deceased is still a part of our life, but we cannot let go of the relationship, either — in a sense trying to act as if the past did not exist. The bereaved find ways to construct connections to their dead loved ones that are both comforting and sustaining (Pincus, 1974; Feldman, 1979; Silverman & Silverman, 1979; Klass, 1988; Rubin, 1992; Silverman & Worden, 1993; Klass *et al.*, 1996; Normand *et al.*, 1996; Silverman & Nickman, 1996; Silverman, 2000a).

Historically, mourners have continued to maintain their bonds with the deceased (Stroebe *et al.*, 1996; Walter, 1999). For example, Victorian widows were not expected to let go and get on with their lives, but rather to live in companionship with their deceased husbands for an extended period of time. After reviewing recent bereavement research, as well as their own, Silverman and Klass (1996) concluded that most bereaved people do not experience death as the end of that relationship.

The view of grief as something that people can get over and the accompanying psychologicalization of grief are compatible with the Western values of individual independence and autonomy. Dependency on others is often perceived as a negative quality (Miller, 1987). Relationships are viewed instrumentally — in terms of having one's needs met — and much contemporary thinking on individual development focuses on separation and individuation. According to this theoretical framework, when a relationship ends, either through death or through other circumstances, it is appropriate for the mourner to sever ties to the deceased.

[Mourning is the internal process we undertake to transform our relationship to the deceased (Attig, 1996). Transformation is very different from detachment, and constructing a relationship to the deceased typically is part of an interactive process with other mourners in the family and in the community (Silverman & Klass, 1996). The support and shared memories of others help shape and direct this reconstruction of the relationship with the deceased (Nickman *et al.*, 1998). In the words of a young widow:

> I find it helpful to go to the cemetery and just go over the day with my husband and let him know how the children are doing. Sometime I complain about how tough things were and I ask him for advice.

[Maintaining a continuing relationship with the deceased reminds us of the important place that the deceased person held in the internal and external lives of the bereaved. Pincus (1974) identified a psychologically healthy process that she called *incorporation*, in which the lost person is internalized and becomes part of the bereaved (p. 124). The processes of denial and negation are central to others' understanding of how mourners maintain their connection to the dead (Silverman & Silverman, 1979). *Denial* is part of the mourner's initial reaction to a death that manifests in various ways when the mourner over time has difficulty integrating this new reality into their lives. *Negation* gives significance to the death by providing ways to maintain a connection to the deceased through memorials and actions that would have elicited the dead person's approval. Yet another conceptual approach helps the bereaved find continuity between past and present by detaching the familiar meanings of life from the relationship and reestablishing them independently (Marris, 1974). Within this framework, a person masters grief not by ceasing to care about the deceased but rather by abstracting what was fundamentally important in the relationship and rehabilitating it, a process of reformulation rather than substitution (Marris, 1974). People do not give up the past; they change their relationship to it, a process that probably continues over their lifetimes.

Marwit and Klass (1996) described how maintaining bonds with the dead has influenced the lives of college students. The deceased have served as role models, provided situation-specific guidance, helped clarify values, and served as a source of nurturing memories. In this way, the deceased continue to play an active role in the lives of those who mourn them. In the words of a young widow:

> I feel his presence. I know that in some way he is still part of my life. But I am also cognizant of the fact that he is not here…. I have this continuous conversation going on with him. (Conant, 1996, p. 183)

An elderly widow described how she created opportunities to talk about her deceased husband:

> He collected ties and so over a lifetime there were enough to make quilted pillows for each of my grandchildren. Then I shared with them the times when their grandfather wore these ties. We laugh and we cry together, and I feel good and they get to know him in ways they wouldn't otherwise.

In the wake of the 9/11 tragedy, those helping the surviving families kept looking for ways to foster healing. As a result, each family received an urn of ashes from the World Trade Center that was intended to bring closure. A woman whose husband died in the World Trade Center on that day told me, however, that this gesture provided little solace to the mourning widows and widowers. In many ways, such initiatives can actually compound the survivors' pain because they know that closure is unattainable. Relationships must change after a death, but they do not end (Silverman & Klass, 1996; Silverman, 2000a; Klass & Walters, 2001).

Playwright Robert Anderson summarized his experience 15 years after his first wife's death:

> I have a new life…. Death ends a life but it doesn't end a relationship, which struggles on in the survivor's mind toward some resolution, which it never finds. (Anderson, 1974, p. 77)

These stories challenge the use of words such as *recovery, moving on*, and *closure* — concepts that the bereaved see as irrelevant to their experiences. To gain a fuller understanding of the need to continue the bond with the deceased we need to consider the social/cultural context in which the mourner lives and which can provide a framework for this continuity.

☐ The Effect of Culture and Society on Grieving

We cannot understand how partners relate to each other, how they express their grief when one of them dies, and what they experience as loss without examining the social and cultural context in which they live and the prevailing attitudes and values of this context. While every person grieves differently, the language of grief, the manner in which grief is expressed, and the ways in which mourners experience their loss change as time, place, and the social context change.)The fact that we all die is not socially constructed nor is the fact that people react to death; however, every society provides its own traditions and rituals, subject to historical and cultural forces, that guide mourners' behavior (Lofland, 1985; Charmaz, 1994; Stroebe *et al.*, 1996; Parkes *et al.*, 1997; Walter, 1999; Yalom, 2001; Rosenblatt, 2001). These attitudes and values are not static.

In their review of the literature addressing what mourning behaviors might be universal, Stroebe and Stroebe (1987) noted that in almost all societies the loss of a significant other leads to tears and sadness. Bowlby (1969, 1973, 1980) suggested that such behavior is programmed into all mammals. In contrast, Lofland (1985) questioned whether the very personal reactions people have to a death may be socially defined.

Grief, whatever its roots, is expressed differently in various cultures. Some faith systems require restraint as proof of the mourner's faith in God's judgment; however, in some communities, women are expected to vent their feelings in public by tearing their clothes and their flesh during the funeral but then to appear reconciled to their loss immediately afterward (Rubin, 2004). In other parts of the world, women are expected to give expression to their feelings and may even be assigned the role of ritual mourner (Seremetakis, 1991). Other cultures, such as the Aborigines, will not mention the deceased for several years after the death.

Writing in the beginning of the twentieth century, anthropologist van Gennep (1960) described a several-stage process involving rituals that facilitate mourning. He identified rites of passage that mark the separation of the living from the dead and observed that the community's initial focus was on the burial of the deceased. Mourners then could visualize the dead at rest in the land of the deceased from which they can never return. This helped mourners to sever ties with the deceased and eliminate the accompanying role obligations that kept the involvement alive. In some societies, however, death and its rituals do not end the mourner's obligation but simply change it. For example, in ancient China, one's responsibilities for and to ancestors continued at least through the lifetime of the mourner; Klass (1996) described similar rituals in contemporary Japan but which are practiced for a more limited period of time. Other societies have developed rituals of mourning that sharply differentiate the duties of the mourner from the duties of that person before the death (Rosenblatt *et al.*, 1976). Routines of daily life are interrupted, and behavior changes are validated. Rituals of re-entry or reintegration into normal life follow later. When the bereaved participate in such rituals, they simultaneously have an opportunity to express their grief as well as feel solidarity with the social group of which they are a part.

In analyzing these rituals, it is interesting that almost all of them place the obligation for observance on the widow or the woman as mourner or helper (van Gennep, 1960; Rosenblatt *et al.*, 1976). Rosenblatt described the role of a ritual specialist, who is assigned the task of helping a widow reintegrate into society after the designated bereavement period. (In many ways, this role resembles that of aide in the widow-to-widow program.) It is not clear what was expected of the men in these communities and how their needs were met. In fact, the indigenous Bangladesh language has no word for widower, as men quickly remarry. In contrast, consider this description of men and women mourning in the Lakota Indian community:

> Mourning is considered natural, and the unrestrained expression of grief is appropriate and regarded as a good thing for both sexes. Women will typically wail loudly; men will often sing emotional mournful songs. (Cook & Oltjenbruns, 1998, p. 105)

In Western society, we have moved from the observance of communal rituals and practices and religious beliefs that framed the mourner's behavior to a focus on the individual and his or her inner feelings and personal reactions (Aries, 1981). Until the twentieth century, religious faith and ritual played an important part in guiding people in their grief, including finding ways to mediate between the living and the dead. In the last century, we developed more rational interpretations of death that minimized the concept of an afterlife and the value of ritual in consoling or guiding the behavior of the bereaved (Parsons, 1994). Rituals focus attention on the meaning of the loss and help to legitimize feelings; the lack of rituals often leaves a painful void, leading the bereaved to return to their spiritual roots. In the words of a young widow whose partner had died:

> I am a lapsed Catholic. I rejected my family's rigid observance. We never went to church, but I am glad, when my partner died, that we had a church service in the traditional fashion. I realized it was what we knew, and I needed that connection.

This move away from ritual reflects the influence of the physical and social sciences on Western religious philosophy and practice, so explaining human behavior with regard to death and bereavement is no longer the prerogative of philosophers and clergy. The contemporary focus on mourners' restraint relegates grief to the private inner lives of mourners. Once grief becomes invisible, others are discouraged from offering consolation and support (Gorer, 1965). Even Western cultures, however, hold onto rituals of burial, such as the moving memorial service for the astronauts who died in the Columbia explosion. We must ask how such rituals meet the long-term needs of the surviving families as they experience the full impact of their loss. Such a memorial is, in fact, only a first step in a long process.

Traditions can guide the widowed over the long term. Jewish tradition involves rituals to console the bereaved and to honor the deceased over the lifetime of the mourners (Lamm, 2000; Brener, 2001). Within the Catholic religion, a memorial mass is often held to honor the deceased on the anniversary of the death. The Hispanic community has extended this tradition into an annual community ritual known as the Day of the Dead. This celebration involves visits to the cemetery and elaborate parades and is especially prevalent in the southwestern United States and in Mexico. This celebration provides an opportunity for families to visit their deceased relatives and to maintain a connection to them. Until recently, the Protestant church had no rituals to facilitate the mourning process or to honor the dead, but individual churches are beginning to develop their own traditions.

In contemporary America, little is offered to help mourners deal with the many changes that accompany spousal death. Few traditions instruct the widowed on developing new behavior patterns to replace their former daily routines that involved or were centered on the deceased. An important part of our culture is the roles assigned to men and women in our society. Another aspect of context and culture that must be considered is gender. The meaning of widowhood cannot be separated from how the roles of man and woman or husband and wife are defined in a society. Some of these roles are associated with biological differences (*e.g.,* childbearing), while others are primarily associated with socially constructed roles. These socially constructed roles defining marriage and marital relationships have changed considerably over time and need to be considered in greater depth.

Widows and Widowers:
Gender Differences

I'm not sure. In some ways we seem to be different. Many women in the group had an issue that they hadn't done enough. A sort of failure in caretaking. Men were more practical. The women also felt that they were "still married" but after two years that wasn't my experience.

55-year-old widower, two years after his wife died

What does it mean to be a widow or widower? Is it different for men and for women when their partners or spouses die? We should not, in any way, gloss over the individual differences between the experiences of the widowed as they suffer spousal loss, but what differences can we attribute to gender and the ways in which each gender was socialized?

☐ Gender in a Societal Context

Historically, men and women have been socialized to fill very different roles in society. By understanding the ways in which these roles are defined, we can gain insight into the meaning of losing a spouse for both widows and widowers. Women's roles, in particular, have been largely shaped by how the role of wife has been defined over the ages. Taking an historical view on how women's lives have changed, Lopata (1994) divided the lives of women into three periods — the *traditional*, the *transitional*, and the *modern* — which still have some relevance today. In her study of the history of women's lives which traced how the role of wife has defined a woman's place in society and her sense of self over the past several millennia, Yalom (2001) made similar distinctions. Throughout history, the men around a woman have defined who she was and how she lived her life with regard to her family as well as to the larger society.

In *traditional societies*, women married and left their parental homes for those of their husbands. In these societies, first the father and then the husband had authority over a woman. These societies were patriarchal in descent, inheritance, and authority and patrilocal in residence. A woman's only option for establishing her place in society was to marry the man of her father's choosing and become a wife. On marrying, a woman moved in with her husband's family, and the relationships established there governed almost every aspect of her life. When she was widowed, her sons (if any) would take care of her. If her husband died at a young age, the widow's place could be seriously compromised. In some parts of the world, this system still defines a woman's place in her home and in society, as well as the consequences when she is widowed (Lopata, 1996a). These women have no economic standing, no vote, and no voice.

The past several hundred years can best be described as a period of *transition* that was witness to many changes in how the role of wife and women was defined. As societies became more industrialized, families left their clans or extended relatives to move to the city. From an historical perspective, this pattern is relatively recent and still characterizes many communities in the contemporary Western world. In these societies, the power of patriarchal lineage is limited, but the wife is still dependent on her husband to support her and their children and for defining her legal status in society. A man's power to procreate and establish a family was expected and respected, although the man's wife did not have to sever ties with her own nuclear family when she married. Beginning in the eighteenth century, the idea of companionate marriage gained in popularity among middle- and upper-class families, and to some extent the trend to define the roles of husband and wife within this context has continued (Yalom, 2001). Most women at that time defined themselves as housewives and mothers, and those who had careers outside the home probably were very much the exception and often did not marry. Typically, a "working woman" still accepted the idea that her personal status in society would be determined not by her own attributes but rather by the characteristics of the man she married. Her true vocation was that of wife and mother, taking care of others in a male-dominated world. As a result, she learned early to make herself attractive so that a man would want to marry her. She was discouraged from developing a sense of herself as competent in any other role. If she did aspire to develop her intellectual abilities or pursue a career, she was criticized, not only by men but also often by other women. Men and women usually could choose their marriage partners, and most often reported that love was the basis for their choices. It was unacceptable for a man and woman to live together without the benefit of marriage; women who became pregnant out of wedlock often were forced to marry to legitimize the child's birth or were secreted away to bear the child and then surrender the child for adoption (Silverman, 1980).

We have to keep in mind that women had limited options for education and work outside the home. These options have expanded only within the last 100 years and in very slow increments. It was only at the turn of the twentieth century that women began to have access to higher education, were admitted to the professions, and were granted the right to vote. Giele (1993, 1998) wrote about changes in how the role of women was defined before and after World War II. During the war years, expectations of women changed as a result of their being needed in the work force; however, after the war, they returned to focusing their primary energies on child care and support of their husbands.

These socially constructed definitions of marriage and marital relationships were reflected in the law; for example, restrictions were placed on a woman's access to her own money and to her ability to testify in court. In the United States, as recently as the 1970s, a married woman could be denied credit in her own name, regardless of her credit rating prior to her marriage. In many states, her husband's authority took priority over her ability to act on her own behalf. She was still considered his property, fragile and in need of protection. If her husband battered her, she was blamed, and the courts rarely challenged her husband's authority. The law was on his side. Women defined themselves, and were defined by others, as being without power, without the intellectual competence of men, and with a position secondary to that of their husbands. Betty Friedan graphically described some of the consequences of these attitudes in her seminal book *The Feminine Mystic* (1964), which marked a turning point in the way in which women viewed themselves. In 1975, I experienced first hand this prevalent perception of a woman's place in society when I gave a talk in another state and my host sent my husband a letter thanking him for "letting me come."

Psychological theory of the time reflected a Western emphasis on independence and autonomy, qualities typically expected and rewarded in men and seen as indicators of their maturity. During the first 60 years of the twentieth century, most of the literature on the psychology of women supported a view of females as being appropriately passive and reliant on their mates for their sense of self and place in the world. Erikson (1950) portrayed girls as being exempt from the identity crisis of adolescent males who struggled to discover who they were in relation to society, because the men they ultimately married would shape the women's self-images. That women express concern for others and openly share their feelings was taken as an indicator of their inherent dependency. It was understood that "healthy" women would not set active goals in pursuit of their own identities, and those who displayed independence or autonomy often were labeled as "masculine" or "aggressive." Mental-health professionals deemed assertive behavior as pathological and inappropriate when displayed by women, in contrast to similar behavior in men being seen as positive indicators of their ability to function well in society (Broverman *et al.*, 1970).

When a married man died in a transitional society, his wife's new role of widow offered her little in terms of status or position in society. She felt empty. A woman who was widowed in 1969 described it this way:

> When I was married I was somebody. Now I am no one.

An older widow reminisced about what it was like when she was younger:

> When we saw a woman alone or with other women we would ask what was wrong with her. A woman would be ashamed to go out alone. It was as if, if you didn't have a man to take you places, there was something wrong with you.

We have now entered what Lopata described as the *modern period*, a time that coincides with the growth of the women's liberation movement. This movement was dedicated to achieving equity for women in most aspects of their lives and has brought about radical social and political changes over the past 30 years. Each decade has furthered women's quest for equity and opportunity as they have joined the work force, become better educated, and moved away from defining themselves primarily within the roles of mother and homemaker. Women began to reflect on the self-perceptions that had guided their behavior and to realize how much they were influenced by societal assumptions and expectations. Today, in modern societies, women can choose to define themselves as more than wife or mother, and marriage is an option rather than a given. Indeed, couples commonly cohabitate without benefit of marriage. Woman who remain single are no longer called "maiden ladies" or "old maids." The rate of divorce reflects the fact that fewer men and women are locked into unhappy or unfulfilling marriages. Both men and women are less constrained by societal expectations, and role assignments are not necessarily gender related. In many nuclear families, husbands and wives share work and often exchange responsibilities that once were gender specific (*e.g.,* caring for children). Realities, however, often reflect older values (Yalom, 2001). Even today, women earn less money than men for comparable work. Aspects of the transitional family still remain, and many women still feel they are defined by their marital status rather than by their strengths and capabilities. In certain communities within the United States, women are still expected to defer to their husbands — even with regard to making everyday choices — and the women accept this as appropriate.

Some of the most dramatic changes have occurred in the years since the original widow-to-widow project and are reflected in modifications of the role of wife. A widow in her early 60s reminisced about the ways in which her view of herself as a woman has changed:

> I was first married when I was very young. By the time you were a senior in college if you weren't engaged to be married there weren't a lot of opportunities for you at the time. It (my marriage) didn't last. I didn't want to get married again. I was in a committed relationship — more of a union, a partnership. We were two distinct individuals who wanted to share our lives. We came to it in a much more adult way.

These changes precipitated a wider examination of women's self-concepts and how their behavior was influenced by society's definition of "woman." Recent research on women's psychology has evaluated caring and other typically feminine characteristics in a new light. Scholars now question autonomy as a general developmental goal and no longer view more emotionally interconnected women as immature (Miller, 1987). Researchers agree that a woman's recognition of the importance of attachments contributes to her unique developmental trajectories. Miller (1987) suggested that a woman's sense of identity or sense of self is primarily organized around her ability to make and then to maintain affiliations and relationships. According to Miller, a woman's involvement with others is not an indication that she is less mature than a man but rather that she understands the importance of relationships and connections to others in her life (Miller and Striver, 1997; Gilligan, 1993; Belenky *et al.*, 1996). Such insights extend our understanding of the way people grieve, adding a new dimension to Bowlby's observations of the importance of attachment and connection and how grief is expressed and experienced (Silverman, 2000a).

Historically, the role of husband has had fewer restrictions. Men typically have enjoyed greater status in our society and thus have experienced greater freedom to act on their own behalf. For most of history, the model for men's behavior, as noted earlier, has focused on their independence and self-sufficiency. When pushed, a man might be expected to react violently; otherwise, masculinity throughout the years has been exemplified by the silent, self-contained type who displays little emotion (Silverman, 1996). It was long accepted that men should hold back their emotions when dealing with a loss. They more easily express anger, aggression, or even joy than sadness and pain. Our society still, to a great extent, maintains certain stereotypes about male vs. female behavior that both men and women continue to internalize, thus sustaining the "macho warrior" model (Thompson, 2001).

Pollack (2000) described a "mask of masculinity" that guides how males are raised. Boys are taught to hide their feelings, to limit the ways in which they share their lives with others, and to deny the importance of others in their worlds, reinforcing the societal values of independence and autonomy. Pollack (1998) observed that boys are still socialized to be competitive and aggressive with each other which spills over into their relationships with girls and, ultimately, wives.

Some of the changes occurring in the way men and women are socialized are reflected in the research that looks at differences in the way in which men and women emerge in egalitarian societies. In a study of the role of fathers who choose to participate equally in childcare activities, Ehrensaft (1995) concluded that men maintain a separateness between self and others that is distinct from women's behavior. Similarly, in research on Canadian families, McMahon (1995) reported that women working full time still thought of parenthood as requiring the woman to assume greater responsibility than the man, that the woman participated to a greater extent in domestic work and child care, and that the woman had a special awareness or focus on their children:

> Men could potentially learn to behave like involved parents, but they didn't feel or think like mothers. Indicative of their male partners' different consciousness, several women pointed out, was their ability to compartmentalize and segregate parts of themselves and their lives in ways women felt they did not, or could not, do. (McMahon, 1995, p. 251)

A widower reflecting on his role with his grown children supports McMahon's findings:

> I can't be there for my children like my wife was which is probably from my being a man. Your mother is your mother and when you lose your mother you really lose a lot — not that fathers are expendable, but we don't have the same kind of bond, language. For me it is like a double loss. I see my children and I know that if I died, my wife would be handling it differently.

In a dualistic, black-and-white world, men are strong and women are dependent. Such a dichotomy may exist in many cultures in the world and in some communities here in the United States, thus placing women at a great disadvantage with regard to their perceived inability to hold their own in the larger society. For example, without the protection of a man, the traditional Hispanic woman often feels stigmatized and uncomfortable in her new role of widow. In a multicultural modern world, we must make room for different perceptions of the marital relationship. Within the context of spousal death, it is important to focus on what the widow herself experiences as lost and what expectations and needs she has as she considers her changed world. For many women, their roles of wife and mother are still central to their sense of self. A young, stay-at-home mom described her life before her husband's death six months earlier:

> I took care of the children. I helped his mother who lived next door. I didn't need to work — that was his job. I loved my life. I didn't need for it to be different. Some of my friends thought I wasn't being liberated, but that's not how I saw it. We had a good life together; we were really partners.

While others might have considered this a traditional family, the widow, in fact, did not. In collaboration with her husband, she made an active choice. She was then forced to make new choices to accommodate her changed circumstances. The fact that she even had a choice is perhaps the critical difference between herself and women of an earlier generation.

We see this dynamic for men as well. Campbell and Silverman (1996) noted the many ways in which the death of a spouse permeates every aspect of a man's life; the man's grief is profound and intense. What do men experience as lost, and how do they identify the changes they need to make? A 60-year-old man, widowed for two years, described the evolution of his marriage:

> Our relationship went through many transitions. Some constants included equally shared household responsibilities and joint decision-making on important questions (child rearing, big expenditures, where we lived, travel, etc.). Still, we both were strong-willed, independent, and opinionated people who had serious conflicts in our marriage. We went through rough times but worked hard and emerged stronger, so that we could be true partners most particularly during the years she suffered from cancer.

Today, women are more likely to have been working and to have careers when they marry. The role of wife may be only one of many they fill. It is dangerous to generalize based on gender alone or, for that matter, on any other single aspect of a widowed person's life. In contemporary society, people become involved in committed relationships for many reasons. The focus now is not on status or position but on the value of a caring relationship. Being involved in relationships is essential to a person's sense of well-being, and these relationships become the defining force in the partners' lives. Thus, the way in which a marriage or partnership is constructed reflects the ways in which its participants were socialized, but a great variety exists in the way these relationships are constructed. Expectations of marriage, in part, depend on when the partners were born and how they were influenced by the changing times around them. The meaning of a relationship is influenced by the way in which roles are defined, by the expectations partners have of their relationship, and by how they live together — all factors that influence how husbands, wives, and partners will react to a death. This relationship is a dynamic changing phenomenon; becoming a widow will move it in yet another direction.

☐ Differences in Coping Styles

As noted previously, men traditionally seem more task oriented, independent, self-sufficient, and proud of their ability to show little emotion:

> I guess I've changed a lot. Before my wife died, I didn't have much to say. I would have this two-minute conversation with my daughter and then I would give the phone to my wife. I often wondered what they talked about.

Today, many men would characterize themselves as "quiet," "non-communicative," and "restrained." Tannen (1990) described the differences in how men and women identify and use language to explain problems. Men want to get to the essence of the issue and solve the problem expeditiously, while women prefer to explore options and talk over what they will do. Men are socialized to contain their feelings, to project control, and to endure their pain (Cook & Oltjenbruns, 1999). Cook (1988) noted that grieving fathers tend to focus more on physical activities, such as caring for the grave, or on activities that distract them from their feelings. Observers might worry that these widowers are not grieving, thus putting them in a "dad's double bind" (Cook, 1988). When men behave in ways that are not consistent with society's expectations, others may insist that they talk more or risk an emotional breakdown.

According to Cook, men use four strategies to handle upsetting feelings without disclosing them to others: (1) thinking about something else, (2) using reason and reflection, (3) taking action on an unrelated issue, and (4) expressing these feeling to themselves. This last strategy could involve a mental dialog between an internalized other who once comforted the mourner and the self who is struggling with his sadness. Such a dialog might even move him to tears. By taking some sort of action, even if it involves closing off others, these men gain a sense of control. In contrast, wives find talking and sharing feelings to be very reassuring and helpful. Women are more likely to receive emotional support for sharing their sadness and pain, while men frequently receive a mixed message about giving in to their feelings (Staudacher, 1989), due, in part, to differences in societal expectations that reinforce any reluctance men may have in sharing their experiences.

There are exceptions, of course. The widower quoted at the beginning of this chapter was overwhelmed by the support of his friends and could openly discuss his feelings and reactions with them, and, as noted earlier, many women have felt abandoned by friends who could not deal with their feelings over time. One way in which researchers have studied how gender affects the way in which men and women grieve is to compare the consequences of their grief.

☐ Differences in Outcome

As noted in Chapter 1, no consensus has been reached on the definition of a "good outcome" following spousal death. Part of the problem is that no one good outcome exists for all. A limitation on such bereavement research is that it is difficult to recruit people to participate, particularly men. As a result, much of the research on bereavement is based on women's reactions (Stroebe *et al.*, 1999); however, one study of older widows and widowers reported the same response rates for both men and women (Lund & Caserta, 2001). In the MGH/Harvard Child Bereavement Study, we found that men and women agreed to be involved in proportion to their numbers in the bereaved population (Silverman & Worden, 1993). The differences in response rates, therefore, could not account for any differences we found in the responses of widowers and widows. It is important to continue to look for factors that might contribute to differences that might otherwise be attributed to men's lack of representation in the research (Stroebe, 2001)

We have little consistent evidence to suggest that either men or women fare better after the death of a spouse. Stroebe and Stroebe (1987) reviewed findings identifying the emotional consequences of spousal death for the surviving partner and found that partner loss tends to be associated with higher rates of mental illness, serious physical illness, and physical disabilities for men than for women. The Institute of Medicine report on bereavement identified other negative consequences for men, such as higher death rates in older widowers and a higher likelihood of dying from suicide in the first months of bereavement (Osterweis *et al.*, 1984).

Individual variations in the ability to perform the basic tasks of daily living have been found to make a difference in adjustment to widowhood. When men and women have had no difficulty organizing changes in their daily lives, they follow similar patterns of accommodation (Lund & Caserta, 2001). This observation could explain why some researchers have found no differences in adjustment between men and women. In the child bereavement study (Silverman & Worden, 1993), similar observations were noted among the fathers who were able to take charge of the daily lives of their families.

Feinson (1986) reported no gender differences in older widowed people in measures of their emotional well-being. In a study of widowers, most felt sad, numb, in shock, and depressed (Brabant *et al.*, 1992). These men handled their pain alone by keeping busy, using prayer, and thinking a good deal about their wives, not by sharing these thoughts with others. They turned to new relationships (new partners) to serve as buffers against their sense of loss, consistent with Cook's (1988) findings on bereaved fathers' coping strategies.

Men and women report different incidences of depression following spousal death. Men have scored lower on grief inventories (representing less dysfunction), perhaps because they use repression, suppression, and denial more often than do women (Umberson *et al.*, 1996). In another study of depression that confirmed these findings, men tended to report fewer symptoms and less affective distress than did women (Klerman & Weissman, 1986).

Men also report becoming depressed in relation to the more instrumental aspects of their lives, such as managing the household (Umberson *et al.*, 1996). Worden and Silverman (1993) found that widowers who cared for dependent children had higher rates of what appeared to be clinical depression than did widows in similar situations, perhaps because the men needed to reorganize their lives around caring for their children and may have felt incapable of assuming the single parent role. Children who lost fathers seemed better adjusted at two years after the death than those who lost mothers (Boerner & Silverman, 2002). Apparently, these mothers already knew how to care for their families; this responsibility by itself did not add additional stress. In the words of one mother: "I went on doing what I always did."

Widows who experience financial strain are more likely to be depressed than their grieving colleagues (Umberson *et al.*, 1996). Women have also reported the loss of a significant relationship as a contributing factor to their depression (Scarf, 1980):

Important figures leaving or dying; the inability to establish other meaningful bonds with a peer-partner; being forced by a natural transition in life to relinquish an important love tie; a marriage that is ruptured ... are among the commonest causes of female depression. (Scarf, 1980, p. 95)

Lund (2001) reminds us that as we look for differences in the ways husbands and wives react to spousal death, we should remember that men and women may be more alike than not. We know that in many ways all widowed people share common experiences. Martin and Doka (2000) observed that there are no exclusively male or female ways of responding to death. We have to keep in mind that, in the long run, we are not dealing with a competition but with respect for differences, while acknowledging similarities as well. Apparently, with regard to the differences noted between men and women, these may not involve the way in which they *experience* their grief but rather how they *respond* to it.

☐ How Do These Factors Influence Change?

The differences in the way men and women are socialized will affect the ways in which they define their roles as husbands, wives, and partners. In turn, these definitions and the resulting sense of identity will influence how they express their grief and construct a new sense of self as widows or widowers. The widowed talk of change and growth, not unlike adolescents who describe themselves as feeling more grown up. A widowed person may not put it exactly this way but may report such differences in him- or herself after the death of a spouse. In the words of an older widow from Great Britain:

If I could have my husband back, I'd go back in a minute. But I like the way I have changed. Here I am running a national organization for the widowed. I'm lobbying before Parliament and in many ways he wouldn't recognize me. It was like I found a new part of me, but I didn't have a choice.

Out of necessity, both men and women begin to see others with new understanding and respect and begin to interact in more complex ways. In fact, it may be that widows and widowers take on new roles that bring their thoughts, feelings, and behavior into closer alignment. Widowers become more communicative and tender, while widows become more confident and assertive. Widows often develop a new sense of self that they proudly describe as more independent and self-reliant:

> Making important decisions for myself was a new concept to me. I now voice my own opinions and I am sometimes surprised that I am doing this, right or wrong.

Widows often feel empowered to act on their own behalf. Coping with bereavement enables them to develop a greater sense of competence and to act in ways they could not have considered before:

> Yes, I experienced a growth that would not have been possible before if I had continued to be a "submissive" partner. In fact, I would not have stepped out. This does not mean that I felt liberated in losing a partner but this is what happened as a result.

In contrast, widowers begin to value relationships more deeply (Silverman, 1987a,b). Men talk about developing their social skills, becoming less anxious in large social situations, trying to understand other people's problems, and becoming more tolerant. A widower in his late 40s (a lawyer and an estate planner) is a good example of such a change:

> I usually meet people shortly after the death [of a loved one]. Before my wife died, I would offer my condolences and quickly move on to business. Now I find myself listening, asking questions, and sharing. I'm making a very different connection.

An older widower elaborated on this:

> I seemed to be more sensitive and caring. My values have changed. I pay more attention to other people's needs. It wasn't that I was selfish before — it's just different. I am determined to live my years in a mood of kindness to others. If I find the right person I will marry again.

Remarrying and developing new relationships are realistic options for most men:

> Just a guy looking for a wife and not being a dreamer. I am looking for someone in my generation with similar interests and reasonably good health.

While both men and women express a new kind of wisdom about life, their direction of change often appears to be somewhat different. Widows do not suddenly detach themselves from their important relationships nor do widowers become less independent. They seem to move in ways that bring their point of view closer to that of the other. Both men and women change as a result of their widowhood and begin to express and respect themselves as well as their need for others in a different way. This in part is what is meant when change is understood as a developmental process in which the widowed begin to see themselves capable of relating to others and responding in a more complex manner with a greater variety of reactions. Not only are they able to see themselves with new dimensions, but they can also see beyond their own point of view. As their perspective expands they find new ways of appreciating others and seeing their point of view as well. Consequently, they move toward each other, becoming in some ways more complete, as described by a 55-year-old widow:

> There was the slow realization that I am really independent and that while I love and am loved by many people, no one really cares what I do on any given day. They have confidence in me — I do in myself and slowly I am trying to shed fear, guilt, and over-concern about what other people think. I am working on many facets of what I hope will be changes in lifestyle and personal growth.

How can we characterize this process of change? One way is to describe mourning as a time of transition.

CHAPTER

Grief As a Time of Loss and Change: The Nature of Transition

There is a rhythm to it. My wife's anniversary was in November. And there are times when it just hurts a lot and then there are times when I can focus on my future. And it is easier to do that. I don't know … it like cycles. It is not a direct line. I had heard too that people say the second year is tougher and I say "My God! I have to deal with even more pain." And then I realized what they were talking about 'cause I am in it. And it is different, 'cause you are not numb. And so some of the things are painful but there is also an ability to embrace new things in your life.

60-year-old widower, 18 months after his wife died

It is difficult to describe the dynamic, interactive process that is set in motion after a partner dies. It is not easy to understand that one minute there is life and then there is none. Dissonance exists between the reality of the loss and the feeling that this person cannot really be gone. How can we accept that life will go on in the face of this death? It is impossible to take away the pain of grief, and nobody can travel a straight line between grief and accommodation to the loss. Creating a new reality is not the result of one action or one activity; it occurs a bit at a time as the bereaved

59

deals with the many challenges facing him or her. Life without one's partner takes time to get used to, according to Adele Cooperband, who started
work as a widow aide in 1966. She said that in many ways bereavement
never ends; rather, it is a process of adaptation that a widow may need to
renegotiate for many years to come. In this sense, mourning is similar to
life. We are constantly in motion from birth to death, whether or not we
are grieving the loss of a loved one. In fact, people who work hard to
stand still and avoid change find that remaining static is impossible.

Several authors, such as Shuchter (1986) and Worden (2001), have identified tasks that reflect the issues with which the bereaved must cope; however, Attig (1996) has questioned whether the term "task" is really
appropriate. He noted that a task is circumscribed and modest in scale and
can be completed. The tasks of the bereaved are not easily circumscribed,
and they are not something that they can finish in any sort of orderly fashion. The widowed, indeed, must attend to myriad issues, such as recognizing their pain, dealing with multiple changes in their lives, and developing
effective coping strategies; however, we must consider the fact that the
widowed return again and again to certain aspects of their experience,
bringing a slightly different perspective each time. Identifying mourning
as a period of transition is one way to map the changing experience of the
bereaved and gives direction to their grief over time (Bowlby, 1961; Silverman, 1966). Looking at bereavement as a period of transition and, as noted
earlier, as an expected life-cycle transition provides a framework that
reflects, for example, the widow's struggle with her grief as she looks for
ways to live with the consequences of her loss both in the present and into
the future (Silverman, 1982b).

☐ Mourning As a Time of Transition

Bowlby (1961) used the concept of *transition* to explain how children
respond when they are separated from their parents, and Tyhurst (1958)
used the term *transition* to describe a person's reaction following a natural disaster. Both men observed that people do not remain in a steady or
static state following parental separation or natural disasters but instead
engage in a process that involves various responses as the situation
changes. Both Bowlby and Tyhurst use the concept of transition to cap-
ture the sense that people move from one place to another over time and
ultimately are changed or even transformed by their experiences. Over
the course of a lifetime, we anticipate making many transitions, such as
growing from childhood into adolescence and young adulthood, entering
school, getting married, or having a child. All of these transitions require

a change of roles and a new way of looking at the world and our place in it. Widowhood is another major transition that is experienced by all married couples or committed couples, because one of them usually dies first.

I defined (Silverman, 1966) three important components of the transition process (*e.g.*, from wife to widow): (1) a disequilibrating event or series of events that initiates the transition, (2) a loss of direction and meaning that involves a role shift, and (3) a series of changes over time in many dimensions of the widow's lived experience. The experience of widowers appears to be quite similar.

☐ Spousal Death As a Disequilibrating Event

A widow's transition begins with the death of her husband or partner. If a wife anticipates her spouse's death, she may experience a foreshadowing of her life to come. Nonetheless, no one can really deal with death until it happens, so a quality of the unexpected is present even with a probable death:

> For 10 months he was on life support. We knew he wouldn't make it. Yet, when he died I felt like something hit me. I went numb and I suddenly was in a whole different place.

Almost every death of a spouse has a disequilibrating impact that leaves the widowed confused and uncertain as to how to proceed. The point was made earlier that, as we experience life's major challenges, we seek to make sense of them, to find patterns that integrate these experiences into a meaningful whole, and that this process of making meaning is affected not only by an individual's unique constitution and development but also by societal values and expectations. People in mourning often find that their ways of mapping or coding the world are challenged or insufficient for the situation (White & Epson, 1990; Neimeyer, 1998, 2001). Stress is typically and unavoidably part of this experience (Holmes & Rahe, 1967).

Some deaths may be more traumatic than others. These include sudden and/or unexpected deaths; those that are caused by war, violence, or disasters; those that result in mutilation; and those that are self-inflicted. Altschul (1988) quoted Freud as saying that trauma is any experience that calls up distressing responses such as fright, anxiety, shame, or physical pain and which challenges the resources of the victim's ego. Van der Kolk *et al.* (1996) defined a traumatic event as one that disrupts and creates great stress in the individual so that his or her resources are inadequate to develop an effective response. By both these definitions, virtually every death, expected or unexpected, can be traumatic as survivors experience disruption and stress they have not previously known (Rubin *et al.*, 2003).

In closed societies, a system of defined rules, customs, and rituals governs all behavior, including mourning. As we have seen, these rules particularly apply to the role of women in these societies. Women in such societies have a somewhat easier time learning to cope with spousal death because cultural traditions direct the process of change in a socially acceptable closed framework. The widow has fewer options for how she may properly react to her loss, and individual variations may not be readily tolerated (Lopata, 1996b); however, mourners typically do not experience the same kind of disruption as they might in a more open society. In more open systems, most commonly found in contemporary Western culture, well-developed ideologies on how to understand and react to death are no longer as prevalent and consequently offer less guidance to mourners. As a result, widows may encounter a vacuum when they try to find ways to give meaning to the death. Parkes (1993) referred to this vacuum as the "loss of the assumptive world." The differences between the worlds of men and women may affect how they experience this disruption. It is not that the assumptive worlds of men have not been challenged; as noted earlier, they may simply be expressed differently and have a somewhat different meaning for them.

Antonovsky (1979) identified four universal stressors: war, murder, hunger, and death. In their non-bereavement-related studies of stress and coping, Lazarus and Folkman (1984) claimed that an event becomes stressful when those experiencing it do not know how to define what is happening or what to do about it, and/or they feel that their well-being is in danger. In related research, Antonovsky (1979) observed that what one person finds overwhelming may be transient and fleeting for another. If individuals do not feel threatened, have adequate resources to address the event, and employ appropriate coping strategies, they will not be overly stressed.

Applying the concept of stress to bereavement, we see that almost any death, expected or not, is stressful and potentially traumatic, even more so in a society where death is not accepted as a normal part of the life cycle. Few mourners can quickly put their lives back together in tidy packages (Silverman, 1985b; Altschul, 1988; Stroebe *et al.*, 1996). A society with an unrealistic understanding of the course of grief often isolates and stigmatizes the mourner because of its own fear of mortality and denial of the survivor's pain (Silverman, 1969b, 1993). All of this intensifies the widow's sense of disorganization and loss of meaning. Stress in this context is a dynamic, changing phenomenon that is part of the experience of losing a spouse or partner. The challenge is not to avoid the inevitable stress that results from a death but rather to recognize it as being appropriate and to learn ways to moderate or ease the pain.

☐ My Place in the World Is Lost

The changes precipitated by the death of a spouse occur in many domains: the physical world in which the deceased is no longer present, the life that the widow now leads in the absence of her husband, and the ways in which the widow remains or becomes connected to (or disconnected from) others. The relational aspects of her grief become clear: A spouse dies, and with that death the widow loses not only her husband but also her relationship to him as well as their shared lives as partners. A woman with a 15-year commitment to the same man described her reaction to his death:

> It's not just the loss of a person. It is the loss of a whole life. You lost a relationship and you lost your life.

In this context, the widow has no option but to recognize the necessity for change. The concept of roles helps us understand what is involved when a widow must make the transition from being "married" to being "widowed" and, in some ways, to being "single" again.

Most cultures offer consistent definitions of the roles of husband and wife and how these roles frame each partner's sense of identity. As noted in the previous chapter, these are usually gender specific. Ideology is transmitted in part by the larger culture's language and traditions. The individual's sense of self and his or her repertoire of responses are embedded in the values and attitudes present in the larger society and the degree to which the individual has internalized these values and attitudes.

How is a role defined? Lopata (1994) described a role as being a set of socially prescribed patterns of behavior involving others in a set of interdependent relationships. Lopata theorized that roles exist between a social person and a social circle; a particular circle describes a specific role and includes everyone with whom the social person interacts and by whom he or she is influenced. This relational process defines the rights, privileges, duties, and obligations of the members of the circle to each other. The individual as a whole is not involved in every social role, and each role has its own circle. One circle or many can exist within the context of a marriage. For example, as Lopata explained it, in the role of wife a woman relates to her husband, their children, other members of their respective families of origin, and even neighbors and friends. As a mother, she relates to her children as their moral, intellectual, and emotional guide and to her husband as his partner in child rearing. Her various roles interact, so that the roles of mother and wife are interrelated and synergistic. In fact, none of our roles exists in isolation; all can be seen as interdependent and mutually influential.

With significant changes in the way the roles of women and, to a lesser extent, men are being defined, the ways in which the roles of wife and husband, widow and widower are commonly understood are also changing considerably. In contemporary society, the role of widow should be temporary (Lopata, 1996a). The widowed person needs to give up the part of his or her former identity that is related to the role of husband or wife or to that person's abstract self-image as a particular type of person, an image that transcends any role and situational context (Lopata, 1996a). In accepting the role of widow or widower, the widowed may lose aspects of the ways in which they see themselves as women, men, partners, or friends. Letting go of such familiar and important roles is not easy, and most people do not eagerly anticipate assuming a new role of widow or widower. As a result, the process of redefinition is quite challenging:

> It was awful when I went to sign my kids up for school and there was no place to say their father was dead. And that I was a widow. It was as if the world had no place for me. I am not married, then what am I? I had to create a category on the form, and I barely was able to finish, I was crying so hard.

When a spouse dies, he or she leaves gaping holes in the circles that once defined the surviving spouse's roles and relationships with others. This space may look different for men and for women. We need to consider how the structure of these circles is altered to define new roles for the widowed. Others in these circles may also experience role shifts, so the overall relational disruption can be quite profound. Still others may need to be added to the social circles. Johnson *et al.* (1986) found that the death of a spouse in a long-lasting marriage creates a great deal of dislocation in the survivors' social relationships — their "social anchorage" — and influences their self-concepts. Talking to the widowed reveals that they rarely are able to reconstitute their lives as they were before.

In contemporary society, roles shift as people move from one social circle to another. While we might anticipate that the disruption caused by the loss of a spouse would be less profound for a person who holds many roles, this may not be the case, especially for women:

> I am a full professor in my department. I always had an active life outside of my family. When my husband died, it took me two years

to get into any meaningful work again. It was as if, in some way, I didn't know who I was.

Compartmentalization clearly was not working for this widow; however, for some men and women work can be a distraction and the ability to compartmentalize is a comfort:

> I got my job after my husband died. People at work didn't know him. It was nice not to have to talk about the death and just be myself, not a widow.

☐ Redefining the Self

A person's role is intimately entwined with that person's identity or sense of self. A social role is the public definition of a person's place in society and the work associated with this position. In contrast, identity is a reflection of the person's inner sense of self, of who he or she is, and how that person internalizes a given role; therefore, the loss of a role is often accompanied by the loss of a sense of self and identity that were part of this role. While "self" can be defined in various ways, Basch (1983) described it as the uniqueness that separates the experiences of an individual from those of all others. At the same time, the notion of self confers a sense of cohesion and continuity to the disparate events experienced throughout one's life. Our sense of self allows us to process and connect experiences, to direct behavior, and to know who we are and what we are doing, but we do not accomplish this by ourselves. The self is formed in relation to others. Mead (1930) claimed that we can only know ourselves as we know others and as others know us. Youniss and Smollar (1985), drawing on the work of Sullivan (1965) and Piaget (1954), emphasized this point by reporting that the study of development becomes a study of the self in interpersonal relations with others, rather than a study of the self-contained person.

Clinchy (1996) theorized that the self is not a finished product carted about from one relationship to the next; rather, our sense of self changes as we differentiate ourselves from others and include new people in our lives. In this way, the self is constantly being constructed and reconstructed within the context of important relationships. This notion applies to the emotional and cognitive place of the mourner (Kegan, 1982; Silverman, 2000a). A death can lead to a shift in how the bereaved makes sense of the world — moving from an egocentric understanding in which the world revolves around that person toward a perspective of greater mutuality.

This model describes an increasingly complex and coherent way to understand relationships between self and other, a model that depends not on chronological age but on interpersonal dynamics. When considering how the widowed cope with the stress associated with the loss and their need to find new ways to make order in their lives, looking at the process of change developmentally provides an additional direction to this activity. An egocentric view of the world constrains the meaning-making ability of the widowed. When dealing with their sense of displacement, the widowed can gain new perspectives by looking at the larger picture. Seeing themselves in new ways in new relationships puts the meaning-making process in a much larger frame, thus expanding the range of coping options.

When a spouse dies, the significant other in this definition of self is no a longer part of the physical world. The continuing presence of the deceased is not anchored in concrete reality but rather is something that the bereaved carry within themselves. This continuing bond to the deceased is one contributor to the widow's evolving sense of self. The death of a spouse can upset a widow's certainty in who she is as a wife, woman, mother, or breadwinner. For the moment, her identity can be seen as "spoiled" (Goffman, 1963; Silverman, 1981; Thompson, 2001). A year after her husband died, a 40-year-old single mother said:

> I am John's mother but I feel like I don't know who I am anymore now that Jim is dead. If I am not his wife, then who am I?

This widow continues to know herself as a mother, but she has lost the self she knew within the context of her relationship with her husband. She has not yet constructed a new sense of self, and only with time will she fully realize all that she has lost and the many tasks that await her in developing a new sense of self. A 48-year-old widow concurred:

> I'm not sure who I've become. I was the wife and then the caretaker. These were defined roles. But who am I now and for what purpose?

A 60-year-old widower described the death of his old self:

> To me there is a death of the self — that's what you have to come to terms with. There is a part of me that says the old self is dead because part of the old self was the relationship with my wife. So for me part of what I have to do is to let go of the old self and not feel that I am not still connected to my wife but it's not in the old way. I've learned that change is inevitable.

□ Change Over Time

The time after a spousal death has been described in many ways. Kubler-Ross (1969) wrote of stages of dying that, in many ways, have been inappropriately applied to the bereaved. Other writers have divided this period of time in various ways. Common to all is the sense that individuals usually move from a state of unreality to some kind of recovery and have varying needs at these different points in time. It is important to recognize that over time movement occurs; however, it is not linear and readily charted in an easily recognized sequence, where one step follows another. In addition, the use of the word *recovery* is inappropriate. Instead, the widowed make an accommodation that involves a shift in roles, the development of a new sense of self, and finding new ways of living in the world as it currently exists. In some ways, to accomplish this, the widow must take a developmental leap that reflects the changes she needs to make with regard to how she relates to herself and to those around her. Over time, the widowed will continually negotiate and renogitiate these changing circumstances. The concept of "recovery," then, is too static.

The three periods of transition during the grieving process that were defined at the beginning of this chapter (Silverman, 1966) are broad and are not meant to be interpreted as concrete stages that the widowed march through in a prescribed sequence. Thinking of grief as a time of transition diminishes the sense that there is a correct way to grieve. The widowed can move in and out of these time frames or even experience them simultaneously. For example, widows and widowers often describe spiraling between feeling numb (often characteristic of their feelings shortly after the death) and feeling sad and anxious (more typical of later reactions). Over time, however, most widowed people gain a sense of forward movement; nevertheless, it is counterproductive to ask whether or not the bereaved is at the right place at the right time in the transition. Although the widowed have their own highly individualized timetables that reflect what they are experiencing at any given time and which must be respected by others, we can still identify some common experiences.

□ Reality vs. Disbelief: "It Didn't Really Happen, Did It?"

The widowed usually report feeling numb when learning of the death of a spouse. They experience a sense of unreality and disbelief and react in a detached, robot-like way. An older widow recalls:

> In the first couple of months I felt like I was somehow in a fog. I was doing only the necessary things, going through the motions. I wasn't eating right.

The intensity and duration of this numbness can vary depending on the circumstances of the death. When death follows a long illness, the widow is likely to feel exhausted and near collapse from caring for her husband and watching him die. She may experience a great sense of relief, and her shock may not be as profound as for a widow whose husband dies suddenly:

> I came home from the hospital. The children sensed that it was over and my son started crying. For three weeks we had known that he could not live. The children and I lay down, and for the first time since we knew we slept through the night.

When the death is sudden and totally unexpected, it is more likely that the widowed will experience pervasive shock and numbness. One widower made the observation:

> I saw it in the group. When there is no chance to talk about it, to say goodbye, there is a different flavor. When you go through something like this (long illness) and see the suffering and so on there is an element of relief.

Few widowers experience the sudden deaths of their wives; statistics indicate that women are not as likely as men to die suddenly. A death that occurs unexpectedly allows no time to say goodbye, to contemplate being alone, or to make even the most rudimentary and tentative of plans, and disbelief is very strong. In the words of a 35-year-old widow not long after her husband died:

> I wasn't there when he died. I kept thinking he was on vacation. If I could have been there, I think it would have helped make it more real. I'm glad I got to see his body at the funeral. Other widows have told me that they couldn't believe it for months and that even a year later they would forget and think of their husbands as alive. They reminded me that it wasn't always because he died suddenly. It is just hard to believe in general.

Many have no idea how to arrange a funeral or choose the type of observance:

> I didn't know what to do. When we went to bed he was fine and here we were in the emergency room and he was dead. I didn't even know how to get him from the hospital to a funeral home. I remembered

that my cousin was a widow and I called her. Fortunately she came right over and took charge. She made a few calls and things started to happen.

The widow's new legal status has no social or emotional meaning to her. Old role definitions and relationships still guide and frame her behavior. The newly widowed automatically think, feel, and act as part of a couple. They know how wives behave and what is expected, and they act reflexively. Being numb or in denial can be adaptive. Such defenses allow the widow to integrate her loss a little at a time until she is ready to understand its many implications. Numbing also allows her to plan her husband's funeral without being overwhelmed by the full meaning of her loss:

> You have to be out of it a bit. How else could you go through the motions of selecting burial clothes and even choosing a coffin? If I hadn't been I could never have stood the pain of the fact that this was for my husband.

Denial might also enable a widow to avert a state of collapse and make difficult decisions that she could not have handled otherwise:

> He didn't want a big wake with an open coffin. His mother was very upset but I insisted on honoring his wishes. I didn't think I had the strength to argue. I never stood up to anyone like that before. It was almost as if I were suddenly a different person — a part of me was somehow closed off. But I had to do what he wanted. I was his wife. I owed it to him.

A widower talked of his sense of disbelief and relief after his wife of 22 years died following a long illness:

> It is partly disbelief, partly where is she? You sort of turn and say, "Well, that's where she used to be." A feeling like she is going to reappear at some point. Knowing in advance didn't matter in a sense.

Although numbness and disbelief may temporarily protect a widow from her most acute anguish, these defenses do not necessarily blind her to surrounding people and events. While organizing her husband's funeral after his long illness, a 63-year-old widow realized that others were worried that she may break down and behave irrationally:

> The doctor kept insisting that I take a tranquilizer. He said that my family was afraid I'd break down at the funeral. It would have been numbing the already numb. I was so angry I almost did become irrational at that point. Now I realize that it wasn't really me they were

worried about — they just didn't know how they were going to deal with me, if I really did let go.

This period of time has no predetermined length nor is it totally devoid of feelings. Emotions come and go; however, because the widowed have many concrete chores, such as planning the funeral, caring for children, arranging financial affairs, or applying for Social Security, they remain connected with others. Numbing gives them some respite from the intensity of their reactions until they are better prepared to face them. Supporters and extended family may be deceived by the widow's outward reactions and outsiders may think that the widow is holding up very well. These friends and family members are unaware, as the widowed may be, that this is but the first step in a long and painful process.

☐ Uncertainty: What Will Happen Next?

Bewilderment may follow the growing recognition of the reality of the loss. The numbness is no longer so pervasive as the widow begins to recognize the fullness of her feelings of despair, loneliness, and pain — feelings that she may have had all along but kept at a distance. The widow may also begin to feel frustration, fright, despair, hollowness, tension, and even anger as she recognizes that her life is forever changed:

> We'd built a good life together. Then it was taken away. I felt so cheated. I kept saying, "Why us?" as if anyone had a good answer.

It is not unusual for a widow to react as if a part of herself has been amputated:

> I just feel as if half of me has been taken away and I am just half.

Widows may experience a loss of appetite or sleeplessness; conversely, they may want to eat or sleep all the time. They may find themselves impatient and restless, not wanting to be with people but also not wanting to be alone. They may feel misunderstood because friends and relatives appear impatient and uncomfortable with their continuing grief.

Some widowed people conclude that by keeping busy they can keep their reactions at bay and avoid thinking about either the past or the future. Others exert increased control over their emotions to feel less overwhelmed. A 70-year-old widow described this process:

> It has been eight months now. I am finally beginning to feel the veil is lifting. I am not crying so much and I can talk on the phone without getting all "teary eyed" — that is, most of the time.

Stroebe and Schut (1999) observed that widows vacillate between moving away and toward their grief. Moving away (restoration-oriented behavior) allows the widow to focus on mastering the tasks that are necessary to reorganize her life and develop new identities, providing her with some relief from the intensity of her emotional reactions. Moving toward grief (loss-oriented behavior) involves the widow dealing with the emotional aspects of the death. The widowed, however, do not necessarily achieve closure within one orientation before moving on to the other, but rather continue to move back and forth between the two, perhaps forever.

Widows and widowers do not stand still in their mourning. At some points in time, the reality of the loss may be grasped very well; at other times, the loss may seem incomprehensible and overwhelming. The widow quoted in the following passage occasionally still imagined that her husband was away and would return soon:

> I used to hear his car pull in the driveway. I still do sometimes. I used to look at the drivers of cars that were like his, trying to see if my husband was behind the wheel. I'd go to the mall and look at all the faces going by, looking for him. Every time I went to church I would feel an incredible sadness, for a long, long time. I would picture his casket in the aisle. My list is endless.

Bowlby (1980) referred to this behavior as "searching," but it is far more involved than that. It is also the beginning of finding a new way to relate to the deceased and to connect him or her to the current life of the bereaved.

The widowed generally are ill prepared to deal with their difficult reactions and must come to realize that there is no easy way around their misery. If a widow recognizes that her suffering is normal and inevitable, she may find it easier to endure. A 55-year-old widow talked about her life a year after her husband's death:

> I was so proud of myself. I thought I was doing so well. I thought that I had everything under control. I was starting to look for a job. And all of a sudden the bottom fell out. I started to cry when my neighbor called, "Good morning" to me. I began yelling at my daughter on the phone when she called. No one had warned me I might feel this way. I called the doctor and he offered me a tranquilizer. Then I spoke to another widow. She was great. She said it was normal. Once I appreciated that I was bound to have bad days and even bad weeks, that I wasn't simply going to put the past behind me, I didn't need the tranquilizers any more.

Stress results from the vacuum that exists when new rules and habits have not yet replaced the old. At this point, the widowed know that they cannot go back but are still not ready to go forward. And, as a widow recognizes that she can no long live by former patterns, she develops a crisis in meaning as the reality of her new situation begins to break through:

> My husband had been dead for six months. I was job hunting. The first time I had to check "widow" on a form I had to hold my hand because it started to shake. Until then I had avoided saying that word or even thinking of myself as a widow.

In the words of a 65-year-old widower:

> The world seemed safer to me when my wife was alive.

At this point, when the widowed most need reassurance and support, they may find themselves more and more alone. A 30-year-old widow explained:

> For a while my life was so crowded that I needed a traffic cop. Suddenly I was all alone. I guess I had become the fifth wheel people talk about.

Even when a widow has not yet developed a new identity, she begins to see the direction in which she must go and starts constructing a self-image as a formerly married, currently single person who needs new friends, relationships, and ways of engaging in the world:

> I had never thought of myself doing any of those things — balancing my checkbook, buying a house, negotiating a loan.... I realized that I had to accept a new image of myself. My world was different now, and no matter how much I may have wished that I could go backwards it was not going to happen that way.

☐ Reconstruction: Building a New Life

Marris (1974) noted that every change entails losses, including the need to give up former, now inapplicable roles. He observed people's reluctance to relinquish the familiar and labeled this wish for constancy as the "conservative impulse." The widowed accommodate change by integrating some aspect of the past into a new role or changed situation. This integration resembles the cognitive process identified by Piaget

(1954). Children who attempt to apply formerly workable strategies to new situations learn that they cannot assimilate certain aspects of the past into the present because they are no longer applicable. Eventually, children accommodate by developing a new schema for dealing with the new situation. Within this new schema are remnants of prior schemas. This, in part, is how development continues and learning takes place. When the widowed develop new schemas, they find room for their evolving relationships with the deceased (Silverman & Klass, 1996). When responding to a death, the widowed should not be expected to give up the past but instead should find ways to incorporate aspects of the past into the present and future. This process will look different for every widow and widower — no one way exists to find a new role and place in the world — nor can the widowed recognize a specific point at which they begin accommodating their loss. They have been constructing a new understanding of the death from the moment it happened and are constantly developing new perspectives on their feelings and experiences, learning how to integrate the loss by living differently in the world.

For example, when a widow remembers her husband and recalls their shared history, she may cry and accept her reactions without becoming frightened, uncomfortable, or ashamed. She can accept her pain as natural and appropriate, even when provoked by the happiest of occasions:

> When my daughter received her cap in nursing, it was very exciting for me. There was the pride I felt watching her walk up on the stage, but there was also the shattering sense of loss I experienced not having her father there. He idolized her and he was not there to share her day, and he doesn't know the fine young man who is her husband.

As a widow develops a different perspective on her loss, her feelings usually become less intense, less constant:

> I very often give the impression that I have it all together, but I really don't. It is a constant struggle and the only way I get by is one day at a time. In the final analysis, I still have trouble believing that he is gone, but I know that I can't change what happened. Life is either lived, half lived, or shelved. I either have to stagnate or go on. It's my choice. We all have the potential and ability to change. It's my decision. We can win or lose depending on our attitude. To lose means to end up totally alone. To have a "win" attitude means that all sorts of avenues can open up and there will be green lights all the way.

This 66-year-old woman learned that she can laugh and that she has things worth living for, that she can enjoy people and look forward to each day.

Repopulating their lives with new friends and becoming involved in work are other ways the widowed forge new identities and roles. As reported by a widower whose wife had received hospice care:

> I decided to become a hospice volunteer. It is my way of giving something back. They were wonderful when my wife was sick and it gives me a sense of doing something important for others besides going to work. I would never have dreamed of doing anything like this before.

Old habits of daily living fade away while new, more appropriate patterns emerge:

> My job was routine and boring. I knew I needed a job where I was needed and where someone was counting on me. I had worked with my husband as an editor, but never for money. I thought maybe I could do that again. I decided that a university might be a place for a mature woman. I was right. I work for a group of people who are friendly and supportive and who need me.

Transition involves a continual negotiation with self, others, and the wider society to integrate the many changes accompanying spousal death. In effect, people learn how to cope with periods of transition, welcome or not, often out of sheer necessity. If these learning opportunities are to be effective, they must help the bereaved reflect on their feelings and behavior and provide new information to expand the repertoire of coping strategies available to them that can enhance their accommodation. When this is the case, over time most people are able to face these new challenges successfully. A setting that seems to provide the most meaningful learning opportunities is when the help of another widowed person is available.

Help in a Mutual-Help Context

I joined the group in March. I get the sense that other people have the same feelings as I ... just knowing that there are other people out there like me made me feel less alone.

49-year-old widow, six months after her husband's death

We cannot prevent the pain of widowhood. We cannot protect the widowed from the disruption that the death causes in their lives. We know that their lives will not look the same as they might have if the death had not occurred, but we can help the widowed cope with their pain and with the many changes that accompany the death of their spouse or partner.

☐ The Nature of Help

The two complementary objectives in helping the widowed are (1) to strengthen their pre-existing abilities to cope with new situations and to provide the needed information and resources, and (2) to help them develop new approaches to problem solving by teaching them new skills and bolstering their sense of empowerment. In either case, help involves creating opportunities for the widowed to learn new ways to meet their needs, thus enhancing their sense of competence. Settings that facilitate learning usually legitimize the widowed person's experience and respect his or her energy, imagination, and strength which serve as the foundation for further development. By making increased competence a goal, a challenge then becomes not what happens to someone but rather what actions the person takes in response.

Competence has been defined as the "quality or state of being or having sufficient knowledge, judgment, skill, or strength (for a particular action)" (*Webster's*, 1968, p. 463). Competence equates with exerting greater personal control over any difficulty that might be encountered, coping effectively with it, and developing and/or demonstrating higher self-esteem as a result. The concept of "experienced competence" emphasizes the importance of the bereaved relying upon their own experience during their adjustment (Allen & Hayslip, 2001; Hayslip *et al.*, 2001). Observing a similar quality that he referred to as a "sense of coherence" in people coping successfully with difficult situations, Antonovsky (1979, 1987) described their openness, flexibility, and capacity to seek new skills and information. All three of these characteristics enhance a person's coping skills, sense of competence, and ability to redefine a situation, thereby mitigating stress. To a large extent, such people are not defined by their widowhood (or other tragedy); rather, they define it and give it meaning.

A sense of competence and coherence is influenced by individual development. When we look at the process of change through the lens of development, we can identify ways in which the widowed need to adapt. This perspective also provides a language for describing these changes and the level of maturation that may be involved. In one study (Folkman, 2001), for example, people who were able to step back and reframe a problem in more positive terms developed a greater sense of control and ability to respond effectively by generating many new coping skills. Such a model allows us to see loss as an impetus for developmental growth (Kegan, 1982; Silverman, 2000a). In the face of disruptions precipitated by death, the widowed are challenged to shift the way in which they make sense of their world. When they approach an event from an egocentric standpoint, they have limited options in how to interpret it. The widowed may need to learn, or relearn, how to "take subject as object" — that is, to step back, reflect on themselves and the situation, see the possibilities, and assume a perspective of greater mutuality (Kegan, 1982). This model describes an increasingly complex and coherent way to understand relationships between the self and others, a model that depends not on chronological age but on interpersonal dynamics. By seeing themselves as capable of responding to and relating to others in different ways, the widowed are able to understand and react to the death in a broader context.

Coping cannot be separated from the bereavement process. Including coping in our understanding of grief expands our perspective as we examine what the bereaved do about their situation. Effective coping strategies acknowledge and develop an understanding of the nature of the stressor and help identify choices about how to react. Coping describes how people manage, master, tolerate, reduce, and minimize internal and environmental demands and conflicts, reflecting how they actively grapple with the event. Each action sets into motion a process of adaptation extending over time, one effort leading to another. In this way, coping involves an evolving set of responses rather than an enduring approach or style, and the focus is on managing and responding to stress as it changes, not necessarily mastering or overcoming it. We are always coping with life events. Even remaining frozen in the moment is an attempt to respond to a perceived change. The ways in which we cope — how we respond to the stresses we experience — may be more important to our overall morale, social functioning, and health than the frequency and severity of episodes of stress (Rutter, 1983).

What are the consequences of employing the various coping strategies available? Do particular coping mechanisms resolve particular problems? Do they redefine the situation so that the mourner can more effectively respond? Or, do certain coping methods create new problems?

Lazarus and Folkman (1984) identified two main coping strategies. The first involves problem-solving strategies such as reframing the problem. This approach addresses environmental or personal threats, similar to White and Epston's (1990) concept of *externalizing the problem* — that is, stepping back from the troubling situation to examine it and its meaning. This is similar to the stage in Kegan's (1982) theory of adult development when one can shift focus to consider and reflect on one's own behavior and its consequences. The second strategy involves the regulation of emotions and, in particular, the distress produced by a threat. Denial and distraction are behaviors that can help achieve a sense of balance, even if temporarily. Stroebe and Schut (1999) have reinterpreted this strategy to reflect the experience of mourners by defining *loss-oriented* and *restoration-oriented* strategies. Loss-oriented behaviors help the bereaved face their grief and the sense of loss that follows a death. Restorative behavior acknowledges the importance of a continuing connection to the deceased and includes strategies for developing and maintaining these connections. Stroebe and Schut proposed that, as the bereaved cope, they alternate between these modalities. The same is true of most people: We all rely upon more than one way of coping. For the bereaved, strategies might include information gathering, taking direct action, using humor, turning to religion, retreating from or cognitively trying to control our feelings, finding ways to construct a relationship to the deceased, or accepting support from others.

Those who are widowed use different responses at different moments in time to deal with various aspects of their experiences, the demands of the situation, their changing understandings of it, and their emerging needs. They need to integrate and move among problem-solving strategies and to apply strategies that respond not only to their internal experiences but also to the social context in which they live. Thus, ways of coping have to change as the widowed face many new challenges. Rather than relying on one set of responses, they must adapt their coping strategies to the demands of their lives in transition.

☐ The Widowed As Helpers

Helping and being helped by other widowed people can provide the widowed with a unique opportunity for change and growth that makes the kind of learning needed easier (Barrett, 1977). The widow-to-widow program has demonstrated the special value of a mutual-help experience in promoting the ability of the widowed to live through their grief and make needed changes in their lives. This kind of help is most often referred to as *mutual aid* or *self-help*. Because the help goes both ways, the term *mutual help* will be used here, as both those being helped and those helping gain from these encounters. In this setting, the widowed use their own experience as the basis of help. These mutual-help efforts build on the resources that people have within themselves to help themselves and to help reach others (Silverman, 1982b).

What qualities of this experience make it so effective? A key quality is the opportunity for the widowed to feel connected to others like themselves. Acts of caring and concern, cooperation, and mutual aid are the cornerstones of the foundation of viable societies (Kropotkin, 1902). We are social creatures, and the need for others is essential to human life. Meyers (1976) pointed out the special connection this need creates for people:

> When a man is singing and cannot lift his voice, and another comes and sings with him, another who can lift his voice, the first will be able to lift his voice too. That is the secret of the bond between spirits. (Meyers, 1976, p. v)

The essence of this simple idea is that in coming together around common issues we find new strength and new opportunities to solve problems. Mutual help binds people together, and probably there has never been a time when the bereaved did not reach out to each other and learn from each other.

People learn more easily from peers when facing crises or emotionally laden situations (Bandura, 1977). Help is offered on the basis of specialized expertise that results from shared personal experience. Borkman

(1999) distinguishes between at least two sources of wisdom: The first results from formal learning and is referred to as *professional knowledge*; the other accrues from personal experience and is referred to as *experiential knowledge*. The latter applies in mutual-help exchanges (Silverman, 1985b).

Learning is easier when the helper is experienced with the problem and is one step ahead of the person in need (Hamburg & Adams, 1967). We talk a good deal about peer influence on adolescents, but we need to consider that the value of learning from peers may be important throughout the life cycle. At each new stage or phase, we seek others who have gone before us to learn what Goffman (1963) called the "tricks of the trade." Relationships available in a mutual-help exchange can be seen as linking opportunities (Silverman, 1980) or as a transition, a bridge between the past and the future (Goffman, 1963). In this type of relationship, the widowed share their common problems, issues, concerns, and experience. They obtain new information, receive validation for their experiences, and discover role models for how to live through their pain and build their lives anew (Silverman & Smith, 1984). This kind of help is often embedded in existing helping networks in which the bereaved are involved. What are these networks?

□ Helping Networks

On any given day, a person might participate in any number of helping exchanges involving various people and issues. These interactions occur in the family, in the neighborhood, at work, with friends and peers, and within institutions such as hospitals and faith communities. These helping networks obviously vary by level of formality, ease of access, remuneration, and distance from recipients. The further removed the system is from the nuclear family unit, the less personal are its services.

The family anchors the individual in a social network and within the larger society (Shapiro, 1994; Nadeau, 1998) and functions as a provider of care, approbation, material needs, and feedback (Caplan, 1974a). Family members connected by marriage, birth, or adoption maintain a system of mutual obligation. Helping exchanges generally are reciprocal and occur, in part, because people feel responsible for each other. The nature of this support can vary (for example, babysitting arrangements, food cooperatives, and family associations) and many helping exchanges are unplanned and spontaneous.

Usually a death leaves behind many mourners, both within and outside the immediate family. This community of mourners often turns to each other for help with the funeral and to manage the new realities of life. They share feelings and memories and offer mutual support as they acknowledge their pain and loss. Extended family, neighbors, and friends provide help as a matter of personal obligation, mutuality, and reciprocity. Within this informal system, a helper's expertise derives from that person's own experiences, value systems, and connections to the bereaved. As we move beyond the neighborhood, the bereaved encounter a more formal network that includes formally trained professionals such as clergy, funeral directors, teachers, police, physicians, and healthcare and mental-health workers. Funeral directors and clergy are invariably involved in every death to plan appropriate funerals and services. In this formal network, assistance is specialized and the division of labor is clear: The bereaved are the consumers of services, and professionals are the licensed providers with a mandate to serve in their particular areas of expertise. Professionals usually charge a fee for their services and do not expect direct reciprocity. The client or patient is responsible for payment and possibly also for complying with the professional's advice (Hughes, 1971).

☐ Mutual Help and the Professionalization of Services

As society has become more specialized, especially over the past century, we have witnessed the professionalization of services once performed by citizens for each other. Today, people can be hesitant to offer help in times of stress due to their perceived lack of credentials to do so. Experiential knowledge often is not recognized as being legitimate or useful. In many ways, professionals have relieved us of our sense of responsibility to each other. McKnight (1995) described the "over-professionalization" of life to the extent that providers (professionals) deliver services to dependent clients (the rest of us). Care becomes a commodity, and people begin to doubt their ability to help each other. McKnight (1995, p. x) defined care as the "consenting commitment of citizens to each other ... care cannot be produced, provided, managed organized, administered, or commodified." In the United States, professional expertise has emerged as the panacea for almost every disturbance known to afflict mankind. This is one consequence of the growing medicalization of grief. We no longer differentiate between times when professional care is truly required and helpful and when friends and relatives might rely on their own experiences to respond effectively to others going through normal life-cycle stressors. The observations of McKnight (1995) and Kleinman and Kleinman (1997) are consistent with those made by Friedson (1970):

> A pathology arises when outsiders may no longer evaluate the work by
> rules of logic and the knowledge available to all educated men, and
> when the only legitimate spokesman on an issue relevant to all men
> must be someone who is officially certified. (Friedson, 1970, p. 92)

The category of professionals could include clergy, physicians, or mental-
health therapists. Unless they have a psychological orientation, clergy
may rely on prayer and concrete advice. Physicians usually prescribe
medication to relieve what have been identified as symptoms of grief.
Mental-health professionals generally focus on the psychological aspects
of the process (Jacobs, 1999). Whatever the source of help, the implicit
message to the bereaved is that they must consult someone more knowledgeable than they so they can get over their grief. These kinds of help
can, indeed, be useful — or, they can imply that the bereaved are doing
something wrong, that their grieving is defective (Silverman, 2000a). A
member of a support group talked about how this situation plays out in a
community that assumes that therapy is necessary:

> My daughter went to a wedding shower last week. The mother of the
> groom came up to her — she knew that her father had died — so
> she said, "How are you doing?" My daughter answered, "Okay." So
> this woman said, "So, you have had counseling?" and my daughter
> said, "No." This women then said, "Oh, then you must not be ready
> to accept it yet." It's like it is a cure all. They just don't get it. They
> mean well, but they don't have a clue. They can't deal with the pain,
> so they want you to take antidepressants and get counseling so you
> will feel better. I had to explain this to my daughter to help her be
> less upset about what this woman said.

In this view of the world, people at all levels of society are disenfranchised from solving their own problems. Yet another example of this can
be found in a popular novel (Lipman, 2001) in which the heroine of the
story ruminates about how to behave after her mother's death and asks a
friend what a grief counselor would advise her to do. She cannot honor
her lived experience as having any value. People today are taught that in
times of stress they need to consult an expert.

Often, a tension exists between those professionals who advocate and
encourage mutual aid and those who maintain the primacy of their professional knowledge and skills. This is very evident in the help offered to survivors of the 9/11 tragedy. At the time, it was assumed that they would all
need professional counseling. At a meeting of 9/11 survivors, a colleague
warned me of the danger of encouraging these bereaved people to turn to
each other for guidance and support. She felt they were lacking in the perspective and knowledge required to effectively help each other. In this

atmosphere, success in coping based on a person's life experience counted for little, and knowledge gained from coping with actual experiences was devalued (Silverman, 2000a; Borkman, 1999). In the professional context, roles are sharply defined between the consumer (recipient) and the professional (provider).

Care for the bereaved, by its very definition, cannot be a commodity. Dakoff and Taylor (1990) have documented that different help is expected from various helpers in a helping network; therefore, the helpfulness of any given act is in part related to its source. For example, in their study, esteem and emotional support were valued from family members and not from physicians. When physicians provided specific information they were seen as being very helpful (for example, to people with cancer). When such a profound and complex disruption as the death of a spouse or partner occurs, no one kind of assistance is usually sufficient. Professionals might better serve the community as partners or colleagues, and many are beginning to see the merits of this approach.

☐ The Influence of Social Support on the Provision and Acceptance of Help

People who are involved in a mutual-help experience talk about feeling supported. What is meant by support? It has two components: (1) the nature of the help itself, and (2) its availability, which facilitates the acceptance of help. These functions are well documented (Folkman, 2001; Stylianos & Vachon, 1993) and go hand in hand. The availability of supportive help from many sources reflects a community's sense of responsibility to the bereaved and the ways in which it expresses its concern. (Support helps when it provides information that allows the widowed to feel cared for, loved, valued, and held in esteem and when it exists within a network of communication and mutual obligation)(Cobb, 1976). Support is reflected in a functioning system, such as the family, that provides its members with feedback and validation of their expectations of others (Caplan, 1974a). This information may offset communication problems within the larger community. A supportive situation treats the individual in a personalized way. People speak that person's language, guiding him or her in what to do, offering feedback on subsequent actions, and, when appropriate, providing money, materials, and other tangible assistance. Family and friends are most often the sources of this kind of help.

In their summary of the growing literature on social support, Stylianos and Vachon (1993) defined support as a transactional process requiring a fit among the donor, the recipient, and the particular circumstances.

Another definition of social support (Stewart & Langille, 2000) focuses on the interactions among family members, friends, or peers and the health professionals who communicate information and respect and provide practical and emotional help; Stewart and Langille emphasized the role of the professional caregiver as the provider of support. Eckenrode and Gore (1981) and Folkman (2001) claimed that it is not possible to understand the value of support without looking at the context in which it occurs and the responses of the recipients. In a professional–client relationship, the roles are not equal. The focus here is on the support available in mutual-help exchanges among equals. Gottlieb (1983, 1990) extended these views by reminding us that support is a process and that understanding the nature and effectiveness of support requires an understanding of the interactions among those involved, how these interactions are expressed, and where they lead. For the widowed, support has to lead to a new way of looking at their world, of coping with their situation, and of living in their world.

If we are to determine if an environment is truly supportive, we must ask a series of questions (Gottlieb, 1981; Vachon, 1979): Who are the actors in the network? How they do they interact? What help do they provide, and what do they expect in return?

For example, Belle and her colleagues (1982) found that depressed, low-income women often were in contact with many potential helpers; nonetheless, these women felt isolated and unsupported because these potential helpers were more interested in taking than in giving, despite the clear needs of others. In another study, those who lost a loved one to AIDS but who retained a positive approach to life and accepted their need for assistance were better able to use the support (Folkman, 1997; Folkman & Moskowitz, 2000). Thus, the existence of potential help is never enough. The helper must reach out in an appropriate way with appropriate assistance, the recipient must view the help as relevant and then accept it, and the help must alleviate one or more sources of stress. A 70-year-old widow explained the need for a match between helper and recipient:

> I think that depends on values. If you come here and everyone feels this way, then you realize that you are fine. But for a while when it is just you — a lot of people who love you and are trying to be helpful, they are giving you what sounds like good advice. You think, "Why am I not fitting that role? There must be something wrong." Then you come here and you find out, no, it is not just me.

In the context of a mutual-help exchange the widowed feel supported because the helper is someone with whom they can identify, they are an equal among equals, their feelings are legitimized, they feel heard, and they see themselves as part of a community of people whose experiences match theirs.

☐ Mutual Help and the Bereaved

The past several decades have witnessed a growing interest in the kind of help that returns control to the recipients of help. This type of help involves people coming to the aid of others like themselves, using their own experience with a particular problem as the basis of their help. Informally and often spontaneously, people have rediscovered the value of learning from peers who have experienced similar problems and who have coped successfully. These mutual-help efforts build on the resources that people have within themselves to help themselves and to help reach others. More significantly, these efforts are demonstrating that mutual help is sometimes the most appropriate and relevant help, as it offers a positive and meaningful response to a very real human need. For example, several years ago interviews were conducted with a sample of ten parentally bereaved children participating in a volunteer-based program for grieving children in which interaction with other bereaved children was a key element in the program (Silverman, 2000a). When asked what was the most important part of this experience, the children (all between the ages of 8 and 10 years) answered: "I met other kids who had the same experience. I realized I was not alone; I didn't feel different."

In times of stress, people need others with similar experiences to serve as role models and teachers (Silverman, 1966, 1969a,b, 1978, 1980, 1986; Gartner & Reissman, 1977; Leiberman & Borman, 1979; Powell, 1987). Stewart *et al.* (2001) found that elderly people who participated in mutual-help groups were more satisfied with the available social support and experienced diminished needs and increased positive affect. Vachon and her colleagues (1980) found that the widowed involved in a widow-to-widow program adapted better and more rapidly than those in a control group. When Videka-Sherman and Lieberman (1985) studied the impact of mutual help *versus* professional help in their extensive study of the Compassionate Friends, they found that the mutual-help experience led to greater positive change than did professional help. Lieberman and Borman (1981) compared the members of 71 They Help Each Other Spiritually (THEOS) groups in the United States and Canada with widowed people who had decided not to join. They found that the more intense a person's involvement with the group, the better the outcome with regard to self-esteem and absence of depressive symptoms. These findings are supported in Lieberman's (1996) subsequent report on his continuing research with mutual-help groups for the widowed. He noted that outcomes seemed related to not only the amount of support but also the sources. He pointed to the value of other widowed friends for some of his respondents as well as the sense of belonging to a group. In general, the health status of those participating in the groups improved over the first year, and the members who were more involved experienced the greatest mental-health benefits as measured in the study. It is not simply a question of attending group meetings but also the strength of the linkages members develop with each other.

☐ What Is Mutual Help?

Informal mutual exchanges go on all the time, and people discover in each other common experiences that until that moment they may have believed were theirs alone. Sometimes people seek out people who have had a similar experience, or they are introduced by a common friend. These exchanges usually do not move beyond the level of informal encounters. When informal encounters do develop into formal clubs or organizations, it may occur because people in the group sense they have a mission to extend their discovery to others like them. The literature on mutual help and bereavement tells us more about the formal encounters. As we talk of promoting competence in many ways, it is the informal encounters that need to be encouraged because in many ways these are the major influence on the way a community responds to grief and is helpful to the bereaved.

Gottlieb (1981), looking at the continuum of help available in the community, considered intentional communities to be places where people seek to meet needs that cannot be met in their existing networks. Some researchers have talked about intentional communities as being natural helping efforts (Pancoast *et al.*, 1983). To the extent that they are often spontaneous, this is true; however, *intentional* seems to be a more accurate term because these initiatives are often consciously designed and carried forward. They are not based on professional knowledge, which is used in the more formal system, but on experiential knowledge (Borkman, 1976). These intentional communities are sometimes developed by professionals as demonstration projects (Silverman, 1966; Caserta *et al.*, 1999; Stewart *et al.*, 2001) and evolve into ongoing mutual-help programs or organizations.

A mutual-help experience can take many forms. The original widow-to-widow program was a one-on-one exchange. When Wuthnow (1994) wrote about the small-group movement that is growing in the United States, he described the growing phenomenon of people coming together in small informal groups around common interests, providing each other with support, care, and connection in communities outside their families and neighborhoods. These are often sponsored by faith communities or meet in people's homes. They may or may not have a professional facilitator. Also growing in numbers are bereavement support groups convened by professionals (often sponsored by hospice) who are responsible for their continuity and agenda. Each of these modalities provides opportunities for the widowed to reach each other, beyond informal exchanges in the neighborhood, within the family, or at work.

A mutual-help organization limits its membership to individuals with a designated common problem. Their purpose in coming together is to offer one another help and guidance in solving their common problems or mutual predicaments. They join together as members of the organization, not as clients. As members, they control the resources and determine what help the organization will provide and who will provide that help. Help is provided by peers. These communities may have a formal structure resembling a club or other type of voluntary association (Silverman, 1978, 1980). Borkman (1999) described the ethos in such organizations:

> "You alone can do it, but you cannot do it alone" is an often-quoted saying in the literature on self help and mutual aid … and produces a special form of interdependence in which the individual accepts self-responsibility within a context of mutual aid — that is, giving help to others and receiving help from others. Individuals can maintain interdependence … the whole of self-help mutual aid is greater than the sum of its parts. (Borkman, 1999, p. 196)

In a formal mutual-help organization, help can be provided by educational seminars, newsletters, telephone outreach, one-to-one exchanges, social gatherings, and sharing during small informal meetings or in regularly scheduled groups that are facilitated by professional mental-health workers. Some organizations do not bring in outsiders; instead, members graduate to assume the helping role as facilitators of these groups.

Alcoholics Anonymous (AA) is one of the best-known, formal mutual-help organizations. Only a former alcoholic who has been dry for a period of time and who was helped by the AA method can become a helper. Helpers are not recruited from professional schools; their expertise comes from their own success in coping with alcoholism. AA relies on indigenous talents and resources for its success.

When a group becomes formalized, in order to maintain its character as a mutual-help organization it must develop an organizational structure, with officers, a governing body, and procedures for continuity (Silverman, 1980). The members determine all policy and control all resources, and they are both providers and recipients of the service. Membership is limited to people who have the particular problem or problems with which the group is concerned. Mutual-help organizations must be distinguished from such voluntary philanthropic organizations as the American Cancer Society, where volunteers usually join in order to help others, not to solve a common problem. Mutual-help groups maintain their identity because of the shared experiences and commitments of their members around the problems that brought them together. They perpetuate themselves when they develop a sustaining organizational structure (Silverman, 1980; White & Madara, 2002). They also perpetuate themselves when people become an informal community providing ongoing support and friendship to each other.

Formation of a mutual-help organizations can be a response to the lack of a match between the needs of a potential members and help offered in their communities. These organizations develop in communities where citizens feel empowered to express their needs and to develop programs to meet them. This impetus is similar to that of the small-group movement described by Wuthnow (1994). Those who take the initiative are responding to many issues they encountered while dealing with their difficulties, such as professional failure, the gap that can exist between technological advances and available services, or rapid social changes (Silverman, 1978).

Mutual-help groups fill voids in our society. They are places where people can go to share their common experiences and to develop more effective modes of coping with their problems in today's world. When they help people to learn to behave differently in different roles during times of transition, they are enabling organizations. In short, their purpose is to help people negotiate a transition — to get from here to there (for example, from a hospital bed back to the community) — and lead as normal a life as possible (Lenneberg, 1970; Silverman, 1978; Borkman, 1999). For the widowed, we can talk of going from feeling lost and overwhelmingly sad to finding a new direction and meaning in life, to move from feeling helpless and alone to finding ways of helping themselves and each other.

☐ Connecting Help to the Motion of Transition

When Lifton (1973) studied the experiences of returning Vietnam veterans, he identified essential factors in the helping situation that facilitated their coping with the transition to civilian life. He found that the veterans were able to help each other in what became a mutual-help experience. He first noted a special *affinity* that developed among them. In the language of social support, this affinity made it possible for these veterans to feel safe and understood. This bond was a result of their coming together to share a particular, and in this case overwhelming, personal experience, as well as the basic perspective regarding that experience for which they were trying to make some sense. Lifton then noticed the development of a sense of *presence*, a kind of being there for each other. A fullness of engagement and openness to mutual impact came from the veterans knowing that the people helping them had shared the experience, really did understand, and could tolerate the pain. New coping strategies were developing at this point as well. He then observed that members began to change roles, a process that Lifton labeled *self-generation*, which is comprised of two parts. First, the veterans developed new insights that led to a process of change in themselves, which occurred largely on their own terms. Even when calling on the aid of others, those who sought help retained major responsibility for the shape and direction of these changes. The second part of this process was the veterans' willingness, in turn, to help others in the same way they were helped. It seemed to me that this process — affinity, presence, and self-generation — explained how the widowed used the help of other widowed people to make the transition from their old images and values to new ones. It suggests why mutual help can be effective and how the helping relationship changes over time.

Affinity: "I'm a Widow, Too"

Initially, when meeting other widowed people, the newly widowed find that such encounters make it easier for them to face their aloneness and the possibility of dealing with change. The newly widowed are usually too numb and feeling too uneasy to know what they need or to consider their new status fully. Some widowed people have asked what other widows could possibly teach them, as if this role did not apply to them. Meeting someone who has been on this road before them and seems to be managing shines a new light on the life of the widowed. They become less fearful about their new situation. Receiving help from a peer tends to minimize a sense of weakness or incompetence in the person needing help. A new widow in the widow-to-widow program talked about meeting the aide for the first time:

> It was very reassuring to meet Adele. Being widowed somehow didn't seem as frightening.

They no longer feel so alone; rather, they feel that their experiences are legitimized and their feelings appropriate:

> I realized for the first time that I am not the only person who has lost a spouse. I realized that the things I was experiencing and feeling were normal.

For widowers, joining a group may be one step in acknowledging that they may need to find other ways of helping themselves, that they might have a need for others that they had not considered before. This is not always easy for a widower to do. A widower who was a volunteer in a program for the widowed talked about what it can take to get a man involved:

> When I was the community representative for the Widowed Person's Service, I got a call from a man. He didn't want anyone to know how much he was hurting. I said he could come over but he showed up at one in the morning.... No one knew how he felt; he didn't want to be seen as a "sissy" at work.... He was a lineman for the railroad.... He finally agreed to come to a meeting. The men meet around a poker game.... Now he never misses one.... I told him, this talking saved my life. I told him I was the same way once. I was lucky I found a phone number.... I, too, was desperate.. You have to identify what you lost. You can't just say I lost my wife. You lost a lot of things: a companion, an ego builder, a counselor who will tell you when you're right or wrong. I was retired and that's a loss, too. (Campbell & Silverman, 1996, pp. 193–195)

Presence: Learning From Others Like Themselves

As things move along the pain of the new reality may become more real. Other widowed persons are able to provide information about what the widowed are feeling and about their need to find new ways of living in the world. A 44-year-old widow whose husband had died 17 months before talked about what she got from the support group:

> They validate where I am at when it does not match my own expectations or those of people around me who have not been through this. Last year, my friends kept telling me I'd feel better in the spring. I thought this, too, as I always feel better when winter is over. Instead, I got worse. It was a complete surprise. Other people in the group brought up that they were feeling the same way. It is a season of new life and the newly bereaved cannot join in. I have tried, but meeting other widows in To Live Again are the only ones who understand; my closest friends who still have their husbands, I can feel they almost think you can do whatever you please and they can't hear me when I try to let them know, so I have stopped trying.

People talk of developing a sense of optimism and hope as a result of this sharing, as well as finding role models:

> I began to see from others who had coped, who looked happy and had made it, that I had something to look forward to.

Information that offers some perspective on what the widowed are experiencing can be as helpful as being listened to:

> The lectures were helpful and the grief workshops were very good.

Learning from peers provides people with whom the widowed person can identify, not only someone they are like but someone they can be like, serving as role models that are real and available. This could be especially important for a widower who wants to keep up his self-image of not needing others:

> I met this guy at the group. I had to force myself to go. I wouldn't have stayed if I was the only one. He seemed real nice. We talked "shop" before the meeting. We did similar work. Then, in the group, as he talked about what he had been through and what he had learned, I decided maybe there was something here for me, too.

Self-Generation: Changing Self and Others

While receiving help from peers is critical to making the transition from spouse to widowed person, so might be the opportunity to change roles and become a helper. Then, as a widow or widower begins to integrate new understandings into a revised identity, he or she starts a different phase of life. At this time, the widowed change their connections to the support group. They become more responsive to each other's needs and they change their focus from sharing each other's pain to sharing ideas for building new relationships and developing a new community. In the words of a widow:

> I can understand the newly widowed because I cannot forget the lost-soul feeling I had. I am better because in turn I am helping someone else.

Men have often found helping themselves by helping others to be a brand new experience:

> It's the secret — by helping others you help yourself. Other than my children, TLA, and the work I do with it, is the most important thing in my life. I feel I am really doing something worthwhile and it makes me feel a sense of real accomplishment.

Most helpers have reported that being needed has given them a purpose in life and an opportunity to connect to others and to themselves: "In helping others, I help myself." This is the real meaning of mutual help — the exchange and reciprocity that take place between people as they cope with common problems.

II

On Helping

Help is not about providing the widowed with a prescription for what to do at such a time in their lives; rather, it is opening doors and giving them options and information they can use as they learn to cope. There is no formula for the bereaved, no one approach to coping, or no clear picture of a "good" outcome or accommodation. Fortunately, most people do not go through life alone and have access to sources of support. The bereaved have family, and friends. There are clergy, and funeral directors who have particular roles immediately after the death. Health professionals are available at this time as well during this period. The bereaved have two other important resources as well: their own energy and imagination. They find creative solutions and ways of being in the world that they would not have previously imagined. They learn that there is no one way to mourn, nor is there one kind of help that will make everything better. The focus here is on the widowed themselves as key helpers in this process providing the opportunities for the widowed to learn from each other's experience about the many complicated dimensions of grief in front of them. The chapters in this section describe the changing nature of the needs of the widowed and the various ways in which other widows and widowers were helpful.

☐ Defining Help

What do I mean by the word *help*? In *Webster's Dictionary* (1968, p. 1093), *help* is defined as "giving of assistance or support, a remedy, cure, to provide relief, extricate, benefit, to be of use, change for better. It is an act of giving aid or support and the resources employed in giving assistance." It would appear as though help should improve the situation for the recipient; yet, help is more than something given. Help is an interactive, complex process. To be useful, help must be responsive to the needs of those toward whom it is directed; a match must be found among the problem, the solution, and the help offered. Any offer of assistance has to be experienced as helpful by those to whom it is directed; therefore, it is important to learn what the recipient thinks or feels is needed and would be potentially valuable. Helpers must learn to listen and must recognize that they are participating in a relationship. They should be encouraged to consider that in the process of giving they themselves may also be helped.

Support for the bereaved often focuses on encouraging them to talk about how they feel. While the bereaved may obtain short-term relief when they recognize and experience feelings, talking about feelings does not necessarily generate a more effective response to the death. Effective help should also provide the widowed with opportunities to learn new ways of thinking that enable them to move from a simplistic view of grief as something from which they will recover to a new appreciation for the complexity of their experience of loss and their own role in coping and effecting change. When the widowed are able to integrate their feelings with their thoughts, they can identify the role they play in coping and effecting change; in effect, they find a new "voice" and grow in how they relate to themselves and to the world.

Mourners find their own individual rhythms of grief, but some aspects of widowhood apply to most people. It is easier to "own" the unique parts when the bereaved feel supported by those with whom they share a common experience to see the similarities between their own experience and that of others. Help in this context is indeed relational: It goes both ways, as the person helping feels a new sense of pride in what he or she has learned and a recognition that out of pain and growth springs insight valuable to others. Relationships with other widowed men and women can be seen as transitional ones that offer the newly bereaved a bridge between the past and the present. The helper and mourner honor the deceased, validate his or her continuing presence in the world of the living, and find ways to build a different relationship to the deceased. In so doing, the bereaved are able to invite the past into the present without precluding the possibility of a rich, viable future.

Just as the bereaved are changing so, too, must the kind of help available change. Initially, the widowed need to learn more about their own grief and develop a language that enables them to acknowledge what they are experiencing. They need to see that they are not alone in the world and that their experiences are not unique. They may need help with concrete tasks associated with the burial, funeral rituals, caring for themselves, making financial arrangements, getting back to work, caring for their children, and the like. They may need information about community resources, as well as about the grieving process. With time, relying upon role models and learning from each other help the veil of grief lift and provide some hope that the widowed can manage their lives and their feelings in a manner that gives them some relief and ease. The focus may be more on their emotional lives. As they make accommodations, the many ways in which change is needed in their lives become clear.

Dividing a transition into stages, phases, or aspects makes it easier to describe how the bereaved and their needs change over time. The chapters in this section of the book show how the nature of the issues facing the widowed shifts with time, as does the help needed and offered. The focus is on how the relationship with other widowed people is effective in bringing about the accompanying change. We need to remember that grieving is a process, and it may look different for each widowed person. A common core to this process exists and is presented here.

In the chapter on transitions and mutual help, three components of the transition are identified: reality *versus* disbelief, uncertainty, and looking to the future, although no clear delineation between them exists. For the sake of demonstrating movement and discussing the common core in the grieving process, a chapter is devoted to each component. Chapter 5 looks at the initial period immediately after the death; Chapter 6 reflects on the period of uncertainty that the widowed experience as they move ahead in time, if not in how they feel; and Chapter 7 looks into how the future is taking shape.

Where the widowed are in their life cycles will have an impact on how they experience their losses. One aspect of the grieving process that clearly differentiates one segment of the population from another is age. We typically associate widowhood with the elderly; however, a large group of widowed are still raising children, some of whom were born after their fathers died. Chapter 8 looks at the issues these single parents face as they deal not only with their grief but that of their children as well. Chapter 9 provides an overview of some aspects of the experience of the widowed who are over age 65, including the way in which the very nature of their relationships with their grown children change.

Could This Really Be Happening to Me?

> What can I say? It is a lot of pain. It takes up a huge amount of space. There is a sort of disbelief. You turn to where she used to be — a feeling like she is going to reappear at some point.
>
> **Middle-aged widower, after his wife's long illness and death**

As noted earlier, the widowed often feel numb and live with a sense of unreality. At the same time, the many concrete tasks that require their attention buffer them from immediately realizing the full impact of the death. While they have not suddenly become helpless, widows and widowers often feel as though they are and that to some extent they are out of control. An older widow explained after her husband's death:

> I couldn't do a thing. We had made all these arrangements but I couldn't remember what we had decided. The hospice nurse helped me mobilize my children to follow through with the funeral plans. I began to get a little bit of order in the chaos I was feeling, and I started to move a bit, but it didn't really get better for a long time.

Help, at this time, is available from a variety of sources — particularly friends and family who can bring food and take charge of basic household responsibilities. People have to be told about the death and funeral arrangements made. The newly widowed are making decisions they never thought they would have to make:

> If someone had suggested to me that I could negotiate a funeral, I would have said, 'Never.'

In the United States, clergy typically are involved in planning the service. For most of the widowed, the burial service is the last public event where the deceased is, in effect, present. In the weeks following the funeral, surviving partners remain grounded, to some extent, by their need to apply for pensions, figure out their financial situations, and maintain the house and family. Some cope by focusing on a task that provides a sense of accomplishment, such as sending thank-you notes:

> I wrote 200 thank-you notes. I had to do it myself. I had trouble finding words and sometimes it took a long time to get even one finished. But it was important to me that I do it by myself. I needed to focus on something that I could do.

While friends and family usually remain close by at this time, they (and possibly even the widowed) do not realize that this is only the start of a long and painful process that will affect them for the rest of their lives. Other widows and widowers seem to understand this instantly. As one woman explained, she "grew up at that moment."

While the widowed find the support of family and friends to be critical at this time, this support may be even more critical for those in unconventional relationships, such as same-sex or heterosexual partnerships not formalized by marriage. The mourner's sense of disbelief about the death is exacerbated by the lack of social recognition of his or her grief. The surviving partner often wishes to have, but is usually denied, status as a "surviving spouse." A woman whose female partner died revisited with me the memorial service:

> The priest didn't acknowledge me as part of her life. I needed to be recognized as a mourner, that my grief was legitimate. Fortunately, my partner's family asked me to do the eulogy, over the priest's objections.

As a result of their invisibility to other mourners whose status is more conventional, many surviving partners appreciate friends who create new rituals that recognize the importance of this relationship in their lives. A young man and his partner had been together for seven years but had never married because she was still involved in divorce proceedings. When she died in an automobile accident, he recalled:

I couldn't be mentioned in the church service. So several friends put together a memorial service. That made a big difference for me. I have been very lucky to have friends who understood, who kept me whole. Being invisible is a big deal. I am beginning to know what is important and what isn't. But sometimes less important things get to you.

☐ Unexpected and Anticipated Deaths

Many believe that a sudden, unanticipated death is more shocking and disruptive than one that is expected. One young widow reported that she was unable to remember much about the death of her 35-year-old husband who collapsed at a church picnic:

> We went out as a family, and the next thing I knew I was in an ambulance taking my husband to the hospital. He was already dead and I guess I knew it. I didn't see my children again until after the funeral. Someone must have taken them to my mother's. That's where I found them. I really didn't know what hit me. Maybe I still don't. Everything is still a blur.

It is no surprise that this type of sudden death left the widow in a state of shock and disbelief. A middle-aged woman recalled:

> We were on our way out to dinner when I suddenly heard this thump in the hall. My husband was on the floor. I don't know who called the fire department. It must have been me. Next thing I knew, I was on my way to the hospital and I can't remember what happened next except that I called my parents and suddenly everyone, including my children, were there.

It is common in these situations for the widowed to feel detached from themselves, to be both aware and unaware:

> At the funeral I just sat there. It was like standing outside and watching. People told me I was in shock. As I look back, I guess they were right, but I didn't know it at the time. I thought that I was fine and in touch with everything. Only later, when people talked about the funeral, I realized my brother and sister had done everything.

In contrast, when partners die after a long illness, widows often are surprised when they react so differently than they would have expected. Despite knowing that their spouses are going to die, many widows experience surprise when it actually happens, even if the couple had talked together about the impending death. Shortly after her husband died, a widow reported:

> He suffered so much. I was glad it was over for him, but I didn't expect to feel this way.

Another reported:

> Even though I knew it was going to happen, I still had this feeling. Even at the funeral I couldn't believe I was really dressing the children to get ready to go to their father's funeral.

An anticipated death still provokes feelings of shock and disbelief. Some attribute their numbness to their denial that their spouse's illness was terminal:

> We knew how serious his illness was. I didn't allow myself to go there, maybe to protect myself and to protect him. Also, we said we weren't going to be like everyone else. We would make it. The hospice nurse said that after he died it was going to be easier. But that wasn't true in my case. I felt like it was a sudden death, like I had no preparation whatsoever.

Another widow said that although she had lived with her husband's illness for five years and was very clear about the outcome, she, too, felt as if his death was sudden:

> Once they are gone, nothing can prepare you for that. Even when he was in a coma I could hold his hand. And that was better than having him gone.

The burden of caregiving often leads to an emotional or physical letdown after the death. Exhaustion may also have generated a sense of relief. A widower with teenage children whose wife died of cancer described his reactions:

> There is an element of relief. You feel like you are unburdened, in a way. The grief has a different flavor, as I see it. There was time to say good-bye, to sort of wrap up things. In sudden death, there is a shock period that I think is different after a long illness.

A widow whose husband died after a long illness agreed:

> His attacks were so bad that he would almost choke to death. It's the worst thing that can happen to anyone. You have to live with it

to realize it. For his sake I was glad it was over, and maybe for mine as well.

This sense of relief, however, coupled with the opportunity to say good-bye, still does not protect the widowed from the real pain of grief. This widower considered his reaction:

> I think that what happened as time went by — the grief took up a lot of space. It's sort of like sitting right there and in a way it's a kind of relationship. I mean it *is* your relationship. It's your relationship going forward after the death. That's a way of being with a person who died.

Several widows have observed that women who have suddenly lost their husbands seem to remain part of an active social network; in contrast, those who have cared for spouses through long illnesses often feel that they have lost their ties to others:

> My husband lost all his hair and didn't want anyone to see him. People stopped coming, except for the children and their husbands. When he died, I couldn't simply pick up and see the people we had once known as a couple.

Not only is such an illness a strain on the wife's energy, but it also impacts her relationship with her husband. After 35 years of marriage, a widow talked about the last years of her husband's life:

> He was in such pain. Physical contact was a very important part of our marriage. Sex was very much a part of our relationship, and for the last years I could not touch him. Losing that was probably the worst part of his illness for me, and maybe for both of us.

Another widow compared her loss to those of women who experienced the sudden death of their husbands:

> He had leukemia, so for a year and a half he was back and forth for treatment. It was a big strain. I know women who have had their husbands die suddenly. It was a terrible shock for them. I don't know which is worse. Not that you're ever really prepared for it, but in one sense, even though the other is a shock, I think it is probably best [to have warning], because you know you have time to think about the idea. But still, they had healthy, normal marriages right up to the end, and I think they were lucky for that.

Some women are angry and feel abandoned by their faith. For others, faith plays an important and affirming role:

> Prayer has been vital to me, both my own and the prayers of others.

Others have expressed a sense of remorse or guilt. A woman in the widow-to-widow program said:

> I felt guilty. He was trying to tell me something and I couldn't under-stand him. Could I have done more? The doctor wouldn't let me by his bed. I felt badly about that. But he said it was not going to be a peaceful death.

With our modern focus on palliative care and the widespread availability of hospice services, this couple might have experienced a very different type of death today. An older widow talking to another group member reminded her:

> What difference does it make? In the end, here we are in the same place. My husband was the ideal heart patient. He did everything he was told. You can't keep beating on yourself because you couldn't get him to go to the doctor. We don't know why — but here we both are.

☐ The Silence of the Grave Becomes Real

The widowed acknowledge the reality of the death in different ways at different times. A 55-year-old widow explained:

> I had to read the notice in the paper before it penetrated.

But, even then, these moments of disbelief continue to come and go as the bereaved vacillate between realization and disbelief, which can occur for the rest of their lives.

Regardless of how their partners die, the widowed still must deal with their feelings and with what it means to be widowed. Some women avoid the empty space in their beds for weeks or even longer or even sleep on a couch in another room. One woman could not sleep in her bed even after moving to a new house. She was comfortable using the bed-room as a dressing room but continued to sleep downstairs. Other women keep their bedrooms exactly as they had been:

> The day before my husband went to the hospital (it was going to be a very brief stay), he brought my breakfast to my bed. I had a cast on

my leg. He went out and got a rose and put it in a vase. That vase and the rose are still alongside my bed. It's dead but it's still there. We each have our own way of getting through it.

Positive thinking allows some people to tolerate their new circumstances. Shortly after her husband died from a long illness, a young widow reflected on her situation. To some extent there was a bit of bravado in her voice but adopting this approach seemed to help her find her way:

> I feel I am a better person for having gone through this. I feel that this was an opportunity, not one I wanted, to meet a challenge and do the right thing. Help my kids, put this into perspective … appreciating what was really of value. And I had the feeling that I wanted my kids to get everything good out of it. There is a lot of good stuff coming out of this awful stuff.… I stayed by my husband's body for a long time after he died. People started to come to the hospital. I felt I had to leave the room and go to greet them. Then the next week, I would tell anyone I was talking to — especially my brother-in-law who was hanging around — that my heart was broken and I wailed to everyone, "I want you back! Don't go!" Then I decided this is just my make-up. "Okay," I said, "let's go on. Now what?" I knew I was okay financially. We weren't going to have to move. I didn't have to make any rash moves. Knowing that helped.

☐ Their New Status As Widowed

No matter how their husbands die, women generally have great difficulty thinking of themselves as widows. Just as a new widow knows but does not really believe that her husband is dead, she may not yet connect her sense of self to her new legal status as a widow:

> I could not use the word "widow." I could not believe that it applied to me and that he was really gone.

A widow with very young children felt this acutely:

> I accepted it. He had been very ill for a year. I couldn't understand why, but I was able to accept that he was gone. What was hardest for me was accepting it. Here I was, 23, girls my own age were just finishing college or out working a few years, and I was a widow.

Another woman with young children was able to consider the meaning of widowhood:

> The day after he died, I went to the library and got out all the widow
> books because that's how I deal with everything. I read up on it. So I
> took out every book that looked interesting, and I read them all in a
> couple of weeks. I also had two very close friends who also lost their
> husbands. So I had a model of good friends and I think that helped.

On the other hand, many widowed people feel the label of "widow" has
no place in their self-images. One woman in her mid-50s whose husband
had died suddenly recalled her reaction to the letter from the widow-to-
widow program:

> I thought, "What an awful word to call me." I threw the letter away. I
> didn't think that the word "widow" had anything to do with me.

Nevertheless, this woman talked at length with the aide on the telephone
on several occasions, demonstrating that a woman's willingness to talk
with the aide has little to do with her ability to actually identify with the
widowed aide or to clearly articulate her needs.

A new widow who knows other women who have lost their husbands
may have an easier time accepting this label. A young mother in the widow-
to-widow program explained how she understood her new marital status:

> Here I was, taking care of three children under the age of five. My
> family couldn't understand why, six months later, I still needed help.
> Mary [the aide] didn't have that problem. She understood and helped
> me find other ways of getting some help — like getting a baby-sitter
> for a few hours one evening a week. I didn't have to constantly feel let
> down by my family. I felt better about myself. I wasn't crazy. I was a
> widow.

☐ Connecting to Other Widowed People

Aides working with the widow-to-widow program have taken the initiative to connect the newly widowed to others in similar situations:

> When Betty introduced me to other widows who seemed to have a
> life, it gave me permission to be a different person. It made me feel
> and understand that there is no written creed that says you have to
> be married to be happy.

When hospice is involved in end-of-life care, the surviving spouse often
is invited to join a hospice-sponsored program for the widowed. A widower described his initial reluctant involvement and how this changed
once he got involved:

My landlady's sister died and she was telling me how her brother-in-law isn't doing anything for himself. To me, the notion of not trying to figure out by finding people who are going through something similar *now* is really alien. I fell into it [the support group], because someone [at the hospice] recommended it. If they hadn't recommended it, I wouldn't have thought of it.

Support groups, under various auspices in the community, provide another opportunity for the widowed to meet. Many widowed people consciously decided to seek out such a group. As one woman explained:

I had been in a support group before he died. So I knew I wanted one now.

A mother of teenage boys talked about why she looked for a group:

I kept thinking, "Don't give up. Just keep calm." I had been in a group when I had my cancer with other people who had cancer, and I felt that's what I needed now. I needed to meet other people in my situation. I also wanted to take it away from home. My sons have done incredibly well. We share a lot, but as a mother I didn't feel I should share the details of my health concerns with them, or about being married. I guess I was thinking about sex and what have you.

However, it is frequently very difficult for the widowed to take the initiative in seeking out a group — at least initially. A widow whose husband had been hospitalized for some time recalled:

That's my biggest complaint. I walked into the hospital with a husband who was sick and I walked out without a husband. And that was it. No support, no follow up. I had to really go searching. I called back the hospital and the operator gave me the name of this group. One place. It's as if the right hand isn't talking to the left. I didn't do anything then. Then my mother died. I was feeling very, very lonely, and then I called to find out more about the group. I thought I was okay but I really wasn't. I learned from the group leader, who I talked to before joining the group, that I was okay for where I was that at point in my life. It was a relief to know that.

A 50-year-old widow reported:

I kept getting sent to one number after another. Then no one called me back. I called a lot of local churches. I'm still waiting to hear from some of them. I found something about this group posted on the bulletin board in my doctor's office.

Once the widowed have found each other, what do they discuss? Much of their talk centers on small events, not those important lifesaving or transforming experiences we might imagine. The widowed helped each other learn to cook, clean the gutters, or negotiate the purchase of a new car.

☐ Financial Concerns

In the early days of bereavement, aides in the widow-to-widow program most often helped with mundane matters such as housing and finances:

> This widow didn't know that she was entitled to VA benefits. I found the address for her and reviewed the procedures. I offered to drive her down, but she had a friend who would go. I warned her that they might make her feel like they were doing her a favor, but she was entitled to the money. To make sure she got everything she was entitled to, I explained how I had handled them.

Widows with dependent children at home are eligible for Social Security benefits. If the widow does not work, she is eligible to receive some benefits for herself as well. These benefits are also available to a widower who has cared for their children and are based on the late wife's accrued contributions:

> My wife's Social Security paid for my babysitter. The funeral director was the first to tell me about this benefit. And then we talked about it in the group.

Social Security and insurance benefits give some widows a financial security they have never before experienced. An aide can help the widow manage her income by showing her how to prepare a budget and plan for the long term. One young woman in the widow-to-widow program whose husband was killed in an automobile accident shortly after he started a new job thought she would have to abandon any hope of buying a home of her own. The aide gave her specific advice and a new sense of hope:

> I told her that with the insurance money she would collect she did have a down payment. It would feel funny normally to go to a bank asking for help, but under the circumstances I told her to go to her local bank and explain her situation to the manager. He would clarify what loans she could get and if she could afford a house. I did the same thing after my husband died.

The widow followed through, received helpful advice, and began to see a way to achieve her dream of home ownership.

In a working-class community, many women depend on their husbands' wages and have limited reserves. Today, it often takes two salaries to make ends meet. If a widow is under 62 and has no children at home, she is ineligible for Social Security benefits. Even if a widow is eligible, some women may not have received their Social Security checks for three or more months after the death of their husbands. Because they might have little money in reserve, many have to develop a budget or must apply for Welfare to hold them over. A young woman whose husband died recently in a work-related accident received workman's compensation for life or until she remarried. Nevertheless, she still had financial problems:

> I applied for health coverage under a state plan for children. I'm not really getting a lot of money. I was told I had too much income. I don't know how they figure that. I'm not sure how, but we will manage. I can't work; I have a new baby.

A health benefit for children in low-income families that is in part supported by federal matching funds is known as CHIP (Children's Health Insurance Plan), but coverage varies from state to state.

Older people over 65 might have health insurance through the federal Medicare program; however, younger women whose families' health insurance had been provided by their husbands' employers often worry about how they can now afford healthcare coverage. Working widows face the same dilemma as widowers: finding daycare for their children. Some women are exhausted from caring for their dying husbands while working to support the family, and they need a respite:

> Now that I have Social Security I'm quitting my job for a while. I need time to rest.

Financial difficulties and learning how to deal with them have led some widows to consider that they do, indeed, have a future:

> It made me think about what was needed to go on living (even if I wasn't sure I wanted to), and it reminded me that in spite of it all, that's what I have to do.

Many women, especially those in the widow-to-widow program whose children were grown, have had to find work. Work holds many meanings for these women. Because many have never worked outside the home, they do not know how to locate suitable openings or even fill out job applications. Some face the double bind of not being able to focus on the job hunt but needing to make money to cover expenses:

> I need something to keep me busy, but I can't really concentrate on anything. Still, I have to pay my bills.

☐ Confronting Family Issues

Families might resent the new stable income of a widow, even when it is not necessarily adequate. One widow in the widow-to-widow program needed to be reminded that, because she had to support her children, she was not selfish for refusing to share her money. Another widow's mother asked her to support her sister, who had trouble keeping a job. These widows had to practice saying "no."

When she made a home visit, one aide found a new widow repainting her apartment while listening to her husband's records. The widow's sister took the aide aside and asked that she intervene. This woman believed her newly widowed sister should not work so hard, and should not dwell on memories of her deceased husband. Rather than agreeing with her, the aide encouraged the sister to be supportive, not critical. The new widow later explained her sister's behavior: "She couldn't understand — she's never been married."

Because the widowed and their children are the focus of attention, the older parents of the deceased are often overlooked. Even though they might be expected to be especially supportive of their grieving daughter- or son-in-law and grandchildren, not all in-laws are helpful to the widowed. An aide in the widow-to-widow program knew from experience that the extended family can often cause problems:

> I think that was one of the questions Betty asked me: "How are your in-laws?" That brought up a lot, and we discussed them for a long time. They were very possessive, old-fashioned. They were just lost in their own self-pity. Nothing I do is right, no matter what I try. It never is good enough. They kept acting as if the children and I hadn't lost anything.

This aide introduced the widow to another young widow living nearby. The two had much to share, including their distress about their in-laws' reactions. It helped the new widow to hear that her new friend's in-laws had also disowned her. Together, they recognized that they were not to blame; rather, their in-laws were grief-stricken over their sons' deaths and took out their sadness and anger on the widows and their children.

A young woman talked in her group about what happened after her husband's death in the past year:

> I have in-laws from hell. We lived near them. They owned the house we lived in. In return for rent, my husband maintained the house, upgraded parts of it, and really took care of it. Immediately after he died, my mother-in-law told me I had to move. It's like she's blaming me for his heart attack and she doesn't even talk to her grandchildren.

Not all in-laws are like this, however:

> My parents and my in-laws are good friends. They couldn't be more supportive. In turn, they come to help. We cry together and we try to help with each other's pain.

A widow's own parents also can be extremely helpful. One young woman's mother came to live with her after her husband died in an industrial accident:

> My mother is a widow. She understands. She moved in to help with the children. She'll stay for as long as I need her. I was much older than my children when my father died. My mother is patient with the children and can be there for them when I still space out.

☐ Beginning To Grieve

Because widow-to-widow aides have also experienced the death of a husband, they understand that shock and disbelief often protect the new widow from experiencing strong feelings of stress. As long as this protection remains in place, the widow can feel good about how well she is coping. Sometimes the aide stands back but remains available for when things start to fall apart; sometimes the aide chooses to warn the widow:

> Things may be fine now, but before they really get better they are going to get a lot worse. I remember that once we sold my husband's business and I had a chance to stop, I fell apart.

The widow who received this warning was grateful:

> It made such a difference. When I didn't think there was going to be a tomorrow, I kept remembering what Dorothy [the aide] said. I remembered she told me nothing would stay the same, that feelings like these don't last forever, and that kept me going.

When a widow wanted to know how she would and should be feeling over time, an aide tried to reassure her but also explained that there is no right or wrong way to grieve. People respond and change at their own pace and not according to some preconceived schedule. Talking with others often helps this process of understanding and change:

> It is a great avenue for pouring out feelings. I think sometime I don't know what I am feeling unless asked and have a chance to talk about it. The group came through at surprising levels. I think you are unaware of something until you hear something from others.

Another widow in the same group said:

> One thing I learned from the group: People think that if you have any pain or angst, or are really miserable, then something must be wrong. And how do you disabuse people of the fact that maybe that's where I need to be right now? I can't change them, but the group makes me feel okay.

Even when the newly bereaved are protected by a sense of shock, this shock is not impermeable. Many women have sleepless nights and find themselves weeping when they least expect it. Women who have gone to their physicians for help often receive prescriptions for tranquilizers, but many are uncomfortable with taking them:

> I couldn't eat or sleep at first. I lost a lot of weight that first winter. The doctor said I was depressed. He wanted to give me tranquilizers, but I refused. I don't believe in them. I knew this was something I had to fight and deal with.

Medication can be helpful if used as a temporary support. Aides encourage those who accept such medications to use them for as long as they cannot sleep or eat. As one widow began to overcome her insomnia and retain food, the aide suggested that she taper off the number of pills and talk to her doctor about prescribing a lower dosage. In one extreme situation, a few weeks after her husband died a widow visited her physician, who then referred her to a psychiatrist. Even though the aide felt the widow was responding appropriately to the stress of caring for an ill husband and then watching him die, the psychiatrist prescribed electroconvulsive therapy. The widow did not think this treatment was helping but did not want to offend the doctor and was afraid to stop. At the aide's insistence, the widow went to another physician for a second opinion. The new doctor told her she did not need such treatment and prescribed a mild tranquilizer. In this case, the widow learned how to advocate for herself in a relationship in which she was accustomed to being compliant.

This widow's husband was an only child, and his immigrant parents feared that she would abandon them once she got over her acute grief. They pressured her (as had her dying husband) to find a new father for their children who would also consider his parents' needs. While she was not ready for a new relationship and did not simply want to marry the first man who proposed, she felt guilt about disobeying her husband's dying wish. The conflict created by her feelings, her husband's wishes, and his parents' pressure was acute, and she had no experience handling such a situation. She was used to others making difficult decisions for her. Her aide was older and became a kindly mother surrogate. The aide gave the widow a new perspective on these various issues and made it clear that everything takes time. Later, the aide referred this woman for psychological counseling; after two years, the widow married a man whom she cared for greatly and who enjoyed the ready-made family of her in-laws and children.

A woman whose husband had committed suicide had difficulty simply getting out of bed. She ground her teeth, which gave her bad headaches. The doctor prescribed antidepressants, but they did not really help. The aide appreciated this widow's need to sleep and identified ways in which this widow was coping quite well:

> With four children, you have to get up and take care of them. She was doing that. She was not running away by sitting in barrooms all day. If sleeping is helping her, good. It's probably what she needs; it's her way of healing. The only thing I tried to discourage her from was sleeping her life away. This is something I think you have to do gradually, and I think this is why she eventually did go out and get herself a part-time job. We had been talking about it for a month.

As the widowed begin to feel validated by the aides, they can begin to acknowledge the impact of the loss on their lives. With the aide's support and approbation or in a group with other widowed people, they can consider what they might do about their changed lives. A widow reflected on the help she got from the aide:

> I never would have gotten out, but when she called and said she was a widow, I asked her to come right over. I didn't think I would be able to get up in the morning. She told me everyone feels that way; she did, too. If she has the energy to help me now, I realized I would be all right. She said it takes time. I needed to know that, too. You have to let widowed people know that there are no quick fixes, no easy answers, that through the hurts and upsets of a big adjustment, one evolves into something that surprises even yourself — that each of us is loaded with gifts and untapped talents.

The widowed begin to see alternatives to how they define themselves and how they live their lives. It begins to feel safe, as one woman put it, "to let herself ride the roller coaster" — the feelings of being up and down in her grief.

6

Uncertainty: What Will Happen Next?

Grief … I think it just goes on. Never ending even a few years later. It has to do with experiencing the sadness and the loss while at the same time trying to move forward. Create something out of it. Create a vision of my future while at the same time acknowledging the changes and the losses.

55-year-old widow, a year after her husband died

In time, the widowed often feel that they need to gain some perspective on their experience:

I needed to know that what I am going through is normal, that other widows feel the same way.

Often, just talking with others helps:

Having Mary [the aide] to talk to, to tell me it was normal, made it easier to survive.

In such discussions, the widowed learn that for most widowed people, the pain can get worse before it gets better.

☐ The Pain Is Still There

At some point in the grieving process, all widows and widowers must revise their understanding of the death in their own unique ways, and when they do so the death takes on other dimensions. Whereas it was once possible to put their pain out of reach, it may not always be possible to do so now. When several widows and widowers considered their current situation several months after the deaths of their spouses, instead of feeling better, as they might have expected, they often found that they had more difficulty managing than when their spouses first died:

> I didn't think of it as getting better. That wasn't the issue. I had hoped by now I would have time for all the things I wanted to do these past years, but I just don't feel like it. It's different now, but I can't explain it. I thought it would hurt less by now. It's like a door has opened and the flood is coming in.

The intensity of the pain may be such that the widowed retreat, to find respite in a return to their earlier state of numbness. There is a different quality to it, however. Nine months after her husband died a young widow described what she was experiencing:

> In the last month or six weeks, I inch toward it (the chasm, the emptiness) every once in a while and retreat, and inch toward it, and retreat.

A support group member in her late 50s who was married for 41 years considered her current situation:

> The grieving is changing. For about four or five months, I was functioning at a very low level. I manage a large staff and I wasn't doing a very good job. Now the grief is less intense but it seems almost more pervasive. I sort of like opened the door to everything that I had been keeping inside.

A widower reflected on what it was like shortly after the first anniversary of his wife's death:

> There is a rhythm. There are times when it just hurts a lot and then there are times when I can focus on my future. I have heard people say the second year is tougher and I say, "My God! I have to deal with more pain?" Then I realize what they were talking about because I am in it. You are not numb. Things are painful, but there is an ability to embrace new things in your life.

At this stage, crying has a different quality than it did at the time of the death when it was more reflexive; at this later point, it expresses the deep sadness that develops when the widowed more fully understand what they have lost and that they are now alone:

> I had so much to do, getting rent money, getting to work, trying to manage. I thought I took his death very well. Then, after six months I'd get to work and I'd start to cry — awhile every morning.

A year after her husband's death, a 38-year-old widow described her son's first communion:

> He was so overjoyed. I had to do everything in my power to put on a big smile. I would have cried all day if I could. Every opportunity I sneaked away to catch my breath. We have a tradition when we say "our Father" that we hold hands. I lost it then. I didn't have enough [tissues] to wipe away all the tears. You look at the people there, husband and wife. Row after row. It was very painful.

A widow may cry out of self-pity even as she recognizes that her husband has lost even more:

> Sometimes I feel so sorry for myself. But then I think, I have my life. I think of my husband and what he lost. He didn't want to die. He so wanted to see the kids grow up.

Crying also reflects anxiety about the future as well as frustration with the present. Many widows resent the lethargy that often accompanies the increasing awareness of their loss, as described by a participant in the widow-to-widow program:

> I can't seem to get started doing anything, even cleaning the house. I feel so empty and lost. I think ahead and the whole thing feels like a black hole. Then I find myself dissolved in tears. It's like a vicious circle.

Disruptions in sleeping and eating patterns and a sense of physical malaise often continue. In the words of a widower:

> Something about the aloneness that gets to me … someone to share my bed. I can't even sleep on that side. Someone said, "Pile clothes on that side." So in some way I fill the space.

In addition to insomnia, some people develop other symptoms of tension. A woman in the widow-to-widow program ground her teeth at night and had to be hospitalized when her jaw locked. If, at the time of death, there is a difference between those whose spouses have died suddenly and those whose spouses were ill for some time, this difference had disappeared by now. All of the widowed seem to experience the same letdown. A widow whose husband died suddenly said:

> I just seem glad to get through one day and then another. One of my married daughters was having a lot of problems, and I didn't realize it. I just wasn't functioning.

Another widow whose husband suffered a long bout with cancer talked about how she felt nine months later:

> I couldn't get myself to do anything without a large effort. It's like cognitive dissonance. You know, cognitively, that you have to keep going, but.... Some people say they feel free. I'm not feeling free.

Many rely on faith and prayer to sustain them through this period. Others are angry at what the fates have brought them. In fact, during this period, guilt, remorse, and anger are more prevalent than at other times. Some widows ruminate over what they could have done to prolong their husband's life or to prevent his death. A widow whose husband was killed in an industrial accident while covering for a sick friend told an aide:

> It kept coming back over and over again: "If only he hadn't gone to work that day he'd be alive." I kept asking myself, "What if I had been more insistent that he stay home?"

Even when the widowed use the word "guilt" they seem to be expressing a sense of remorse or sadness — or even anger and frustration over their impotence, as if they could somehow undo the death and regain control over their lives. They struggle with their powerlessness to change history and their reluctance to accept a new reality.

The widow of a man who committed suicide was clear about her efforts to get help for her husband. Before he died, she had gone to his employer and to her priest for help. When she described her husband's erratic behavior, they put her off, belittling her concerns and suggesting that she was provoking such behavior. For the time (1969), this was not an unusual response; typically, women were blamed when their husbands abused them. After her husband killed himself, she kept asking, "Could I have done more?" She expressed no anger toward the employer and priest, but rather turned her feelings inward. The aide listened and reflected with her on what actually happened.

The aide, whose own husband died very suddenly, responded to this widow's sense of responsibility for her husband's death:

> A widow has to develop a philosophical point of view that allows her to appreciate that none of us has control over who lives and who dies. We need to realize that a person's time had come. Otherwise, we would go crazy. Some people jump off a roof and survive; others are crossing the street and are suddenly dead. We have no control. A widow has to come to accept this as part of what life is about.

Gradually, this widow recognized that she had done all she could and that her husband's suicide had kept him from hurting her, as he had threatened to do so many times.

☐ A Place for the Deceased

The widowed still need to talk about the deceased but often find it difficult to get others to listen. It is not simply a question of maintaining a place for the deceased in the widow's life, but friends often cannot find such a place in their lives:

> If I wanted to say my husband would have enjoyed this play, everyone became uncomfortable. I pulled back, and their invitations became less frequent. But my needs changed, too.

Family is often no different:

> We can't call our families if we feel like talking about our husbands. They don't want to hear it. They think we'll hurt ourselves by talking about it.

The widowed talk to the deceased, dream of them, and feel their continuing presence. It is not unusual for the widowed person to feel the presence of their spouse or partner. One widow "heard" her husband's car pull into the driveway or his key in the door:

> At night as I'm lying in bed, I hear the wind blowing, and if something bangs I think it's the door. I have all I can do to keep from getting up to greet my husband.

One woman described going shopping and thinking her husband was with her:

> My husband used to drop me off first and I'd start shopping while he parked the car. I'd wait to buy meat until he joined me. Once, I turned around and there was this man who looked like my husband, and I started to ask him what he thought of the meat I had in my hand. I have this sign in my kitchen: "I experienced yesterday. I am not afraid of tomorrow because I have lived today." I am trying to get myself to believe it.

In their dreams, the widowed sometimes experience their spouses as if they were still alive:

> For months afterward I dreamed about him as if he wasn't dead. Then I'd see him in his coffin or lying there where he died. I'd wake up in tears. I think it took over a year before it stopped.

One widow dreamed that her husband had come back from a trip, and in the dream she told him, "No, you can't come in. You're not supposed to be here now." Other women set their husbands' places at the table for up to a year and report how upset they are when they realize what they are doing.

Many widows continue talking with their husbands for years, as they sort out problems and imagine how their spouses would have responded. Some women worry that these conversations, their dreams, and feeling their husbands' presence are indications that they are going crazy. They are comforted and reassured when they learn that most other widows have shared these same experiences.

☐ Seeing Beyond Family and Old Friends

At the same time that the widow is reacting more intensely to her loss, family and friends often are paying less attention or becoming impatient with her continued grief. Their relationships begin to change. Sometimes they feel invisible:

> You have the feeling that, no matter where you go and no matter what, you are an extra. At a wedding not long ago, a neighbor said there were just 10 of us, so we could all sit together. She forgot about me. I was the 11th. I could have screamed.

While some family members remain supportive and helpful throughout, they still may not always understand. One young widow spoke of her family's attitude months after the death:

In the beginning, everybody was very patient with me. And now it seems that even my sisters and my mother are losing patience with me. They think that I should be over my bereavement, that I should begin to go out, that I should begin to meet gentlemen and remarry.

Often outsiders incorrectly assume that remarriage will fix everything. Many widowed people find themselves facing many "shoulds," as a widower described:

It's been a year, but I am still in the stunned stage, when people say that you should be going out, you should be dating, you should be going on vacation by yourself.

Occasionally, people offer support that is intended to push the widowed into feeling better much sooner than they are able. Others may be critical in ways that are typical of them regardless of the circumstances. Frequently, the widow and her family experience miscommunications, as in the case of an older woman who said her children called her only when they needed a babysitter and did not think of her needs at all. Another widow reported that her parents criticized her for marrying a man who left her with no money. Some families can be overprotective, adding to the widow's feelings of isolation and inadequacy. A widow reflected on her family's reactions to her various needs:

Some people think I'm better off now than when he was alive. He had been drinking, but for the last year he was in AA. Things were great. People don't understand the void in my life. My parents think that I shouldn't complain. I have the house, an income, my children. They don't see why I need pity.

After seven months, one woman moved in with her mother, leaving her old neighborhood and friends:

It didn't work. My mother had no sympathy for me, and my daughter wasn't happy. Everyone kept saying, "Find another man and get married."

Others felt protected by their helping network — at least to the extent possible:

I never felt abandoned by my friends. They always included me. They called, they were there. But in many ways it couldn't be the same. My needs were different.

A widower tried to understand his friends' difficulty:

> Death in our culture is still something to be avoided. It is hard for
> people to deal with it. They are afraid it could happen to them. There
> aren't many people who can be with you who haven't had the expe-
> rience themselves.

☐ Others Like Me

Ultimately, sympathy or material support may not be enough to combat a
widow's growing sense of isolation. As a widower explained:

> The amount of space, energy, and time that the grief occupied was
> declining. It left me really lonely. I didn't know what, but I needed
> something else. That's when I called about a group.

One woman who initially was reluctant to get involved with the widow-
to-widow program told her daughter:

> I don't care what kind of a racket it is. I need to get out.

Being involved with another widowed person, either one-on-one or in a
group, allows the widowed to look at where they have been and where
they are going. The benefit of being with other widowed people becomes
clear:

> I went to a gay and lesbian group dealing with all kinds of losses. I
> found I needed something focusing more on being a widow because
> that's who I was. I joined this group for widowed people, and they
> were very welcoming. It was hardest in the first couple of meetings.
> We were hearing the pain that everyone else in the room had experi-
> enced. I wonder why, if I feel so bad, it was good for me to go into a
> room and, and, like, hammer my head? I didn't run. I learned that
> once you get through the initial pain, you start drawing the connec-
> tions that make it worthwhile.

It is with other widowed people that they at last can find someone who
understands and who is available to listen. They need someone they feel
they can count on ("I feel as if everyone but Dorothy [the aide] has
deserted me") and who could hear them ("There is no one else since my
husband died who I can talk to like you"). When others say they understand, the widowed know that this does not ring true if these others are

not widowed themselves. A widow in the widow-to-widow program explained to the aide the meaning of her visit:

> Since you are a widow, too, when you said you understood, I knew you meant it. And that was important. I can't stand sympathy, and that's all anyone else could give me.

A widower expressed why talking with other widowed people was so important:

> This is the only safe place to laugh. You could be crying in your grief, but there is salvation in laughing. Where else can you laugh about picking out a tombstone?

They learn different ways of reacting and find that humor can be a very effective coping strategy:

> Every time I got a phone call from someone asking for my husband I would get upset. I learned from the group.... When I get a call now and they say they will call back I tell them if you find him let me know.

Feeling safe makes a difference:

> What makes this place safe is that you are not judged at all. If you are a part of the group, no explanation is necessary. And if you are not part of the group, no explanation is possible.

One woman initially said that she could not stand widows and that their talk made her sick. Within several months, weeping and lonely, she called the aide and later reported, "I've talked to Adele about things I've never said to anyone before. Not my best friend, not my sister."

Not everyone finds participating in a group helpful. Some people try it and do not return. Often, more women than men are involved. One widow explained:

> That's true. I said, "I'm not going back." My son said, "Why are you going back if you get so depressed?" I said I would give it three weeks and after three weeks you can't not come. It is amazing. On the other hand, I just met a woman who has been widowed for five years. She said she tried the group for a few months. It made her more depressed, so she stopped going. Not just men. Women, too.

The widowed often have to be ready to take advantage of the opportunity. One woman lost both her husband and mother within three months. Another bereaved woman's widowed sister also died. Both of these widows became depressed. The sister of another widow committed suicide. Such multiple losses placed great burdens on these widows. As noted previously, these are times when the widowed begin to see their need for additional support:

> There are too many people leaning on me now since my mother died. I need a place where I can talk to someone who will listen to how I feel. Mary [the aide] gives me this. I need a sense of belonging. She gave me moral support and self-confidence, especially when I needed to look for a more suitable job.

Connections to, and support from, other widowed people allow the newly bereaved to more readily accept that their deceased partners are no longer there to share their daily lives. Often, they experience a new awareness of themselves, as a 48-year-old widow with two young-adult children still living at home explained:

> I was the wife, the caretaker. I had defined roles. But who am I now? And for what purpose? Everything changes. I've lost meaning, purpose, and direction. Many questions: How will I support myself? Who will I share my life with? While I am overwhelmed at what I have to do, with no one to share the burden, at the same time I have a new appreciation of how competent I can be. I never thought of myself that way.

After talking to others in similar situations, many widows and widowers develop a new perspective that allows them to change and grow:

> I was in such a hurry to be better, and now 20 months later I'm realizing that it is going to be a long road and that's not disturbing to me. I see things will continue and it will be different. People talk about growing, and I do see change.

When they join with other widowed people, the newly bereaved learn that their grief is normal and legitimate. The results can be stunning. One widow who had been physically ill looked so much better and happier after joining a group that her doctor asked if she had been to Florida for a holiday:

> I told him simply I had met a group of widows and found out my problems were not unusual. Everyone has the same difficulties. It made me feel better. I plan to go to everything from now on.

Widows find new friends, develop new social lives, receive help finding jobs, and identify role models who respond creatively to changes in themselves and in the world around them. A member of a support group added to this list:

> We also create new memories. It's all about being together and learning about each other as people. I have new people in my life now, a new community. We get to be known for more than just being a widowed person.

☐ Finding New Friends

At this time of reconstruction, the widowed need understanding friends more than ever. Who else could accept the myriad difficulties they face? For example, some widows find it so difficult to come home to an empty house that they doubt the wisdom of going out at all. One widow said it was like going to a party and then having no one with whom to share the experience.

Within the first year, many women recognize that their old social networks are inadequate and start looking for new relationships:

> I really didn't have too many friends. I was wrapped up in my husband and children and didn't have girlfriends like so many others have.

Sometimes the need to find new friends is a response to not feeling accepted by old friends:

> Weekends were awful. I needed new people in my life, friends who wanted to do things together. We needed something in common, but we also needed to be able to hear each other. I wanted friends who would understand if I talked about being lonely or about going back to work.

Aides in a widow-to-widow program cannot and do not try to satisfy all of a new widow's needs for companionship; rather, they become the conduit for bringing the newly widowed together by arranging for them to meet at small social gatherings such as cookouts, discussion groups, or informal livingroom get-togethers. The aide can also arrange meetings between two women she thinks would be compatible and helpful to each other:

Betty gave me the name of this widow. She was young like myself. She had three young children, and as a result I had more in common with her than with Betty. She had lost her husband about a year and a half before I lost mine. She was still having a hard time, but she helped me a lot. We used to call each other at 11:30 at night and talk until 1:00 a.m. She was the same way. She would just sit and talk.

And from another widow:

We lived within two blocks from each other. If Dorothy hadn't introduced us, we'd have never met. My house is so empty now. It made me feel good to help someone else.

Sometimes the two widows might be neighbors who can look out for each other:

I keep an eye out for her. When I see the light on, I'll drop in.

Several churches in the greater Boston area began sponsoring social clubs for the widowed when their widow-to-widow program ended. Some aides regularly attended these meetings and invited new widows to join them. Some widows were naturally shy and needed more urging. Their efforts have often paid off, as one aide described her involvement with a late-50s homebody:

I had to call her many times before she agreed to come. She finally made it when I agreed to pick her up. She had a good time and promised that next time she would get there on her own. She even took two phone numbers to call other women she met.

It is not easy for some widows to take this first step, a step that outsiders may view as obvious and risk free. They need to feel sure that they will be accepted and they can say what is on their mind:

I was really ready to get out of my box, but I needed to feel safe, to be sure that I would be accepted. And that if I wanted to talk about my husband, it would be all right.

Timing is also critical, and widows sense when they can make use of the offer of help. After receiving several phone calls from an aide without agreeing to meet, one widow finally accepted an invitation to a cookout. At that point, she recognized that her needs had changed and that she had to find new ways to meet these needs. She was pleased with what she found once she arrived at the gathering:

It was very reassuring. I wasn't a fifth wheel and I felt that I belonged. It was helpful to share my feelings. Everyone was friendly and willing to listen. They lived in my neighborhood and I looked forward to seeing them again.

A widower in a support group described the special quality about her particular group:

Not all groups are this cohesive. We go out for a drink every week after we have a meeting. We have traveled together and meet frequently for dinner. It's a real showstopper when people ask who we are and we say, "Widowed!"

☐ I'm Not the Same Me!

Many widows do not know how to drive and had depended on their husbands to run errands outside their neighborhood. With encouragement, widows have learned to drive:

It's good to have a car, even to get away from everything or just to take a little drive. To see something different when you get uptight about something at home. I live near the beach. I very often just get in the car and drive over there. There's something about the water. I just look at it and it sort of relaxes me. Then I come back and I can face things. I never would have done that alone before.

Being mobile changes a widow's attitude about herself. The following exchange took place between widows in the widow-to-widow program:

Tomorrow night is the first widows' meeting at the Espousal Retreat House. One of the widows is coming with me. I called her the other day. Since her husband died, she has learned how to drive. They had a car and she never drove. I had told her it was crazy to have a car and not drive. Last spring she started to take lessons. When I called to invite her, I offered to pick her up. She said, "No, I have a license. I'll meet you at your house." She was as pleased as could be. This was a whole new thing for her.

Obtaining reliable transportation to and from work can be key to holding a job, and widows are often willing to help each other out:

Dee is trying to get me to go with her to get a part-time job. She figures we can get a job someplace together and she would drive.

Women participating in the original widow-to-widow program not only made new friends but also shared resources. First, however, some widows need to learn how to develop their internal resources. One woman who constantly called an aide with questions and requests gradually accepted her need to find another widowed friend. Her family was appropriately supportive and helpful, but she needed to develop self-confidence and a sense of competence. After making a few more connections, this widow relaxed and became more receptive to opportunities around her but continued to need the same type of encouragement a young child needs from a mother. This same woman put considerable energy into meeting men. Although she was not yet ready for a new relationship, she believed that a romantic liaison would take away her pain and loneliness. After about nine months of widowhood, she collapsed because a man she had met did not call as he had promised. As an aide explained at a meeting with other aides:

> I guess the man did not call her, the weather was getting bad, and she does not have enough to do. She does not work full time, and just being alone in the house is not doing the right thing. Her family feels she should go out and circulate more, and not just with men. Her brother finally bought her a secondhand car. I said, "That will be wonderful, because if you are lonely you can pick up and go someplace to visit or to shop." The problem is that she really needs someone there constantly to tell her what to do. I don't think that she has ever made a decision alone since the time she was married 25 years ago.

Eventually this widow recognized that, as needy as she was, she also had many strengths. With the support of her family and the aide, she recognized that she had to learn to manage by herself and to appreciate her ability to do so. She learned, too, that she would sometimes feel depressed, and that this was all right. Little by little, as she learned from other widows, this woman began to change:

> When I saw all those other women making a good adjustment, I decided I had to pull myself together. I realized that I was not the only one to whom this happened, and that helped me get going again.

By observing the responses of other widows, this woman began to see that she had options and that she was in charge of choosing among those options. Another widow whose husband had died about a year and a half before concurred:

I kept thinking of myself as helpless. Every time someone asked me to do something for another widow, I said, "No, I can't do that." I was really getting more and more into a hole. I looked around me and thought that I could die. Like the [80-year-old] widow up the street who died right after her husband died. I realized that I did not want to go that way. Then I looked at Dorothy [the aide], and I saw I had a choice. I could be like her, and that seemed like the way I wanted it to be. It was my choice. I felt like an alcoholic. They say you have to hit bottom before the change. I guess I did crash, but when I was ready to get up, there was someone there to show me the way.

A very articulate widow elaborated on her experience with change and the value of the group:

I feel like it is more like a child in kindergarten where you think you can be Superman. You put on the cape and get on the couch and you think you are going to fly and you hit the wall about five times and you know you can't fly. You need a place to go where other people can help you. It is something of an invisible problem. It doesn't show to the world. The world sees you trying and they say great, but they don't know what it feels like to have a little thing and you know it is little and you know that if your husband was alive, it wouldn't be a big deal, but guess what it is a big deal. I don't want to do this one anymore and I can't face it and you know if you tell people when you focus on this one tiny thing, they are going to say what is upsetting you? Yeah, that's it and it's a melt down. But if I tell you people in this room, you will say I KNOW with a heart and if you take that one little piece it doesn't look big, but in the context of everything that has happened it is BIG. I went through this period, now I don't feel like the person I was. I am feeling more whole.

A more recent widow pointed to the new direction that was beginning to frame her life:

There were very deep changes, in a spiritual way too. But on a more pragmatic level, real-world side of change, I know that 20 months ago there were two people doing the same things I am doing. I would even say that I am more tolerant in many ways and I am kinder. I am also more intolerant, and I am much more pragmatic. I took down five trees that I wouldn't let my husband touch while he was sick. I couldn't deal with these trees. I can deal with losing my electricity, with the clean up, and it was an emotional decision to take down the trees at the time. But it is the real world, and I think some of the changes we have to accept and that's who we ultimately become in this new role, but it is the real world we have to live in.

Looking to the Future:
The Fruits of Help

> People are different in terms of what they are looking for after the death … but all widowed people are on some path to create a new life.

58-year-old widow, two years after her husband died

To say that this chapter focuses on what can be seen as the last phase in the transition to widowhood would give the reader the false impression that eventually mourning comes to an end. This is far from the truth. We can talk about the direction that this helix of change has taken and is taking, but, in fact, the changes never end. Perhaps the best way to describe this time in the life of the widowed is to see it as a continuation of grieving that now also incorporates the future. From their experiences of loss and their understanding of it, the widowed learn and feel empowered to take action and to live their lives differently. This is very much a part of the grieving process. The widowed help each other not only by acting as role models and sources of information but also by serving as facilitators to help them mobilize their own resources and learn to use them on their own behalf. Betty Wilson, one of the aides in our widow-to-widow program, reflected on the help she offered:

> I see it as a very rewarding responsibility for us who have managed to cope with and establish a different pattern of living to help those who have not. One must know what is really needed and how to go about getting it before one can move in a constructive way. Waiting for someone else to do it is never a good response. We know what our needs are, and by doing for ourselves and each other these needs can be met. Since everything seems out of whack for the new widow, [offering] help with decision-making by presenting alternatives can lend some perspective to the situation. (Wilson, 1974, p. xiv)

Looking back over the four years since her husband died, a widow reminded others like herself that they should not try to go through this alone:

> I think it really is important for people to find some really good source of support — whatever it is that works for them. And I'm sure for some people a group isn't what works. But there has to be some place with someone who really gets it, that you can talk to. I can't imagine just having no one, and it really either has to be someone who has gone through a very similar experience or somebody professional who is trained in that area extensively. Because friends can be well meaning. But it's just not the same, unless they are widowed, too.

Professional help has become more acceptable over the past decades, always with the reservation that the practitioner refrain from trying to fix the problem. Professional help, for the most part, cannot be a substitute for the support offered by other widowed people nor is it in competition. A member of a support group emphasized the importance of talking to someone who really understands:

> Well, I think they [other widows] understand what the other person is going through, the pain, the loneliness, the fear, and the confusion. Everything. The emotion that comes daily even after one, two years. It doesn't make any difference. Everybody knows what you are going through. Whether it is a confirmation or a wedding or a child is sick, or a financial decision. We learn from each other. Then it is easier to know what to do as we step back into our "other world."

Some members found that it was helpful to meet people who have been widowed for different lengths of time. This may, in part, explain the success of widow-to-widow programs: The aides become role models and offer inspiration for what the future might hold. In the words of a woman whose husband died in New York on September 11, 2001:

> All the widows I met from 9/11 are in one place. I made a decision to separate my grief from the incident because it is just too much. I just really needed to focus on that fact that he died, and focus on my feelings. And I needed to see what other widows were doing.

Support groups allow the widowed to reflect on the value of the support they are receiving. Their fears, confusion, and trouble moving back into the "real world" are legitimized, not minimized. The key question is not only how people use help at this very difficult time, but also what they learn that leads them in new directions. A widow summarized her experiences with this process:

> The shift is from sharing each other's pain to how do I build a new relationship, develop a new identity.

A widow described how the group focus changes as they begin to look at their experiences through a different and ever-expanding lens:

> I think there are different issues. We started [the support group] two years ago, and now we meet by ourselves once a month. The first months we talked about the loss issues, the guilt issues, the shock. I think that over the year, people are more into the life-building and relationship-building issues. I think people are now at the stage of "What am I going to do for me? Am I going to move? Will I find new friends? Will I be in a new relationship? What kind of relationship? What am I going to do about money?"

A widower with grown children put it more succinctly:

> There is a way in which we are all trying to help each other. How do you build the next part of your life? I don't know, and there are no easy answers.

How *do* you build the next part of your life? There is no easy answer. For some widows, looking to the future is an act of will. Others contemplate the future more gradually as they become aware of and find ways to cope with their changing needs. As one widow dramatically expressed it:

> How do I get the fun back in my life? Through that first year, the acute agony of the grief — of that person being gone, starts weakening. And now, as it gets a little easier to cope with, how do I rebuild my life? I don't know what you think you are going to do. You just have this plan that it's going to get rebuilt. That's when I realized that I am getting just as depressed now as I was after J's death, because I am not just grieving for him, but I am grieving that there is this big

hole in my life and I can't figure out how to plan it. I recognize that it can't be him, but now I know I can't figure out what does fit. I had put in all the "tinker toys" and none of it seemed to work. Now I am in a different place.

With appropriate support, understanding, and information, the widowed become more deliberate and less desperate, as they actively change their relationships to the past. A widow whose children were about to leave home provided her perspective:

You begin to realize that tears won't bring him back. You can miss him and there's many a night that I hug the pillow and say, "Oh, I want you so bad." But you can't bring him back, so there's no sense in crying. You've got to make a life for yourself. You have to go on, and you just have to make the best of it and accept life as it is.

With time, the widowed accept that their recurring pain and sadness are appropriate and that they continue to grieve not only for their spouses but also for the way of life they have lost, as well as for what their spouse or partner has lost. They change in such a way that they can hold their grief, look at it, and allow themselves to visit it from time to time as needed. When feelings or memories are stirred up one, two, or even 10 or 20 years after the death, the widowed are not expressing unresolved grief but rather are interpreting their layers of loss in different ways:

He should have been at her wedding. My daughter told me that afterwards she went to the cemetery and left a special bouquet she had made on his grave. The pain was so palpable when she told me. We had a good cry and she was so glad I understood. She was afraid to tell me at first — not to upset me. But how do I explain it? The pain felt "right."

The widowed come to accept their feelings and their occasional despair. They learn that grief is neither fully present nor fully absent. Even when they are in a new place, they still harbor a sense of disbelief:

There are times when I need to see the grave marker. When I am with other couples — it's now three years later — then it hits me that he's really gone. It is still hard to believe, and I guess I will always feel that way.

Faith can help for some. Many formerly devout widowed people lose their faith when first becoming widowed:

My husband was a minister. He loved the church. His one idea was to make heaven his home. I feel that's where he is now. At the beginning that didn't help. Now it helps me a lot to think of him there. He's in a better place.

For many, their belief has always been a large part of what gives meaning to their lives. A widow whose husband died very suddenly at a picnic reflected on how her faith provided her with a degree of comfort:

I realize now that it was the benevolent hand of God. A half-hour sooner when we were all in the car, and we would have all died.

Religion can sustain a widow through the low points:

My faith makes a real difference for me. You need that kind of belief to keep going. I find prayer very comforting.

No one relationship can meet all the needs of the widowed, but the clergy can play a variety of roles:

I learned to talk to God. It was interesting. I didn't find going to church helpful. Too many people didn't understand. I found a priest who was understanding, and he gave me support in how I was making sense out of the situation. He could listen and he had good ideas that were helpful. He also helped me learn to pray again. I felt understood and it gave me a special strength with the children and as I got involved in school.

☐ Not Everyone Is Helped

As part of this discussion, we must recognize that a small number of people who are involved in mutual-help programs do not feel helped. In many ways, they are unable to relinquish their attachment to their lives as married people. For example, one woman in the widow-to-widow program continually called to complain about her empty life, her deep despair and loneliness, and her children's insensitivity to her needs. Her children were grown but still lived at home. They were quite attentive but unwilling to devote their lives to entertaining their mother. They talked about this with the aide, who supported them in their need to live their own lives. The widow continued to live as her husband had wished, insisting that "he didn't want me to work and I won't work now." She would go to lunch with friends during the day, as she had done when her husband was alive. She would not even consider volunteering at a local hospital that needed help on weekends, as she felt this was inappropriate for her. She would not make any accommodation that forced her to confront her widowhood. She taught the widow-to-widow aides an important lesson: It is not possible to help everyone.

A widower who was very involved in an organization for the widowed expressed his inability to change:

> When my wife was alive, I was fine. Now, six years later, the only time I am okay is when I am with other people. Otherwise, I am always depressed. My life was so good when she was alive.

It is as if these widowed people are caught in a time warp and are not able to move beyond their previous but no longer available lives. They cannot take advantage of the resources available to them. It is beyond the scope of this book to address the complexities behind such responses; instead, we have focused on those who have found that life, while different, can still be exciting and rewarding.

□ A Revised Definition of Widowed

The widowed continue to have difficulty with what to call themselves. Initially, they might believe that the word *widowed* symbolizes the end of joy or pleasure in life — the end of hope for the future. Over time, however, the meaning of this word changes for them, and with it the widows' and widowers' relationships to themselves and the world around them. At one point, they were not able to conceive of a time when they would experience joy again or feel any excitement about life. They often are faced with a difference between what this word has come to mean to them and what it means to those around them. A young widow offered one example:

> People keep telling me how I should behave. I am only 28 years old. It's been two years. I am beginning to think about having some fun. Does going on living make me a bad wife? I will always love him, but …

At this point, the widowed need to learn that they cannot always please others and that perhaps they should not even try. They begin to realize that seeking the approval of others may not be consistent with their needs or the way in which their relationship to themselves is changing. How they learn to react to others in a different way is reflected in this widow's comment on how she reacted when people responded negatively to her rediscovering joy:

> Yeah, I felt guilty for singing and dancing for about eight months. If I had a good time, I would step back out of myself and say, "Something is not right here." And now it feels good. And if someone does say something because I am having a good time or enjoying life, I learned from the group thatI can look at them and say, "Oh!"

Eventually, the widowed try on other labels to see if they suit them better:

> My life has changed dramatically. Now I consider myself a single woman. I'm very social and now I'm on a health kick. I'm trying to get back some of my old energy. If I have to get used to taking responsibility for my own decisions, then I will. I sometimes call myself a "formerly married woman." I tried "unmarried." That didn't work, and I don't really feel "single." I guess "widow" it is.

☐ Reorganizing Their Daily Lives

Daily activities and routines tie a husband and wife to each other:

> No one else cares what the children said. It was only important to the two of us. There is no one to complain to, to share the small things with. But mostly I miss being cherished. It really was a 50–50 marriage, long before women's liberation. It was more than love. We cherished and cared for each other. He used to leave my birthday cards in out-of-the-way places. My son does the same thing. We couldn't afford big things, but he knew how to make me feel good. I really miss that and I know that I won't have it again. I am happy for the fact that I did have it, and that is very important to me.

One woman who lived alone after her husband's death talked about the need to change her dependence on her life's former rhythm:

> I have reorganized my day so I am not waiting at home for him at 4:30. I try to get out for lunch at a nice restaurant. I may do a little shopping to distract myself. When I get home, I feel satisfied to settle in and watch TV. The neighborhood isn't safe, and I don't like to go out at night. I used to enjoy knitting, but I find that boring. I think I will get a part-time job to meet people, even though I don't need the money.

This woman needed new activities to replace those connected to her husband, so the aide recommended the Center for Adult Education as a potential place to meet people and learn new skills. She signed up for a class but eventually became involved in a church charity that gave her a good deal of gratification.

Working widows and widowers lead more structured lives; however, even work does not fill all the hours of the day nor does it eliminate the need to observe holidays and other special occasions. Many widowed people find that they must change the way they approach day-to-day and cyclical routines. They learn from each other creative ways to deal with special occasions:

> It takes a lot to just make the plans. Mother's Day I decided, "I am not going to stay home and feel sorry for myself," and I went out to UMA to see my son. I have had so many times when I am in my house alone and I am so upset. I had to make a plan on how to get out of that and it works.

The widowed have to explore new ways to do things with friends and family. Married friends tend to include widowers in their plans more often than widows, who might be invited only for daytime activities such as lunch or when their friends' husbands are out of town. Often the widow must take the initiative to find creative ways to engage with family and friends:

> I did something for myself after I had a lot of activity. Weddings, etc. I booked a weekend at the Cape with my folks and the kids. We used to go down there all the time. We danced and sang, etc. with the children and my parents. It felt great just to be able to do that. Last year when I had graduation, the prom, etc., I went home to an empty house and I just felt depressed. On Saturday night I was happy, and last year all I felt was the pain.

For many, their friendships with other widowed people remain central in their lives. These friendships often develop beyond their initial premise of sharing the experiences of being widowed:

> I'd be lost without some of these activities. I'm going to Florida with a group this winter, and last year I went to Ireland. I had always wanted to travel, and I thought I would never have the chance once my husband died. We have a good time together — just the women. I'm not saying that it's all a bed of roses, but at least I am enjoying things and doing things I never thought I'd do.

Now the widowed can focus on their own preferences and seek each other out to share these new and varied experiences. While their widowhood may have brought them together in the beginning, friendship now keeps them close.

The widowed also find strength in new relationships and activities that often lead to a new view of themselves — a view that extends beyond their role as widow:

> I can't make this [being widowed] my whole life. I have to find other interests and other things. I see all kinds of options in what others are doing in the group.

Trying new activities becomes easier as the widowed gain self-confidence and feel empowered to develop other interests. Two widows who were very involved with their husbands' activities reported changes they were making in their lives to put the focus on their needs and who they are:

> I was always "his wife" in the church we belonged to. I needed to find a new church. It is difficult to make new friends. I hate to go alone, but I do. I have found another church where no one knew me. I've become very involved and so have the children, and I have made new friends. Maybe it is better to call them special acquaintances at this point.

> We were always together. I'm glad to be at work. I'm more friendly with the people there now. I'm making new friends.

Another illustrated the benefits of reaching out and taking advantage of new opportunities:

> If I am lonely, I can call up two or three people now. There is always someone to go to the movies with, or to just talk. I would never have done this before. A neighbor called me to come to a survey she was doing for a cereal company. I had such a good time. The kids teased me when I boasted that I earned seven dollars. We're not going to buy a stereo with that kind of money. We all enjoyed my pleasure in getting out and doing something different. You'd be surprised how it changed my attitude. I found out there were things I thought I could never do, and I am doing them. It's a very good feeling. I don't even mind being alone. I used to be afraid of that. It is better now. It's my choice. I can choose when I want to be alone.

One widow in the widow-to-widow program whose husband had had a drinking problem joined Al-Anon when he joined AA. For 18 months after his death, she kept going to the meetings. Finally she decided to stop:

> Drinking was his problem, not mine. I don't want to go to those meetings any more. That's not where I'm at now. Now that all the kids are in school, I'm going to go to school, too. I always thought I would like to go to college, and I found out about a program that will give me some credits for life experience. My sister says I'm not smart enough. I used to let that intimidate me. Now I keep hearing Dorothy's advice and now I see it as a challenge.

This widow went on to get a Master's degree in human services and had a long career in the field.

Like the women quoted above, many widows begin to think about how they will deal with the rest of their lives now that they are alone. Typically, for widows served by our widow-to-widow program, their husbands had been the primary breadwinners, and often they had not worked outside the home. Once they were widowed, many quickly realized they needed to find jobs, as previously noted in Chapter 5. At this point in their bereavement, however, work takes on a different meaning. It becomes a path toward independence and self-sufficiency:

> I have a few years until I get Social Security. When I realized that my husband lost his pension by several months and I lost the benefits as his widow, I knew I had to get a job where there was security. I could get more money elsewhere, but this company has good benefits. I have to think about that now, so I'm staying.

> For me, the hardest thing to get used to now is budgeting. My husband always used to take care of the household. I had freedom with whatever I earned on my own. Now I have to live within my means. I have some insurance money, but still I have to think ahead. You have to have some savings. Rents are going up and God forbid if I ever got sick!

Widows today are more likely to be involved in work or have a career. One problem for widowed people currently in the work force is the lack of flexibility in the workplace to accommodate their grief when they become newly widowed. A widower in a support group added it up:

> I was shocked when I heard stories here. From my quick arithmetic I think about 20% of us were pushed out of our jobs because of our grief. If you told married people about 20% losing their jobs they

wouldn't believe it … they would be carrying signs that this is a big atrocity. In big corporations they assume you aren't going to produce as well. They give you 2 days off and they are afraid to let you go while you are going through it, but right afterwards …

A widow was told by her boss that he did not want her on the job until she could function at 100%:

I pushed my hand and used politics so they were afraid to let me go. It was one month after my husband died. It was a loss even though I stayed on. It was my livelihood and a place to go.

In contrast, a new widow who worked in a professional agency was able to take sick leave. As she felt more in charge of her feelings she was able to start work again on a part-time basis. Work in a supportive environment can actually be a positive experience:

I had a skill they needed; they knew I was a new widow but they needed me. At first I had trouble concentrating but in fact the work is fascinating and it is a nice place to lose myself, and at the same time it is really good work to be doing. It's not just killing time.

☐ Life Looks Different Now

The widowed slowly recognize that life will never be the same. Two widows in our widow-to-widow program discovered what they had lost — and gained:

I lost my best friend. Who will I share my life with? I lost a sense of meaning, and direction, and a sense of security. Everything changes, but I begin to see a new light at the end of the tunnel.

I can do things on my own. They [the group] gave me suggestions, not rules. It became clear that I was going to have to make a new life for myself.

Children are constant reminders of other ways in which families have been wounded:

I think that they are growing up to be … well, I think he would be very proud of them, and that's what really hurts. Like when my daughter learned to dive and my son to swim. These are things that you'll never get over, because then it will be graduation and their weddings. You know, there is no replacement. Even a stepfather is not their father. You can't replace people.

Nonetheless, mourning now has a different flavor:

> I don't think that you ever finish mourning. I mean, you don't brood. There's a difference. But as far as mourning the person, you mourn them the rest of your life. You reminisce, but you don't brood or dwell on the past. I think you have to learn to look ahead a little to the future. I used to feel such self-pity. Why was I picked on? You have to pick up the pieces. I just don't know how or when — but somehow I overcame these things.

The widowed find new directions, new friends, and new ways to connect to the deceased. Their creativity begins to emerge as they grow in many different areas of their lives, often without even knowing it. This process can be likened to an active apprenticeship. To successfully integrate the past with the present, the bereaved need the examples set by more experienced widows and widowers. By observing these role models, they develop new ways to make meaning and to define who they were and how they related to others. They begin to accept that they need to act on their own behalf:

> You just can't live on grief forever. If you do, you'll find yourself cutting paper dolls or something else. I had a long road to walk before I felt that maybe I could face the world. All of a sudden it dawns on you that if I don't go out and really work, I'm not going to have a roof. You have to face the world in a way that you did not before, because a wife working is in cooperation with her husband for the extras. Now it's for real.

☐ A New Sense of Self

Reinterpreting their status as "widowed" represents a step in the broader process of developing a new sense of self; however, this process is not always easy:

> I think a big part of it is learning that if you are going to have any self-esteem, you have to do it yourself — which maybe you will or you won't. But it's a pain. It is not the same as someone else saying, "You are gorgeous, you are wonderful, you're fabulous." So it kind of sucks … to start all over again. That's a word we use in this group a lot.

Two years after her husband's death, another participant in the widow-to-widow program was pleased at who she had become:

> I have to keep fighting the family image of me as the "village idiot." I was the baby and they never believed I could do anything. They always said, "Don't tell her, she'll forget. She doesn't know how to do anything." Here I am, standing on my own two feet, taking care of my children. I have to remind them that I am doing it. I've taken responsibility that I never had before. I didn't need to before, but now I'm doing it, and I'm proud of myself.

These changes are profound and real, allowing the widow to relate differently to those around her. She is, in essence, growing, not only in her role as a widowed mother, but also in her role as a competent adult. The family has to deal with these changes, as well:

> My family had to learn it was a new me. It took awhile.

Other widows and widowers have offered their own examples:

> I have to live with me every day. I much prefer to live with the old me, who was much more carefree and happy and secure and playful. This me is more mature. I think "maturity" is the perfect word to describe it.

A widower discovered a new quality in himself:

> I'm a more caring person. Grieving and sharing it with my dear friends and family have made me more open and deeply appreciative of the need to share and to be sensitive to the feelings of others.

A widow was amazed at her new-found ability:

> I never believed I could have done it, but I found this house. I looked over my money and decided to buy it. It was a smart move to a better neighborhood and better schools and was closer to my family. I have everything I want. I work. I think it gives you a little self-confidence in yourself. I think that confidence is the most important thing of all. If you have confidence in yourself, you can get by with anything. I enjoy my home and I try to enjoy myself.

The widow's growing sense of confidence and competence often is accompanied by an equally powerful feeling of increased independence. As they slowly begin to recognize the importance of their own needs, they begin, at first tentatively, to advocate for themselves. While it seems natural for today's woman to be assertive and confident, the participants of the original widow-to-widow program often had to handle situations that they would never before have considered trying on their own. Yet, even today, a newly widowed woman who was proud of her independence said:

> I'll go to a concert alone, a movie. But I wouldn't travel alone. Depending on my mood, I can eat out alone.

Other women today find that going out on their own, which had seemed easy and natural when they were married, takes on new meaning now that they are widowed:

> Because of business and night school and a million other things, there were lots of times when my husband wasn't there. I had to eat out alone, travel alone. I wouldn't think twice about it. I was on my way to school, so I stopped to eat. But now, I think, I still do it. I am much more conscious of the fact that I am alone. While before I just wouldn't even think about it. The first time I went to lunch by myself in a real fancy restaurant, the person seating me said: "Ohhh, you are alone? No one is joining you?"

A widower revealed that he sometimes got the same reactions but he viewed them differently:

> There's a difference in perception. I eat out alone all the time. I don't think anything of it. But I get the same reaction: "Oh, it's just you!" But I don't even give it a lot of thought.

Other widowers agree that going out alone is easier for men than for women:

> You know, a guy can go and do things by himself. And I think a woman should be able to…. If you need time, what's better than walking the beach rather than staying at home in the living room and crying?

Driving and the independence it allows often produce dramatic results, as reported by an aide with regard to one of her widowed clients:

> She had such a hard, closed-in expression. She was negative about everything. I met her at the meeting the other night. I guess her husband must be dead about two and a half years now. She looked stunning. The best-looking woman in the crowd. She was talking to people, reaching out. Her whole manner was changed.

Of herself, the same widow said:

> I am more involved and more outgoing than I ever was, even before my husband died. You were right. Once I learned to drive, things really started to change. I never thought I could do anything, and now I'm taking people to meetings, and I see how helpful I can be. That's also a new experience.

☐ Dating and Remarriage

Taking off a wedding ring is a major turning point for the widowed and for many indicates their readiness to consider other relationships. Most often the widowed wear their rings on chains around their necks or move them to the other hand. Others have made their rings into another piece of jewelry or put them away for one of their children.

Cameron McDonald, a young widow, sought a way to change her relationship to her dead husband without severing it. At a ceremony attended by her friends she took off her rings and read the following poem she had written for the occasion:

> I remove these rings to set you free to be at peace with God.
> I remove these rings in hopes of creating a new
> Union between us in the Spirit.
> I remove these rings in prayer that I will be willing to be open to new
>   life,
> To be the woman you want me to be,
> And to walk in the joy you gave.

Most women are clearly ambivalent about dating and remarriage. Some do not actively seek male companionship or hope to remarry: "I'm satisfied with my family and my friends and my children." Another widow reported:

> I think maybe sometime in the future I might think about it. It doesn't seem impossible, but not any time soon.

One woman who said that she did not want to remarry was nevertheless excited when a friend arranged a date for her with a widower. As another widow stated, "I miss male company."

The widowed often have not had much experience being friends with members of the opposite sex. A widow learned that it is possible to enjoy another's company without necessarily dating:

My husband's company was having its annual holiday party and they really expected me to come. My son had a conflict and couldn't accompany me. I mentioned it in the group. One of the men volunteered. We had a wonderful evening, as good friends should. It was a new experience for me. A lot of heads were turned, and people at the party learned something new about friendship between members of the opposite sex.

Men and women wait different lengths of time before starting to date. Lieberman (1996) found that men were much more likely to be involved in a new relationship (80%) shortly after the death of their spouse or partner than women were (20%).

One woman, a lesbian, who was self-conscious about having met someone she was interested in dating six months after her partner died asked the group if people in heterosexual relationships waited longer to date. They did not see any connection. They said that what was important was that she was not trying to simply replace the relationship she had lost with this new one, to which she responded:

It's interesting. This is a really a very different relationship. I'm not replacing anything. Something new is here. We can talk about my partner and that is important, too. I can't be pushed to make a commitment. It's too soon. But this relationship is important to me.

Children also influence the timing of dating. A widower with children about to leave for college talked about their reactions to his seeing a new woman:

My son [a high school senior] said, "The happier you are, the better it is for me." My other son asked, "If Mom came back, would you go back to her?" That's an interesting way of putting it. Obviously there is an intense loyalty, but I think they knew there was no answer to that. He knew his mother and I had a good marriage that neither of us wanted to end. I tried to explain that no one can replace his mother. This is a different relationship. My friend's children are giving her a hard time. We are not rushing…. It's something I think about all the time because finding another person at this age and the experience is completely different. I feel like I'm in a different life, almost. I have said to people, "It's not that I have two loves in my life. It's that I have a love in two different lives. Like I am almost in a different life now."

Some women seek social outlets where they can meet men. Both men and women visit websites and have other ways to meet people. As they begin to date, many widowed people realize that they are out of practice and revert to the habits of teenagers:

> I was grateful for Adele talking to me like that. I was acting as if I was 16 years old again. That was the last time I had a date. I would sit by the phone and wait. I was so afraid to be alone. But I didn't need that pressure, as if being married was everything. I needed to learn that I didn't need a man to take care of me. Now maybe I am ready to get married if I meet someone I really like.

In-laws often cause problems when their daughters- or sons-in-law start dating. Sometimes this is reflected in the widowed person's own feelings:

> The first time I dated, I felt guilty. I was sure my husband would find out — as if I was cheating. Then my in-laws started on me about being disloyal to his memory. I don't know if they thought that I should sit home in black all the time. Mary [the aide] was really great in helping me understand my own feelings and that it was all right to enjoy myself. She also helped me see that I had to live my life and that I would never be able to please my in-laws. At least now I don't fight with them.

When the widowed become more comfortable with themselves and more confident about their ability to deal with the world, they relax and come to accept that remarriage is only one possible outcome of their changed circumstances:

> I never want to be tied down by marriage again. When I want to go out now, I can go. My life is really my own. I find that I have this freedom. If I have a chance to go out to dinner with the girls at the office, I do, and I enjoy it. This is not just sour grapes. We had a good life together, but now I think it is time to be alone. Maybe later I'll change my mind.

One young widow met someone she wanted to marry. Her children were excited, too. They were too young to remember their father and they wanted a new dad. This woman had not planned to remarry and did not want to marry simply to fill her loneliness. She talked for hours with the aide, wanting to be sure that she cared for the man in his own right. As a practicing Catholic, she could not afford to make a mistake. She also needed support in dealing with her dead husband's parents, who were afraid the children would not remember their father. Her own parents were most supportive. She finally found comfort in her decision to remarry:

When we did marry, I knew I loved this man, who would be a good father to my children. I really looked forward to having his children as well. He's understanding of my in-laws' feelings. If they can accept him, he wants them to feel welcome. I just know that we can work it out for us.

Women who have had good marriages tend to be more willing to consider remarriage, although some believe that there could only be one man for them. Widows often talk about remarriage as one way to address their need for love, respect, and financial security:

I think if anyone has a chance to remarry, then they should. While my children are single, I will never marry. But after they are married, that's different. You can't live your life for them, and they can't live yours. If I found someone who's nice, with enough money so that we won't be destitute, then I'd have someone for a companion.

Difficulties in a previous marriage, however, can add to fears about future commitments:

I miss him very much. We had lots of good times. But he did drink, and we lost out on lots of chances to get ahead because of it. In some ways it is better now — although I wouldn't admit it to my family. I don't think I want to take a chance on marriage again.

Social mores have changed considerably over the last decades, and it is now more acceptable for men and women to have intimate relationships without being married or committed to each other. Sexually transmitted diseases motivate others to be more cautious. It is also not uncommon to see couples of all ages living together without the legal obligations of marriage. Widows have to be sure of their own values and how to protect them:

A man at work seemed inclined to go out with me, but I was disgusted when I sensed that all he wanted was sex. All I wanted was some good companionship, and certainly no sex outside of marriage.

In contrast, another widow said:

Sex was an important part of my marriage. I have a steady friend. This is an important part of our relationship, but I am positive we will never marry. I would look for someone different then.

For widowers, remarriage was much more likely. The death rate for men is much higher than for women, giving men the advantage in finding a suitable mate (Campbell & Silverman, 1996). Widowers who live in retirement communities often talk of being courted as soon as their wives died and joke about the "casserole brigade." These overtures often lead to friendships and sometimes marriage. A second marriage does not replace the first, but ideally it reflects the ways in which the widowed person has changed and grown. A second marriage is a very different relationship in many ways (Campbell & Silverman, 1996).

☐ Establishing a New Relationship with the Deceased: Continuing Bonds

Many widows find comfort in the memory of their husbands or partners. Sometimes they actively seek out these memories; other times, these memories arrive, unbidden. Sometimes the widowed want to cherish their memories alone; other times they need to share. They find various ways to connect to the deceased:

> I get lonesome, especially at night when the kids are gone. If I can't sleep, I sometimes take the bus and go up to the cemetery. I sit there and talk — sometimes to myself, sometimes to him. One day last winter, it was cold and windy. It felt good to walk up there and stand in the wind. I came home and I felt much better.

> One thing I learned [in the group] was that it was okay to talk about my husband. My friends and family sometimes wanted me to act as if he hadn't existed. They didn't want me to be upset. I needed permission to be sad from time to time, and we [other group members] exchanged information about ways to remember and to help each other on anniversaries. In a way, we all got to know each other's spouses and that felt good.

> As the kids have gotten older, they run [for cancer] with me. They get sponsors in the neighborhood and from the family, and it gives us a chance to talk about their mother. And it feels good to think we may be helping others not suffer the way she did.

☐ Helping Others

Much of what this book is about is based on the ability of people to help each other with their common problems. We are talking about a mutuality and an exchange. The widowed described in this book all were involved in committed relationships that involved them in an intimacy and an exchange that sustained them in very special ways. The help they offered each other had some of these same qualities — perhaps less commitment and care but nonetheless an involvement with others. For many, being widowed allows them to connect in a personal way with strangers. The experience of helping becomes an important part of the way they come to see themselves and of how they make meaning out of their being widowed. A widower described his experience:

> When I was first widowed I couldn't deal with anyone else's pain, I couldn't see past my own pain. On the other hand I made a call to someone who had been helpful to me and my wife about something going on in the community. She said "I am very sorry — my husband died," and she wanted to get off phone. I ended up talking with her for over an hour. It was so rewarding to be able to help ... so different from how I felt a year ago. Anyone who came with any kind of pain ... I just wanted to get out of there and now I can be there for that person where as before I couldn't be there for anyone.

Both widows and widowers report new ways of becoming involved with other widowed people. They are able to find a new sense of mutuality and satisfaction as they discover a new-found ability to be involved with others in a new way. They are able to put to use what they have learned. These people have rediscovered Pearl and Riessman's (1965) observation that helping others is a very effective way of helping oneself. In the words of one woman who learned how to drive and had discovered a new side of herself:

> I feel really good — something is changed in me and I really like it. I never thought I could help anyone other than my family and here I am. I'm encouraging them and getting people out.

Another widow had a list she developed in a hospice support group that she eagerly shared with others. She believed it was important to remain upbeat and this was her message:

> I have learned it is extremely important to keep your spirits up. I learned in the group "deep" breathing and relaxation techniques. It is comforting to know that others are in the same boat. We all came away stronger and learned from each other. Everyone seemed to have a different input — but similar in a strange way. I have a list for how to stay upbeat. I recommend: paint your toenails bright red (it's great fun to look at them), take a bubble bath, continue to make

yourself feel special. At Christmas, I decorated the house without a tree, put lights in the window. I found the brightest red tablecloth and I kept it on the table through this awful winter. I feel as if I have turned a corner. I hope what I am telling you will help others a little!

Other widowed people shift roles to becomes helpers in organizations from which they received help. Many of the volunteers for the Widowed Service Line, which grew out of the original widow-to-widow program, had been recipients of help in the earlier program. A widow who had been helped by an organization for the widowed talked about the shift in roles she made:

Working with my chapter has given me a purpose in life. It keeps me busy and allows me to give service to widowed persons, especially the newly bereaved. I need to be needed and I am.

For many women, this new role is a continuation of the one they fill within their families but now they have found a new way of being a care-taker:

I can understand the newly widowed because I cannot forget that lost-soul feeling I had. I am better because in turn I am helping someone else.

Men talk of helping themselves through helping others as a brand-new experience:

It's the secret — by helping others you help yourself. Other than my children, TLA, and the work I do with it, is the most important thing in my life. I feel I am really doing something worthwhile and it makes me feel a sense of real accomplishment.

A widower noted how helping others has brought out a new part of himself:

My wife was my social secretary. I never thought about it. I'm learn-ing to reach out. I've discovered I'm a good listener. I like to help in ways I never wanted to do before.

Most people find that the feeling of being needed gives them purpose in life. In the role of helper, people find a valuable and meaningful way of being connected to others and to themselves: "In helping others I help myself." This is the real meaning of mutual help — the exchange and mutuality that takes place between people as they put to use their lived experience:

I don't know how to describe that feeling, but it is amazing. It is wonderful. It is so helpful to be able to give to others and to be able to share with others the knowledge you now have.

A widow summarized this experience:

I think we all realize that, rather than have it be such a negative in our lives, we should try to very consciously be better in some ways for it.... It's true in many ways that we take on the role of being a teacher and in fact I know that I have had many opportunities.... My dad is very ill and I do not have a problem talking about death. He does, but I certainly open the door as often as I can to allow him should he choose to do so; at least he has someone with whom he can broach the subject. I have a friend who has lost her son and I had no problem this week.... Every day I have reached out to her.... I have another relative who just lost her husband the other day. I was on the phone with her this morning.... It is difficult but it is very satisfying: loving, giving, feeling to let someone know that you truly understand and give them the opportunity to talk if they choose to or not. We (in this group) all know that no matter what the circumstances the grief process is very similar. I think we have all learned that and I truly believe we are better people for it.

Parenting Alone: Widowed with Dependent Children

Our children are exposed to the facts of life, just as I was. No one could have predicted this outcome when I was first married. But you learn that you can't really protect them, and I couldn't have really been prepared.

A mother widowed in 2001

The widowed are not always elderly. Any widowed population includes younger grieving spouses caring for their dependent children. For example, in the original widow-to-widow program, 64 participating families had children under the age of 16 at home. More recent data from the U.S. Census indicate that the death rate in younger women is likely to be approximately 60% that of men. While our society pays a good deal of attention to the needs of children and families of divorce, the same is not true when a parent dies. Death brings an unexpected and premature end to what was usually a good relationship, leaving the surviving spouse to deal not only with his or her own grief but also that of their children.

This chapter focuses on the needs of widowed parents raising children in a single-parent household. The issues facing widowed parents today are not very different from those experienced by participants in the original widow-to-widow program, even though today's parents have more information and resources available (Silverman, 2000a). Surviving parents need help understanding their children's reactions and finding ways to respond appropriately. They need to hear that their children's lives will be different but not necessarily bad. The widowed have to accept that in many ways their children will learn the "facts of life" long before their parents would have preferred. They need to learn more about how the age and gender of children affect their grief and their understanding of death. Widowed parents also have to appreciate how they influence their children's understanding of and response to the death. In time, they must recognize how their own growth will affect their children's coping strategies. Of utmost importance to grieving children is to have their grief validated and to feel safe in their world.

Bereaved children need *care, continuity,* and *connection.* They seek reassurance that their physical, emotional, and social needs will be met. Care includes all the elements of social and physical support described earlier in this book that help meet these needs. Continuity involves the children's need to be certain that their lives will proceed — not exactly as before but with some consistency. Bereaved children do not always trust or have the experience to know that tomorrow will come even though today their world has fallen apart. They also need help maintaining an appropriate connection to the deceased that can give them comfort and solace. In addition, children need to be respected as important members of the family, to be connected to the family drama as legitimate mourners whose grief is as real and valid as that of the adults (Silverman, 2000a).

☐ How Do I Tell My Children?

From the moment a surviving parent becomes aware that his or her spouse might die or has already died, questions arise regarding what to tell the children and how to explain what is happening. The parent might be aware of the need to be open and honest, but doing so often proves difficult, as described by a widowed mother:

> I had no idea what to say. I didn't want to scare her, but she could see he wasn't doing well. My doctor wasn't any help. I finally called hospice, and one of the nurses there made some good suggestions like, "Daddy's not getting any better and we aren't sure if he will get well." The nurse said if she asks if he could die, say "Yes." When I had the words, somehow it became easier to talk to my daughter.

Even when others provide some guidance, it is difficult for a parent to find an easy or "right" way to tell the children that their mother or father has died. This is especially true when the parent dies suddenly:

> My husband died in the emergency room in the middle of the night. I asked the hospital chaplain to come home with me. I had no idea how to tell the children.

> My oldest son was there when he collapsed. He knew. When I got home, I just blurted it out to the others. There is no easy way to say, "Daddy is dead."

A widower recalled how his plan to break the news to his son, who had been away with friends for the day, fell apart when his son walked in the door:

> I had a lot of time to think about what I was going to tell him by the time he came home. He walked through the door. I asked him to sit down and I started crying, and I think he sort of guessed. He knew she was in the hospital. All that I planned to say went out the window and then he started reassuring me that we were still a family. We had each other and we would be alright. Quite a statement from a ten-year-old! He then got on his bicycle and started peddling furiously around the block.

Many widows in the original widow-to-widow program could not remember how they told their children that their father was dead, as the events were a blur:

> When I told my five-year-old that Daddy was dead, he wasn't coming home from work tonight, he crawled under the bed and wouldn't come out. I wish I could have gone there with him. I wanted to hide. Maybe it would go away. My thinking was no better than my son's.

A father whose wife had died at home with hospice care talked about the death:

> Even though we all knew what was coming and my older boy was in the room when she died I don't remember how my eight-year-old found out. My older boy says that he told him. I do remember him slamming around the house. Knowing what was coming didn't make it any easier.

Most children cry when they hear the news, and nothing can console them. Some children try to deny the death or simply cannot believe it has happened. For example, a ten-year-old child hit his older sister when she told him the news as he arrived home from school. He thought she was teasing him. He understood what it meant to die; on some level he hoped his sister was joking, but he knew better. A three-year-old child who did not yet have a clear understanding of the finality of death kept asking when Daddy was coming back; for him, death was temporary. Parents often needed reassurance that they have appropriately handled the situation at the time of death:

> My husband had been sick for some time. Hospice told us he would probably die that day. I gave my seven-year-old the option to be home or go to a neighbor's. He didn't want to be home. He didn't want to see the body. We are in this program for bereaved children. The children were talking about how their parents died. Now that he is 11, he is a bit upset that he wasn't home when Dad died. I explained he did what he needed to do when he was seven. If he had been older at the time, it might have been different. I started to think I had done the wrong thing, but the parent group reminded me he was seven at the time, and he needed to recognize that he was different then. And so did I.

☐ Attending the Funeral or Not

Many parents wonder whether or not their children should be involved in the funeral or memorial service. In the original widow-to-widow program, many parents did not take their children to the funeral because others told them it would be too upsetting. In contrast, I found that 95% of the parents in the Child Bereavement Study did take their children to the funeral, regardless of the children's ages (Silverman & Worden, 1993). Over the past 30 years, funeral directors and clergy have begun to provide more support for parents with respect to their children. Television shows today show children attending funerals and grieving the loss of a loved one. The recent unexpected death of the actor John Ritter serves as a good example. The situation comedy in which he played the father was rewritten to acknowledge his death and the grief of his television widow and their children. For younger children, programs such as *Mr. Rogers* and *Sesame Street* have provided role models for families dealing with a death in the family or neighborhood and have made it easier to initiate discussions of death and dying.

In the original widow-to-widow program, families often pressured their children to be strong and not to break down at the service. One mother told an aide that she and her adolescent son had a signal that they used to remind each other not to cry during the funeral. Another mother remembered worrying that her 18-year-old daughter would not look into the coffin because she wanted to remember her father as he was. In fact, children often are glad they have seen the body but they also want to hold onto an image of the parent as healthy and well. A teenage girl remembered her mother's wake:

> The funeral director was very nice. He had time for us to visit before the wake. But when we saw our mother, we realized that they had gotten her make-up all wrong. We didn't want to hurt anyone's feelings, so we didn't say anything. But it was just like my mother to have something out of order. We laughed, and we were glad to remember the funny things she did.

One widow recalled her own fear as an adolescent at her mother's funeral and did not take her six-year-old daughter to her husband's service or the funeral.

Parents also have to deal with the expectations and needs of family and friends, who sometimes have even less tolerance for being around grieving children. A widower recalled:

> My six-year-old wailed though the entire funeral service. I comforted her. Her grandmother was there, and they sort of cried together. But my friends were very upset with me, that I brought her. I didn't need that. They thought there was no reason to expose her at such a young age. But it was her mother!

When asked later if they should have attended the service, most children have expressed no regrets about going ("It was my father. I belonged there. I needed to be there for him"); however, one child whose father gave him a choice of attending the services later reported that he was not sorry he chose not to go to the wake or the funeral — he liked remembering his mother when she was well.

☐ We Are All Grieving

The widowed with dependent children at home must deal with not only their own grief but also that of their children. At a time when they may feel least able to attend to other people's needs, they must be available to their grieving children. In the original widow-to-widow program, widows with dependent children were more likely than other widows to ask to see an aide as soon as possible after the death. They cited two reasons for their eagerness to talk to someone: "The children are good, but it's not like talking to a grownup" or "I'm worried about my kid — the teacher says he isn't doing well, and I don't understand what I should be doing." They need to talk about the special difficulties of parenting in the midst of grief. These parents have pressing responsibilities and cannot take their own time adjusting to the reality of the death of their spouse. Every day they are faced with reminders that they are now widows and are solely in charge of their families and households. They experience a difference kind of loneliness than do childless or older widows. While they are grateful to have children to provide a reason for living, the continual demands of parenting these mourning children can leave surviving parents with little time to address their own needs. They are struggling to accept the death, and their children's questions and needs often aggravate their own pain.

Many widows find the long evenings after the children have gone to bed and the house is quiet to be particularly unbearable. A recent widower with young children lamented:

> I miss my wife. This is when we would talk. Now I sometimes wander around the house after I get the kids in bed. There is a lot that needs doing, but I can't get into it. Not now!

A recent widow described her dilemma:

> I had five children. If one of them got sick, I sometimes took all of them to the doctor. I have good neighbors and my parents nearby, but it didn't always work that one of them could come over. I had to keep my wits about me all the time. I was always on duty, and at the beginning I felt like it was all a dream.

Another woman got up each morning to get her children to school and then went back to bed to sleep away the day. Women who both work and care for children often are too tired at the end of the day to do anything outside the home. The widowed find that they need to be better organized than they were before the death so they can respond to their children's needs as well as to their own often-immobilizing feelings.

☐ The Daily Routine Changes

While both widows and widowers can have trouble keeping the family going, the Child Bereavement Study found that children in mother-headed households experience fewer changes than those in father-headed households (Silverman & Worden, 1993; Boerner & Silverman, 2002). One possible reason is that women seem to be better at multitasking. Many women have always assumed primary or total responsibility for taking care of the children and the house, so when a father dies the children experience fewer changes in their daily routines. As one widow put it, "That was the easy part. I just continued to do what I always do." In contrast, a widower emphasized the impact of his wife's death on several aspects of his life:

> My wife was the glue that held the family together. I'm really floundering. I'm lucky. I changed my work so I am home more. But it is very hard to keep it all together. With two kids, if my mother wasn't helping me I don't know what I would do. Even so, can I really meet these kinds of needs? I have a daughter to raise now!

An older teenager reminisced about what it was like when his mother first died:

> When my father put supper on the table, and I helped clean up while my sister did the dishes, I had a real good feeling. I was so worried that we wouldn't be able to go on as a family now that my mother was dead.

His father told the group what it looked like from his perspective:

> My kids were worried if we were going to stay here. The younger one was worried about what happens if … what happens if something happens to me. How will the laundry get done? You don't even know how to run the washing machine. I couldn't let it happen by default. We couldn't talk a lot about my wife being dead, but we did talk about what jobs were needed.

A widower whose wife died suddenly, leaving him with three children ages six to 16, said:

> I'm lucky. I have flexible work hours. I had to learn to do everything: laundry, shopping — you name it. I really appreciate what my wife was able to do. It didn't seem so hard then. I can't stand it when I meet people I know in the market who are always asking, "How you doing?" It's not my time to socialize. I go late at night now, when it is quiet and I can get through very quickly.

The majority of widows and widowers find that they cannot consistently sustain their parental roles. They need time off and sometimes ask family or friends to babysit. The eating habits of most families change quickly, with more dinners eaten out and on the fly. Preparing meals often requires more energy than the surviving parent can muster. Some surviving fathers already know how to cook; others have learned how to cook while their wives were ill. Nevertheless, families tend to frequent local fastfood restaurants in the early months of bereavement, which solves the dual problems of cooking dinner and sitting down to eat at a table where one family member is painfully absent. A widower, six months after his wife died, found a way to handle this empty-chair dilemma while on a car trip with his children:

> The first time we went on a trip as a family, my oldest daughter sat in my wife's usual place, beside me. I found myself very upset. The children seemed to need to be able to sit there, and I finally decided that we would rotate so everyone would have a chance to sit next to me. When I saw it as a chance to be close to me, and not taking her place, it took the pressure off, and we all felt better. I started to do the same thing at dinnertime.

Several widows report that, although the title is accurate, they hate being called "single parents." While they recognize that this label acknowledges, to some degree, the increased burden of ensuring their children's well-being, they often feel that the phrase brings up unfair or irrelevant associations. As one recent widow put it:

> When people hear I'm a single parent, they think I'm divorced or perhaps never married. That's entirely different. I prefer the label "single but not by choice," but I really don't have the energy to think about labels.

When a father dies, questions often focus on the family's ability to survive financially. One widow talked about the range of reactions in her eight children:

> When we settled down after the funeral, my oldest boy broke the ice. "Can I go back to college?" I tried to reassure him we would manage. Even if there isn't going to be a terrible change, they realized that there will be a change. My youngest, seven at the time, offered to give up her allowance. This was her way of making a contribution. She enjoys the dramatic, and I think that she saw this on TV once. They needed to know that we could go on, and they needed to see that we could work together to make it happen.

If the family's health needs have been covered by the husband's insurance, the widow must now quickly find work to secure health coverage. When widows work, the need to juggle routines, manage a household, and earn a living parallels the experience of single fathers; however, it is clear that widows do not have as much to learn about keeping a family together as widowers do.

☐ Protecting Their Children From Their Grief

Parents need to learn that they cannot shelter their children from the pain of a parent's death and that when they do they are, in reality, protecting themselves as much as their offspring. Over time and by talking with other widowed people, these parents learn that when parents feel supported in expressing their own pain they usually can do the same for their children. A parent's fear of losing control in front of the children continues long after the death. Although they usually do not deny their thoughts and feelings, the widowed do not want to express emotions that they do not know how to manage in front of their children. Parents rationalize that witnessing their grief would upset their sons and daughters, so they try to refrain from crying in their children's presence. They might say it is the children who are afraid of losing control, and sometimes they are right, but often it is their own fear of losing control and bring overwhelmed. One widow recalled that her children became paralyzed when they saw her cry on the anniversary of their father's death. Another acknowledged that this stoic approach made her feel lonelier, but she also claimed, "You can't go around mourning in front of grown boys."

In many cases, taking the strong, silent approach has helped the widowed avoid their own intense feelings of grief; however, in trying to hide their grief, these surviving parents often withdraw and stop talking, giving their children the sense that they have lost not one parent but two. A father reported that one of his young teenagers told him to get remarried because "then I would have my father back."

Unwittingly, many parents communicate the message "don't show me you're upset." When one boy found his father's driver's license two years after his death, he started to cry and left the room. In another family, the widow reported that her daughters stopped talking about their father when they saw how distressed she became. This same widow worried that her 13-year-old son had become very quiet since his father's death and never even brought up his name. Only when another widow pointed out the connection between her response and that of her son did she realize that his silence was an obedient response to her implicit request for silence and denial.

James Agee's novel, *A Death in the Family* (1957), vividly captures how a child senses his parent's difficulty discussing a death:

When you want to know more about it (and her eyes become still more vibrant) just ask me, just, just ask me and I'll tell you because you ought to know. "How did he get hurt?" Rufus wanted to ask, but he knew by her eyes that she did not mean at all what she said, not now anyway, not this minute, he need not ask; and now he did not want to ask because he too was afraid; he nodded to let her know he understood her. (Agee, 1957, p. 253)

Children can misunderstand a mother's silence, erroneously concluding that she does not miss or care about their father:

I was shocked to discover that they thought I didn't care. This came out when I was talking to my seven-year-old son's teacher. He had managed to explain to her how he felt. I had to force myself to talk about their father and to help them keep their very good memories of him. I don't want them to ever forget their father, but I guess that's what they thought I wanted when I didn't show my feelings. My kids finally asked me if I didn't love Daddy. I couldn't figure out why they thought that. They told me that since I had changed all the furniture and put away all of the mementos that belonged to Dad, what else would they think? I learned something then, and in spite of the pain, I put back some of his things.

Most widows find that avoidance does not work over the long run and are grateful for an intervention that interrupts their tendency to mask or deny their reactions:

I tried to keep my feelings from them. A friend, a priest, told me not to, and so did Dorothy [the aide]. In the end, I let them see my sadness and crying. Now we each share our feelings more honestly. It has brought us closer together.

Another widow expressed her regrets that she had taken her 11-year-old to the first-anniversary mass because he became so upset that he could not stop crying. At the time, she saw no positive value in his emotional outburst. Only afterwards could she admit that he seemed more relaxed, and she understood then that her son needed to express his feelings. When other widows in the group asked about her own grief, she realized that she was not responding to the child's needs but rather to her own desire to protect herself from pain. She, like most grieving parents, had a difficult time balancing her needs and grief with those of her children.

☐ Understanding Their Children's Grief

Many widows expect their children to express their grief with tears and sadness and do not always connect other unusual behavior with mourning. Some widowed parents who have talked about their children's reactions do not understand that these feelings and behaviors take on different meanings at different ages. They need a basic understanding of child development so they can assess the appropriateness and potential meaning of their children's reactions. They do not always recognize, for example, that young children cannot always make a connection between what is happening to them and how they feel; rather, they communicate their thoughts and feelings through their behavior. Older children are more likely to have the relevant language to express their feelings and needs directly.

One father could not make the link between his four-year-old son's clingy behavior and his mother's death a year before. This father needed order in the house and insisted that the child follow rules that were impossible for a child this young to understand. The father was in a support group, and the members tried to help him be more flexible, to see the limits of a four-year-old's understanding, and to realize the importance of feeling secure in this young boy's life. Unless parents can see this type of connection, they have a hard time being supportive of their children.

A grown woman reminisced about her reaction to her father's death and her attempt to visit him in heaven:

> When I was three, I got a ladder and put it up against a tree in our backyard. I had started to climb when my mother found me. I explained that I was going to visit Daddy in heaven.

While this behavior might seem foolish in a 12-year-old, it vividly illustrates a young toddler's common perception that heaven is a physical place that can be visited and that the deceased live there in the same manner as they did on earth. A child of this age is not able to comprehend what it means when told that death is final and universal.

Older school-age children and young teenagers begin to think about the meaning of death and see its implications for their own lives. A father of four talked about his son's behavior on the anniversary of his wife's death:

> My son is 13. He talks the most about it. The week of the anniversary, he was looking at his mother's picture with a friend and said something to him about his mother. He then goes on to talk about

Roger Clemmons and baseball and other things in his life. Then one day he asked me, "When I die and I see mom again, is she still going to be 39? Is her face going to be 38?" I'm like, "Oh, crap, I have no idea." "Is her hair still growing?" He has a ton of questions and then bounces right back. He did that for a whole week. The girls don't talk much about it. My youngest was so little, she doesn't say much.

As this boy found a way to think about his mother, he also recognized that he, too, would die some day.

The widowed sometimes interpret a child's initial denial or shock as a sign that the child does not understand or appreciate what has happened. In some ways, children's reactions are no different from their own, which vacillate between belief and disbelief; however, adults have words for what they are experiencing, and children often do not. Parents come to understand that children communicate their responses through their behavior and that a lack of talk does not necessarily represent a lack of understanding. One surviving parent observed her children and interpreted their feelings from their actions: "They were crushed ... he became very quiet ... he couldn't sleep nights ... they were heartbroken." Typically, children either ask too many questions or remain silent. Either way, this creates problems for the surviving parent. One widow said that each time her children asked a question about what happened to their father, it felt like "a knife being stuck in my throat."

Surviving parents can be confused by their children's behavior and begin to wonder which behaviors can be attributed to grief and which ones to the child's stage of development. A mother of a five-year-old reported:

I was surprised at the questions he asked about what happened to Daddy. "Where is heaven?" "What does he do there?" He seemed so mature, and then he would have an angry outburst for no reason. I learned from the other parents in my group that he really didn't have the language for what he was trying to understand. He was frustrated, but I was almost relieved when he finally stopped asking questions for which I had no answer. It hurt so much to watch him struggle with what happened to his father. I guess I had to help him develop a language.

A mother widowed for the second time said:

I would like to think that he is an adolescent, not that he is reacting to his father's death when he gets quiet and sullen. But I think that is to reassure me, to keep me from getting too upset. It didn't take much for me to start crying.

Parents learn that expressions of grief and behaviors associated with development influence each other and it is very difficult, if not impossible, to make clear distinctions between the two.

Regardless of age, children are usually able to convey their reactions to a parent's death one way or another; however, surviving parents often cannot respond appropriately, in part because they do not understand what grief looks like in children. Another reason, as discussed previously, is that they may be having a difficult time dealing with their own grief. Most parents hate to see their children in pain. They want to believe that their children are fine and keep looking for signs to reassure them of this. They are not able to handle seeing a child break down and cry:

> He wanted to play with his friends, and I said, "Fine." His older brother had disappeared on his bike to a friend's house. We all knew it was coming, but now that she was dead it looked like it didn't matter to them. All they could think about was being with their friends. Maybe that was good. I needed time for myself. I could barely handle my own feelings, never mind theirs.

At such times, children seek confirmation that the world has not completely fallen apart. If their friends are still there and the sun still comes up in the morning, then they can enjoy some sense of stability and continuity. While surviving parents might be upset by their children's apparent lack of concern, they are also relieved that, for the moment, they do not have to face their children's pain.

In contrast, an adolescent girl from the original widow-to-widow project reacted with a dramatic renunciation of her childhood, as reported by her mother:

> Her room had been plastered with pictures of the Beatles. The day her father died, she went upstairs and took them down. She said, "I'm not a baby any more." I tried to explain to her that she was still a child even if her father had died. But I guess when you go through something like that, you never feel the same. The pictures never went back up.

In a sense, these children seem to grow up overnight. Some children have reported becoming impatient with their high school peers' apparently frivolous concerns and feeling older and out of step with people who had once been close friends. At the same time, preadolescent and adolescent children do not want to appear different from their peers by focusing on their loss and try to blend in with the crowd:

> I wouldn't talk about my father dying that summer. At all costs, I wasn't going to let anyone know — I was in 7th grade — that I was in any ways different.

Children find a good deal of comfort in meeting with other bereaved children. In the words of an 8-year-old boy:

> The best thing was meeting other children. I didn't feel so alone or different.

A mother talked about a family history project her nine-year old daughter completed in school:

> They had to draw a time line. She left out when her father died. When I asked her about that, she said, "I didn't want anyone to ask me about him. It would make me feel different. This way, our family looks like everyone else's." I have a lot of learning to do — at first I thought she didn't care. She seems so young to worry about being like everyone else. But I guess this is where it starts. She said in the children's center it was different. Everyone understood.

☐ Worries About the Children

Almost every surviving parent worries about the impact of the death on the children. Will they develop emotional problems later in life? Will they be able to enjoy their childhood and find happiness as adults? Will they fear for their own or the surviving parent's health and safety? These parents universally feel unprepared for the challenge of raising their children alone. For many women, the shift in roles from wife to widow and single parent is difficult. Children, too, experience a role shift in that they now have only one living parent and often must take on added responsibilities. In some cases, they must learn to relate to the surviving parent in an entirely new way. For example, some fathers are concerned that they have never before talked to their children about personal needs:

> My son was used to talk to his mother about school and school problems. He talked to me about football and what he was doing in sports. I had no idea how to talk to my daughter about her growing up. She's 12. A neighbor promised to take her shopping when she needed sanitary napkins. And then I never got another offer. I got used to people promising and then not being there. I don't talk much to the kids, and

I am not always sure how. But we get things done. I don't know how it looks to the children. Sometimes I think they are trying to protect me. I guess they sense that I am all they have. We talked about this in the group. Other parents had the same experience.

By the end of the first year or two, many widows begin to worry that their children need a father. This concern is often associated with an emerging desire to date. Some women have emphasized the children's need for male companionship, while others have sought help with disciplining and managing their children. In the original widow-to-widow program, the aides often referred these women to a Big Brother organization or suggested involving another male member of the family with the children on a regular basis. Doing so becomes even more important when the extended family does not live nearby to provide surrogate relationships for the children.

By voicing their concerns, the widowed demonstrate their ability to focus on others outside of themselves, and, in time, most are able to meet their children's needs. They are eager to talk with others about how to manage the children, to clarify what it means to be a single parent, and to learn new ways to handle family issues. When they share in this way, they are better able to meet their children's needs instead of spending their energy on protecting themselves from their children's pain.

Surviving parents have to learn to put their children's behavior in perspective, which sometimes requires that they relinquish their preconceived notions about child rearing. For example, some widowed parents are reluctant to indulge their children for fear of spoiling them. Put another way, they worry that, with one parent gone, the children will think they can misbehave with no consequences. This is often true in families where the father had been the disciplinarian and where control was valued. Parents learn from each other to reevaluate this concern and to focus instead on what their children's behavior might mean given the loss of their sense of safety and security. In some families, the deceased might have been the more supportive, loving parent — father or mother — and the surviving parent has to develop some of these supportive qualities that were not necessary when the family had both parents.

Younger children may experience sleepless nights and might wet their beds for brief periods. One six-year-old boy who became eneuretic talked a great deal about his father, who had been killed in an automobile accident. He played out crash scenes with his cars for several months. His mother did not immediately connect his bedwetting to his reaction to his father's death nor did she realize that sleeplessness is often a manifestation of night fears. Fortunately, he had a sympathetic teacher who encouraged him to talk about the loss and who suggested that he join a program for grieving children, and this made a difference in his behavior at home. Another new widow instinctively sympathized with her young son and daughter:

> I could sense his fear of being alone at night. I had no problem with his sleeping with me, and then his sister would want to join us. Some people worry about my spoiling them. I can understand their not wanting to be alone. Neither do I. Spoiling isn't my issue — not now!

Most mothers in the woman's support group agreed with her. Over time, those who are initially uncomfortable with being more indulgent with their children become more relaxed and are better able to understand their children's need for security and reassurance. One 12-year-old boy, whose father had been murdered in his front hall, refused to go back and forth to school unless his mother escorted him. She recognized his real and legitimate fears of the neighborhood but also saw that his clinging symbolized his fear of losing her. It took her awhile to realize that having such fears was reasonable and that her fear of indulging him was counterproductive. One young boy began withdrawing immediately after his father's death. This behavior did not last long, as his mother realized that he was having trouble coping:

> He's the only man in the house. He must feel picked on. His father used to protect him from me. I was the firm disciplinarian. I see I have to go easy on him.

Widowed mothers generally recognize that a child might develop difficulties in school and that teachers and administrators should be made aware of the loss. Sometimes a child wants to return to school immediately, even before the funeral has taken place. In these instances, the child has usually told the teacher what happened. Many teachers are attentive to a child's needs at such a time; in one instance, a teacher called home when she noticed a first-grader's unusual sadness and withdrawn demeanor. Another teacher phoned a mother in the original widow-to-widow program to share with her what her 11-year-old son had told her in school — that he was the man in his family now. The teacher now could link the boy's recent poor behavior to his father's death. Although it is not uncommon for people to tell boys that they now must care for their mothers, this mother had not conveyed such a message:

> I was so glad the teacher called. I guess his uncle at the funeral had told him that this was now his new role in the family.... I talked it over with Mary [the aide], whose own son had also been given that message. I told him that I was in charge. I did need his help and I

would ask as it came up. But his job was not to take care of us. His dad would be very proud if he did well in school, in Little League.

Assuming some aspects of the father can be very affirming:

> My oldest boy takes on more responsibility. He has absorbed his father's goodness. He is always asking me if I am all right and if I am happy. But I am trying to make sure he is not trying to take his father's place. He is still a child in the family. I think he understands the difference.

Teachers are not uniformly supportive, however. A 16-year-old girl reported that her teacher told her two weeks after her father died that she could not expect any special consideration and must keep up her work or be penalized. Her mother got support from other widowed parents who suggested that she go to the school and talk with this teacher and even the principal if necessary. Without this help, she would never have had the nerve to speak up for her child in this way. Children, too, need their own groups or activities to help them find the language to describe their grief. They achieve this in play, through stories, and in sharing with others children. As they talk, they feel comforted, supported, and understood (Silverman, 2000a), relieving some of the burden carried by the surviving parent. Children also are glad to discover other children who have had the same experience. One mother described her son's reaction when they went to a support group for the first time: "Mom! Look at all the kids here! You mean all their dads died, too?"

☐ What Will I Do If Something Happens to You?

The focus of group discussions often turns to a child's need for continuity. Some women have mothers or in-laws who can help with child care while the mothers work, thus eliminating the need for another separation into day care. One mother arranged for her daughter to come after school to the nursing home where she worked; the child could work on her homework and gained a sense of comfort knowing where her mother spent her days. In another family, a six-year-old only child expressed her fear of losing her mother by insisting that she walk her home from school every day. The group helped this mother to see how she could reassure her daughter so that in a short period of time the young girl was more comfortable walking with her friends again.

Children are quite aware that they now have only one parent. Younger children often solve this problem by asking the surviving parent to remarry, thus securing a second parent. While these children grapple with the finality of their loss, they are also able to look ahead to the possibility of finding a substitute. As children grew older, they come to understand that it is simply not possible to find a new parent. These children need to know that a plan is in place for their care if something happens to their parent. The surviving parent must make a will and find a friend or family member willing to assume legal guardianship should the need arise. It is important to talk this over with the child.

At the same time, parents need to reassure their children that they are taking very good care of themselves and that they will do everything they can to be there for their children; however, these children tend to have a wisdom beyond their years. They already have learned that the unexpected can happen at any time.

A child's fear of losing a surviving parent can take many forms, depending on age and personality. A younger child who was not afraid of speaking out was blunt: "Who will take care of me if something happens to you?" Some children have nightmares in which they imagine the surviving parent's death:

> I don't know how I took care of the babies that year. I relied on my six-year-old to help. Sometimes I had to let her watch the babies if I had to run to the store. About 10 months after my husband died, she had a dream that I was lying on the couch making noises. She got pills which did not help. I tried to reassure her that I wasn't going anywhere.

Other widowed mothers are not always as intuitive about the meaning of their children's dreams or they do not connect the dreams to the death:

> She [eight-year-old daughter] had a dream about me being taken away from her, or she couldn't find her way home, or it always seemed as if she found herself alone at the end of the dream or nightmare.

This mother began to realize the connection between her daughter's dream and her husband's death. She also eventually understood why her ten-year-old middle daughter would not let her leave the house unless she knew where she was going, who was driving, and when she would be home:

> If I came home five minutes late, she was a nervous wreck. I guess that's how it affected them — not in the usual way with the tears and crying and the grief you naturally expect.

As a result of the aide's prompting and group discussions, she and other surviving parents began to consider talking to their children, their families, and their lawyers about making wills and planning the children's future guardianships.

☐ Children Help, Too

Children can give their parents a good deal of comfort at this time and provide a focus separate from the parent's grief. They express genuine concern for their parents, as well. One 12-year-old girl told her mother, "Don't cry while we are at school." Another mother described her children's response to her:

> They didn't want to go to school at first. They worried about me at home alone. When I insisted they go, I think they were glad to get out of the house. They also said that my middle girl, who is closest to me, would always stay by me so I didn't have to be alone when they grew up.

In follow-up interviews with widows from the original widow-to-widow program, we learned that the girls who planned to stay at home to care for their mothers nevertheless finished high school and went to college; they did not seem overwhelmed by what they had promised their parents, in part because these were reciprocal relationships. These mothers were able to reassure them that they would continue mothering them and consider their needs even as they attended to their own. Older children, especially girls, are often protective of and helpful to the widow:

> They try to get me out, over my depression. I'd be lost without them. They protect and baby me from all the sadness I feel. I almost had a breakdown after my husband died. Working helped me, too. Everyone there worked at keeping me busy and occupied.

One woman said her older girls "became women and were very brave and very helpful." She thought it must be very difficult for a woman with no older children. The woman who had agreed with her son not to cry at the funeral saw him as a "charm":

> He's never been anything but courageous and encouraging to me. If he cried, which he did with his older brother and sister, he never let me see it.

This last point bears further exploration. Siblings are often very support-ive of each other during this time of stress, even if they previously have been rivals.

☐ Problem Children, Problem Parent

From a developmental perspective, some parents relate to others from a self-centered orientation (Silverman, 2000a). They are not able to consider their children's needs outside of the impact of their problem behavior on themselves. These parents can be considered as being *parent centered* as opposed to *child centered*. The latter orientation allows a parent to view a child's behavior on its own terms and to understand its meaning for the child. These parents also recognize that they play a role in helping their children and that their own behavior affects that of their children.

The troubled children in the original widow-to-widow program tended to be boys, usually from nine to 14 years old, although the group did include one girl. With one exception, the fathers had been very involved with their families. Some were gentle with their children and left discipline to their wives. Others were the family disciplinarians and pacesetters, and their relationships to their wives seemed good. Several of the mothers talked about their sons' need for discipline and for a father:

> If his father was alive, he would have made him work. He was more scared of his father.

These mothers saw the role of father as being part policeman and felt the need to pressure their sons to perform up to the standards set by their fathers. The underlying problem in these families was not that the chil-dren needed the control of their fathers, but rather that the fathers' deaths had changed the mothers' views of their sons. In effect, in several families the widow had shut out her sons; with their fathers gone, these boys had, in a sense, lost both parents. It is not clear if these mothers could have changed their behavior in some way to make a difference for these boys.

All of these boys had enjoyed special relationships with their fathers. One child even asked his mother, "Why couldn't it have been you instead of Daddy?" Another tried to be like his father:

> He idealizes him. He still talks about the way his father punished him as better than the ways his friends' fathers treat their children now. He really worries me. I think some of his answering back is adolescence, but he is becoming a loner. He won't go to Scouts any-more, and he's withdrawn and talks about wanting to be an artist.

Another, an adolescent girl, at first withdrew completely from school and then from all activities outside of the house. Her brothers fared better:

> They had a rough time. One was his father's alter ego. They had a sense of responsibility and kept going. My daughter just stopped living.

This girl told her mother, "I am closer to Daddy than you are." This girl had spent much of her free time at home caring for her terminally ill father while her mother worked, which is not unusual when the mother is employed outside of the home and the father is there when the children come home from school.

Widows are often perplexed by a child's fixation on the father and simultaneous withdrawal from activities and performance that the father would have valued:

> He is very emotional. He drives, and every once in a while he goes to visit his father's grave. He talks a lot about his father. I keep saying to him, "You'd better grow up and be like your father," and he says, "I will, Ma." He's not like his father, though. My husband was so quiet, but in sports they were alike. But his grades have gone down. He's stopped paying attention. He seems to live in a world of his own.

This pattern of withdrawal and ineffectiveness seems to be related to the child's position in the family (usually the only surviving male) and to the way his grieving mother has parented. Many widows rely upon the children to give their lives purpose and meaning, which helps keep them going; however, they may not be fully sensitive to their children's need for attention. In our study, the full implication of their sons' behavior was lost on their mothers. Only one mother in this group sought professional psychiatric guidance for her child. This type of help was not as readily available for bereaved children at the time; today, schools are becoming more involved in getting help for these children.

None of these mothers in the original widow-to-widow program talked easily about their feelings, and they found it difficult to allow a new person (such as an aide) into their lives. They often normalized their son's difficulty by attributing part of it to adolescence. Other mothers did nothing but worry but could not confront the real issues. One mother, who never really felt in control of her situation, blamed several teachers for not talking to her son or her about his difficulties. Feeling overwhelmed, she finally took someone else's suggestion and placed him in another school. She herself never talked with her son about his problems and their possible causes, just as she never initiated any conversation with him about his father.

☐ Connecting to Their Dead Parent

Over time, most widowed parents and their children find ways to temper their sense of loss. Building a connection to the deceased helps. Shortly after the death of her husband, one widow said, "We talk about him often, but it is like he is on vacation." With time, they find other ways of remembering and other aspects of their life together to talk about. Many young parents begin to date after several years. Children who have difficulty with this new development are reassured when their parents tell them that they are not trying to replace the dead parent, that this will be a new and different relationship, and that the deceased will always have a place in their lives. One couple, both widowed, said:

> We keep pictures of our first spouses in conspicuous places in the house. We talk about them, and we count on the older children to help their baby brother who has no memory of his mother.

Religion helps some to acknowledge the reality of the death and to find an appropriate way to remember. One young adolescent comforted his mother with the thought that his father was "with Jesus" and by telling her there was no reason for so much sadness. He astutely recognized that his mother could rely on her faith to help her cope. Three years after her father's death, one girl still prayed to him every night, hoping that he was watching over her and would be proud of her. In some families, children go to the cemetery regularly. One adolescent who had given up religion began to attend Mass each month on the same day of the month on which father died. Other children visit the cemetery, either by themselves or with their parent. When the cemetery is nearby, they might stop on their way home from school or bring along a friend. They talk to the deceased and share their day with him or her. These are some examples of developing a new relationship with the deceased, or a continuing bond.

☐ Conclusion

In general, the surviving parent's failure to deal with the children's grief is a result of preoccupation, not neglect. Fortunately, most widowed men and women are eager to find some help and guidance as they struggle with their own and their children's changing needs, and they are able to use the available help quite effectively. Most of the widowed parents in my research stated that their children had given meaning to their lives at a time when they were despairing and hopeless. For some, this meaning came from their having to be alert and involved in order to respond to their children, while others found meaning in having someone to lean on, someone who could get them up and out of themselves. Even those with young children may have received more than they gave. The interface between the children's needs and those of their surviving parent became clear when we focused on the responses of these families. The need to parent dependent and grieving children is an overwhelming responsibility. Both parents and children value the support they receive from meeting others who are also coping with the death of a loved one and are able to expand their views of the possibilities of living together in a meaningful and positive way as a single-parent family.

9
CHAPTER

The Older Widowed

I intend to wear out not rust out.

83-year-old widow

Most people who are widowed are over 65 years of age, and the number of widowed naturally increases as people get older. By the time they are 65, 8% of men and 31% of women are widowed. By age 75, 23% of men and 60% of women are widowed (U.S. Census, 2000). While longevity has increased such that 72% of women over age 82 are widowed and 44% of men are, these numbers are deceiving because we do not know how long these people have been widowed, nor do we know how many who were widowed have remarried (men are much more likely to remarry). It is no myth, however, that widowhood is more prevalent among the elderly and that the widowed are more likely to be women. The current generation of the elderly are longer lived, healthier, and more active than previous generations. Age does not limit learning and growing (Doress-Worters & Seigal, 1994; Jacobs, 1991). Once the elderly become widowed, few differences in their behaviors can be identified compared to those who are younger (Thompson, 2001). The general levels of distress and depression are no higher in older widowed people than in those who are younger (Gallagher-Thompson *et al.*, 1993; Caserta & Lund, 1993).

Moss *et al.* (2001) listed the many losses older people experience: spouse, siblings, friends, and members of their extended family. Some live to bury adult children, which may be the most difficult death they have to face. While they gain experience in coping with each new death, each particular death may require something different from them. When they become widowed, they are concerned with dealing with the reality of the death and the changes in their lives, maintaining their independence and their health, and managing their finances and their relationships with family and friends, as well as finding new directions for their life (Johnson *et al.*, 1986; Utz *et al.*, 2002).

☐ Dealing with Their Grief and Changes in Their Lives

Initially, the elderly widowed experience a very real sense of disorder and numbness. A 75-year-old widower expressed his angst, albeit for the moment:

> When my wife died I was unable to speak. My throat contracted and when my lower jaw moved no sound came out.

A woman married for 47 years (and whose reflection opens this chapter) recalled the first months of her widowhood:

> I lost my self-confidence and I worried about the future. Even now, I can't understand why I was not more prepared.

A sense of disbelief is common:

> I really have faith that he hears me, and that he is with me and that helps … but there are times when I turn to say something and then I realize that I can't.… I think for a whole year I pretty much felt sorry for myself.

When it was a long, painful death, the widowed's feelings are tempered by a sense of relief for both their spouses and themselves. A widow who was married almost 50 years told me:

> I felt alone, there was an emptiness, half of me was gone. My friends were great but when I came home, I was alone. But he was in such pain. He couldn't move. Hospice was great but in the end he couldn't move off the bed, he lost control of everything. It was awful. I just feel such relief that he is no longer suffering, not only the pain but the indignity. This strong, athletic man wasted by this illness. Knowing that he is not suffering anymore has made it easier for me.

They have a growing awareness that they cannot live their lives as before:

> Now I am lonely and frightened. I'm confused — I used to be sure of myself, independent, active alert, moving all the time. Now I have nothing left, but I am trying to stand on my own two feet.

The need to change involves many aspects of their lives. In the words of a 76-year-old widow:

> How hasn't it [her life] changed? After 43 years of habits and sharing life with another — even your thinking changes.

☐ Many Changes Are Involved

Generally, elderly couples have a longer history of being together. Lund and Caserta (2001) remind us that older men and women are more likely to be retired or planning to retire and spend increased amounts of time with their spouses. With the centrality of the nuclear family, the death of one of them might leave them more isolated, limiting the number of resources available to them. A widow from the original widow-to-widow program saw this very clearly:

> My husband and I did everything together. When he died I was very much alone.

Carr *et al.* (2001) observed that men and women who are over 65 are less likely to end a bad marriage than younger men and women, and their tasks of daily living are more likely to be divided into gender-specific activities. Widowed men, for example, are more likely to need help with maintaining their homes, while women generally seek help with house repairs; however, as usual, there are exceptions to this rule (Moore & Stratton, 2002). In the words of a 79-year-old widower:

> I took care of my wife's every need as she got sicker and sicker. There is almost nothing I can't do in the house. She was a bookkeeper and I had to learn to do the books, too. Not what we planned for our retirement.

While men of this age are not typically seen as primary caregivers in the family, this changes when their wives become ill and often with the help of hospice they assume new roles. In the words of a man married 53 years:

What else could you do — when you love someone … and she would probably say you are not doing that right. It always gave me a chuckle when I knew she felt critical of me like she was saying "I didn't teach you to do it that way." The hospice nurse taught me how to take care of my wife. She died peacefully … the whole family was there. Now I guess I'm pretty good at taking care of myself and that makes a difference now.

In the early 1970s, we expected that women between the ages of 30 and 35 years would be largely dependent on their husbands and would have difficulty managing alone. It was not that they could not manage alone but often they defined themselves entirely by their relationship to their husband and the popular definition of the role of wife. A woman who was a leader in an international organization for the widowed explained how she has changed:

Before I was widowed I had to subvert my personality in order not to hurt my husband.

Many accepted "truths" were challenged. While these women may have deferred to their husbands, they often redefined some of these boundaries without necessarily talking about it. In fact, they were involved in various types of partnerships that hindered any effort to stereotype their relationships. A more recent widow described her balancing act:

I was a wife and mother for 47 years. My husband was a very strong man, and I lived as he wanted even though I am a strong person myself, but we achieved a happy medium.

A 69-year-old widow, married for 50 years, reflected on changes she had seen in the role of women over the years:

I wasn't affected by the women's movement. I worked a mother's hours. I was home for my children and my husband. I placed his needs ahead of mine but on the other hand he placed my needs ahead of his. I was always doing what I wanted to do, and I am continuing to do that on a different level. Without my best friend, without my love.

☐ A Changing Sense of Self

Age does not limit the older widow or widower from developing a new sense of self and a new place in the world. In the words of a 79-year-old widow:

> I never thought I would find myself speaking up this way. I always deferred to my husband. Now I find that if I don't speak up, no one will do it for me. I have a new voice and I am getting used to people reacting differently to me. I was even able to explain to my children what I need and how I have changed so they can understand and be supportive. I began to see their point of view and could explain that I didn't need that much protection, even at my age.

Her new sense of self made it possible for her to negotiate with others which grew out of a new ability to take their point of view as well. A 70-year-old widower described his own evolving sense of self which involved his greater awareness of others and their needs:

> I worry more about others. I am not so concerned with me. I'm different, I can't always explain it. If I want a social life, it's up to me and I'm reaching out.

A 72-year-old widow who was involved with the Widowed Person's Service in her community described how she had changed:

> I am a different person than I was when my husband died. I am an independent feminist rather than someone's wife (lovely as he was). I feel I have learned to face up to things (most of the time) and to stand on my own two feet.

☐ Help From Another Widow

Lund and Caserta (1992) found that the needs of older widowed men and women for reciprocal sharing and support are alike; however, men had a more difficult time accepting an offer of help or reaching out to other widowed people. In general, they are often more responsive to an offer of a hot meal or a game of cards; however, there are exceptions (Campbell & Silverman, 1996, p. 205):

> I went to a local group that was formed two months after my wife died. I went and I tell you that was something. I didn't know a soul, but I felt an instant rapport.

Widows on the other hand were more generally more accepting of opportunities to talk:

> When she said she was widowed, I said come right over.

Anther widow recalled a friend encouraging her to talk to a widow from the Council on Aging:

> After my husband died, a friend who was widowed visited. She looked so good, How did she manage to get where she was? She became my role model. I didn't think I needed to talk to anyone, but I found myself asking how her husband died, how she managed her house, her money, her family. I realized that this was the first time I met someone who really understood, and I had all kinds of needs I had been keeping down.

☐ Remaining Independent

A key issue for the widowed is their wish to be independent, which depends on their being able to maintain their health. The widowed elderly are more likely to have a chronic, debilitating illness such as diabetes, a heart condition, arthritis, or Parkinson's disease. One widow in the original widow-to-widow program had Parkinson's disease and was completely disabled and in a wheelchair; a homemaker cared for her. She was pleased to see the aide; when she was hospitalized for awhile, the aide visited her regularly. This woman had a good attitude toward herself and her situation:

> At first I felt as if the whole world came down on my shoulders, but time dulls the pain and you get used to it. By now I'm used to being a widow.

The aide's visits gave her moral support and an opportunity to talk about her husband. She planned to return home with a homemaker continuing to care for her.

In contrast, the woman quoted at the beginning of this chapter (whose plan is to wear out rather than rust out) made it very clear that she was doing all she did because she was in good health. Many of the widowed express concern that they will not be able to manage as they get older and more infirm. An 80-year-old widow who was a leader in a national organization for the widowed was aware of her need to attend to how things were changing for her:

> I'm learning to pace myself so I can stay involved as long as possible. I can't ignore it when I don't have the energy I had before.

Some of the widowed initiated major changes before the death that make it easier for them to remain independent:

My husband could not manage the steps so we moved to a condo-
minium before he died. I am so glad we did. I couldn't have cared
for the house or afforded it financially. I can manage this by myself.

In 1990, 69% of the widowed lived alone, reflecting changing attitudes
about the value of privacy, lower fertility rates, and a society that encour-
ages people to be independent (Kramerow, 1995). Higher incomes resulting, in part, from Social Security payments and Medicare, as well as other
government subsidies, although still frequently inadequate, are contributing factors toward making this independence possible. For those without
other income, the increasing costs of health care and prescription drugs
place their good health in jeopardy.

Subsidized housing for the elderly has made it easier for many elderly
widowed people to live alone on limited incomes. Within these communities, the widowed often form informal support groups. Van den Hoonaard
(2002), however, found support for the newly widowed in retirement communities to be unpredictable, as evidenced by one widow who was confused by her neighbors' lack of responsiveness:

I couldn't understand it. No one called me — friends and people in
condos around me — to say wouldn't you like to go out for dinner....
I couldn't believe that. I would always say to them let's go out to dinner ... and no one called. I can't understand that.

The ability of people to reach out may in part depend on the receptive-
ness of the widow or widower, but it also reflects their own discomfort
with dealing with another person's grief. For those not already widowed,
the risk is very high that one of the partners will be joining this community soon enough, and for others they may not necessarily feel ready to
cope with another widow's feelings.

In some families, the same lack of understanding can be evident. Some
widows and widowers may feel that those closest to them do not always
understand their situation, and they are not able to share their concerns
and feelings with them. On the other hand, many appreciate being surrounded by family, children, siblings, and friends who are trying to be
helpful and most often succeed in doing so.

☐ Role of Adult Children

In many parts of the world, the widowed count on being cared for by
their adult children, and in some societies this role is assigned to the
eldest son. In immigrant communities in the United States, this may still

be true; however, the wish to remain independent is reinforced by the general ethos of American culture. Kramerow (1995) found that over the last century the number of elderly widowed people living with their children sharply declined. Nonetheless, adult children are involved in the widow or widower's life in many different ways. For many of the widowed they are a primary source of support. The widows served by the original widow-to-widow project talked about the importance of their adult children in their lives. Men and women widowed more recently offer similar reports. Sometimes an adult offspring experiencing marital difficulties returns home, grown children who are not yet married still live at home, or adult children who have lost their jobs come back home to live for awhile. Other widows are caring for children with various physical and emotional disabilities who are not able to live on their own, and a significant population of widows are raising their grandchildren (Silverman, 2000d)

Most children are solicitous of their surviving parent and are involved on a regular basis in her or his life. A man in his mid-70s reflected on his children's concern:

> Camping became an important part of my life. When my wife was alive she never would consider it. At first my children argued with me. I know I have a heart condition and could die in the wilderness when I am alone. I knew the risks and the kids finally accepted it.

Given the fact that today large geographical distances often exist between adult children and their surviving parent, some parents consider moving closer to their children. For example, a woman, in the original widow-to-widow program, not quite 60, told her son that she would move into a neighboring suburb close to where he lived but not into his house. She had a heart condition and hoped to get disability assistance, but she could still care for herself. She was denied benefits but found a job, through a friend, at a telephone answering service. This paid the rent, and she managed. Her son was comfortable with this compromise.

Sometimes the children are the first to recognize their mother's need to make new friends. One daughter, who still lived at home, encouraged her mother to remain in touch with the widow-to-widow program and to get involved. The mother explains:

> It was my wedding anniversary. I wanted my daughter to take me to the cemetery. She agreed only if I would go to the widow-to-widow cookout afterwards. I had been talking to Mary for a long time, but always on the phone. She and my daughter had both been telling me I had to get out of the house. Best thing I ever did was to go to that

cookout. Mary introduced me to several other widows right in my own neighborhood. Now I am involved in planning a trip to Ireland — a dream come true.

Some older women find that their children intrude so much that it is difficult to stay in charge of their lives:

My daughter decided that the neighborhood was too dangerous. I couldn't go out shopping alone. She packed up my things and moved me to her house. I didn't have the energy to argue. Now I am really lonely. Everyone is out of the house during the day and there is no one to talk to. I'd move back to the old neighborhood in a minute if I could find a place I could afford.

In this instance, the daughter's being protective and assuming a parental role with her surviving parent limited the widow's options. With housing for the elderly available in many communities, it is possible for the widowed to live in the same town as their children but in a community of peers.

Occasionally, in the original widow-to-widow program, children would come across the aides' letters and ask the aides not to bother their parents, that they were caring for them. Initially, the widows in these cases cooperated with their children, but one gradually became aware of her own needs:

I went hunting for the letter. Fortunately my daughter had not thrown it away. I reminded the children that they were all moving out and that I had to take care of myself. I was going to talk to this woman and find out what it was all about. As I talked to Dorothy, I realized that there were many things I wanted to talk about and I could not share them with the kids. They didn't understand. At 65 I wasn't old. The children really weren't going to support me, no matter what they promised. I needed to find something to do outside of my home and Dorothy was very encouraging. Smartest thing I ever did was to make that phone call.

In many ways, this protectiveness is similar to that of young children who try to protect their surviving parent by not crying in front of the parent. Ultimately, of course, this overprotectiveness does not work. The children also have experienced a loss and need to attend to their own feelings as well. One 75-year-old widow stood up to her daughter's plans for her:

My daughter flew in from California. She began to run my life, telling me how I would manage now. The next thing I knew she was talking about packing me up and moving me out there with her. I don't know where I got the energy. I was still in a daze but I sat her down and I made it clear to her that I could run my own life. I appreciated that her job was to be helpful and I thought perhaps she had some crying to do. I was right. This was her way of avoiding her feelings. We both had a good cry and then we could talk, as friends, and discuss what I was going to do now. I did need her advice.

Some women feel that they cannot share their grief with their adult children. The widowed might observe that their children are rarely sharing their tears or their sadness with them. When he realized this, a recent widower noted:

I worried about my boys, who were not talking to me about their mother. I noticed though that they sometimes talk to each other and I think their wives are very supportive. I guess that may be enough for now. I should relax.

One widower had no experience sharing his feelings with his children. Over time they learned to talk with each other and gradually could share their grief. This was a new experience for all of them. This same widower had no experience with male friends. He had always turned to women for support. In a group for the widowed, he met another widower, and they began to realize the value of having someone to go out with for a cup of coffee or to a movie, as well as the benefit of sharing some of what they were learning as they developed new skills in living alone.

Sometimes in their eagerness to be independent, the widowed do not want to burden their children. A recent widow commented:

My children are grown and I don't know how they are doing. They don't talk about it much. My husband only died a year and a half ago … so they probably need help as much as I do but they are too busy with their own lives to really reach out and I don't want to burden them. We see each other regularly but we don't say much about our feelings.

Some of this hesitance to share is related to culture and patterns that may have been established over the years but have not yet changed given the new circumstances.

Rosenblatt and Elde (1990) noted that adult siblings can be very helpful to each other in dealing with their grief; for example, they can help each other construct memories of the deceased parent. Campbell and Silverman (1996) noted that parents often do not have a great deal of experience sharing their personal feelings with adult children, and children are not always able to share their grief with the surviving parent. This is something they have to learn to do, in addition to learning to recognize the range of responses that can be related to the children's grieving. They also need to learn to appreciate their ability to comfort each other. For example, in one family, the married daughter began to have difficulty with transient depression a year after her father died. Her mood concerned her mother, who was not sure how to make sense out of it. Eventually, the daughter saw that her depression was related to her father's death and to the unexpressed feelings she had because of her family's preoccupation during her adolescence when her father was first diagnosed with cancer. A widow-to-widow aide perceived the widow's concern and supported her in her efforts to be helpful.

How do children help? Helping in small ways with concrete tasks is one way of being involved. A widow reminded me of how helpful children can be in honoring the deceased's memory. This widow was delighted that her son was going to follow the tradition in the Jewish community of naming her grandchild after her husband:

> It was a boy and we named him after his grandfather, in the Jewish tradition. We realized that my husband had done it again. He had given us one of the most special days of our lives, as we gave this child his name. As he grows up we can tell him what a special man his grandfather was and bring him to the garden dedicated to his grandfather and we can tell him that he was athletic and he loved to run. Every day we are thankful that we get to both think of and be reminded of grandpa.

This was the most important thing her son could have done for her.

Children can also be the confidant of the dying parent. A dying father wanted to protect his wife and only shared the fact that he was dying with his son. After his death, the mother explained:

> My son told me that Da talked to him about dying. He didn't want to talk to me because he had always said he would take care of me and he didn't want me to know that he wasn't going to be there to take care of me.

The son realized that his father's secret made no sense in view of how sick he was, but in his own way he was protecting not his mother but his father.

Children can play a role in addressing the long-term needs of the surviving parent:

> My son talked it over with me, that I needed to think about who might care for me as I got older. I agreed, but I wasn't there yet. He wanted me to consider moving to a retirement community or a condominium. I explained that I like my home. I have some help in maintaining it and I want to stay here. It is easy to manage. He could hear me and was okay with what I planned. I can trust him; there isn't much we don't talk about.

Some of the widowed feel an inconsolable sadness and have no desire to do anything, partly due to a feeling of not being needed anymore. A woman in her late 60s described her dilemma in trying to keep going despite her fatigue and depression:

> No one needs me — not even my daughter. My friends aren't interested. Maybe I could get a job? How could I get a job? Maybe I could volunteer?

This widow was not ready to act; she was just beginning to explore her options but not in a very organized way. She sensed that she might need to do something but needed some help in finding the appropriate outlets for her energy. Eventually, as a result of an aide's recommendation, she found a number of places that interested her and who could use her as a volunteer.

A widower found being alone intolerable and realized that he, too, needed to be needed, so he invited one of his sons to live with him:

> I was married for 57 years. The last 7 months I am going crazy. My son and his wife are moving in. I will have my own apartment downstairs. I can do things for them … laundry, dishes, It will give me something to do and I'll have company, and they'll be able to save money.

He goes to a group for the widowed at the Council on Aging:

> I like the group and I still drive and I pick up several members to take them there. But I really need someone at home. My son being there will help me feel less lonely. We can help each other.

☐ When My Children Don't Need Me

Mothers of older children begin to worry about being too dependent on their adult children:

Mary pointed out to me that I was clinging to my children because I was afraid to be alone. They really didn't need a full-time mother anymore. I needed someone to show me what else I could do. I became friends with a group of widows, and they encouraged me to go back to school.

Today, many widowed people participate in active educational programs for the elderly in local universities or in elder hostel programs. These programs open up new horizons for them and offer new opportunities to find others with whom they can develop a new social life:

My children are good to me. I'm looking forward to being a grandmother. That will give me pleasure. The hardest time is the loneliness. I seem to have lost a lot of incentive, but I am moving ahead. I'm learning to drive, although I never wanted to. I'm learning to stand on my own two feet. The kids have their own lives. I have to find friends to do things with on weekends. I was so grateful when Mary told me about the programs at Arch Street.

A widow whose children were out of the house had moved to a more convenient location after her husband's death and reflected on her current situation:

Now that I've moved and settled in, I'm looking for ways to find new friends and fill my life. That's where I am at. I love my work and I am not ready to retire but I need much more. Essentially, I'm looking at being alone, and I have to decide what I want to do with my life.

Grown children can be a comfort, but they also have their own lives to live:

I have to show the children that I can be independent. They have their own lives. I'm too young to let them think they have to take care of me.

For their part, children react in a variety of ways. Some are responsive and respectful of their parent's needs, but others continue a life-long pattern of taking. One widow's son wanted her to sell her home so he could receive his share of the inheritance. This woman had to recognize her own needs and learn to set limits that in some ways redefined how she interpreted her role as mother:

I always thought of the children first, but now I know I have to think of my own needs and my future. I'm alone, and all I have is what I earn and the house.

This lesson is repeated over and over, as the widowed learn to step back, evaluate others' advice in light of their own needs and perspectives, and allow themselves to say "no" without the guilt.

☐ When You Need More Than Family

Even when the widowed have children who make regular visits or telephone calls, this does not replace the need of the widowed for other types of relationships. They may need to share their grief with an aide in a widow-to-widow program, but they also want help in making new friends. In the original widow-to-widow program, several of the women had recently retired with the idea that their husbands would retire soon, as well. These women particularly needed help building a social network. Some women discover, as noted earlier, that they have become a fifth wheel. They had not anticipated that their friends who were still married would be uncomfortable with them.

Women who have no children can be especially lonely:

> I am very lucky. My friends are there and I make sure my niece comes to visit on the holidays. I'm an upbeat person and I make the effort. I couldn't get out much when my husband was so sick. I am finally able to think straight and get involved.

Many widows have had satisfying marriages; they have nieces and nephews who are like children to them, and they are close to their own sisters and brothers. In contrast, in the original widow-to-widow program, a Holocaust survivor talked endlessly to her aide about her husband and what a poor relationship she had had with him. She complained bitterly about how the neighbors did nothing to help. Her own anger served to isolate her further from people. She could not accept that she might in part be inviting this response. Finally, she moved to her sister's home in another city. The sister was a widow, too.

The widow mentioned earlier who had moved in with her daughter became more and more depressed and was not eating. She was alone in the house during the day when her grandchildren were at school and the adults were at work. She maintained contact with the aide, who suggested she come back to her old neighborhood to participate in a hot-lunch program once a week and to play cards with some of her old friends. The daughter was able to drive her there and arranged to have someone bring her home afterwards. Her mood changed as she rediscovered her old friends and met other widows.

The physical needs of many widows and widowers are exacerbated by their aloneness. When their spouses were alive, they could help one another and were able to be quite independent, but now the surviving partners find themselves in need of some helpful interventions. They need help finding adequate housing where they can feel safe. They want help getting to medical appointments and becoming involved in some activity outside the home. Help for them involves connecting them to other community services, particularly those provided by the local senior center. Outreach programs in senior centers make it simpler to connect the widowed to appropriate resources.

Older men and women often do not like to go out at night or they no longer drive, so group meetings are usually scheduled in the daytime and carpools can be arranged when necessary. A widower who consistently refused the offer of help from another widowed person from the senior center finally gave in and agreed to accept a ride to visit the center for at least a hot lunch. After that, his attitude changed:

> I really appreciated coming to the center for a hot lunch and then meeting the other widowed people. It became an important part of my week. Someone picked me up which made a big difference. At first I was embarrassed that I couldn't get there myself. But I soon got over that. People there really cared.

For many older widows and widowers, grandchildren are very important, giving them pleasure and a chance to be helpful:

> I have a four-year-old grandson, and one is almost five. Those children really saved me, I take care of them when they need me and anytime they call I say "yes." It's been great.

Many older widows are still working:

> I thought of retiring, but what would I do all day? I am used to being very busy. I talked it over with the group and finally decided to cut back my hours, which was possible. I really like what I do; it's demanding and challenging, but I'm lucky that I don't need to be there full time to do what needs doing.

Others find themselves involved in a variety of community activities:

> I decided to try taking a course on art history at the adult learning center at the university. It was something I had always been interested in. I went with another member of my support group who had been talking about it for weeks. I was the only one who decided to find out

more about it. Then I met several new widows there who I began to meet for lunch before class. I was getting an education at the same time as I was making new friends.

A widower reflected on how important the outreach in the local Widowed Person's Service was for him:

It gave me a whole new social circle and a new focus for my energies and a whole new way of being alone, accepting and enjoying it. I am beginning to think that I am young enough to date again.

While many widows might consider dating to be a possibility, it often is not an option available to them. Widowers are more likely to remarry, women outnumber men, and older men often get involved with younger women. Campbell and Silverman (1996) talked with several widowers who married within the first year after becoming widowed. They married women who knew their wives, and often they knew the woman's deceased husband. These marriages seemed to work because the partners knew they could not replicate the past but instead had to make a new relationship. Moss and Moss (1996) noted that when these relationships allowed a place for the deceased spouses (*e.g.,* they could be remembered and talked about) the marriages were more likely to be successful.

While some widows do not want to consider dating or remarriage, they still might enjoy the company of males and are likely to seek out groups that men were likely to join:

Church is very important to me. Prayer and my faith have kept me going. We organized a Sunday brunch group of men and women who are all active in this community. Most of us are widowed and it has become an important part of my week.

Another widow declared:

I am an upbeat person. I like being with people. I am very involved in all sorts of things, I liked being married. I am beginning to date. I don't feel too old to think of getting married again.

☐ Children with Problems

Women whose adult offspring are still dependent on them face special problems. In many ways, they are still involved in the caretaking and caregiving of their children. One widow whose son was mentally disabled and quite helpless had an aide who came in daily to help bathe and dress him.

Neighbors came to exercise him and to babysit so she could go out for a few hours a day. A priest from a local church came to help put him to bed. A social worker encouraged the widow to place her son in an institution now that her husband was dead. Her husband had been ill for a long time and she had cared for him at home as well. The widow asked the widow-to-widow aide for help in advocating that she keep the child at home. Without this dependent son, the widow's life and home would be empty.

In two other families involved in the original widow-to-widow program, the children had major mental illnesses that required the widows to assume continuous caretaking roles. It took the aide a long time to learn what was happening with these women. They were eager to be involved but reluctant to have her visit their homes. The children involved were paranoid, verbally abusive, neglectful in personal hygiene, and negligent about taking their medication; they found it difficult to maintain a relationship with a mental-health clinic. In one of these two families, the widow was exhausted from caring for her sick husband before he died and protecting him from their son's abuse. The son was an only child in his late 30s and had been ill for many years. His mother met the aide outside the home. Only much later did the aide learn that this widow was embarrassed by her son's behavior and never had people visit. The widow explained:

> I never know what condition I'll find the house in. He's a chain smoker and has burned holes in the furniture. He's there all day and when I walk in he can start yelling verbal abuse at me. He won't take his medicine, he won't see the doctor, he can't work.

In the other family, the woman's husband had died suddenly. He had been able to set limits for their disturbed daughter, who was the oldest of five and suffered her first breakdown six months before her father died. Now the widow, not quite 62, was ineligible for Social Security and had to think of working for the first time. At the same time, she had to learn how to live with her daughter and how to get her to participate responsibly in the family. The widow feared her daughter's anger and to placate her usually did everything she asked. This widow talked with the aide on the telephone about her daughter but did not agree to meet the aide for almost a year. On the phone, the aide was able to help her by offering some support for her job search. The aide was finally able to get her involved when the widow-to-widow program had a group activity. In time, she was able to share her concern and felt less stigmatized by her daughter's behavior, which was certainly isolating her from others. Unfortunately, this is a problem for many families today. The National Alliance for the Mentally Ill (NAMI) is an organization that offers its members support in much the same way as the widowed are helped by widow-to-widow programs.

☐ Conclusion

As people age, dealing with the business of living creates new challenges. The death of a spouse forces the widowed to deal with a changed living situation alone, in addition to confronting the difficult feelings that must be legitimized and lived through. Those who are widowed grieve but learn to find new ways of living in the world that ease their pain and give new direction. Age by itself adds to the challenge but does not have to limit the outcome. The grief of a younger widow who is still raising children is colored by their need to respond to their grieving children as well as to themselves. In an older population with grown children, the children see themselves in some ways as responsible for their parents' well-being; however, it may be equally important to consider how the grief of adult children affects the widowed and the influence of their interaction on the process.

Conclusion

I walked a mile with Sorrow
And ne'er a word said she;
But Oh, the things I learned from her
When sorrow walked with me.

Robert Browning Hamilton

In thinking about how to end this book, I became involved in a conversation with myself to decide what needed to be said at this point. My first thought was that the poem with which I began this book belongs here as well. We are all students of life, and we have to be open to its lessons whether we are ready or not. No widowed person is ever ready. In revisiting the themes of this book, I was reminded that perhaps life-cycle events lack endings. I have described here a time in a man or a woman's life that begins with a death. In essence, the impact of this death will affect the rest of the newly widowed person's life. In this sense, the widowed experience no "closure," to use a much abused word in our contemporary vocabulary. I also realized that, in many ways, during this dialog with myself I was probably mirroring a process most widowed people go through. I was reminded of the movie *Hello Dolly*. The widow heroine has a continuing dialog with her deceased husband and with herself, as she tries to sort out the meaning of his death and the direction her life should now take. In her day, to deal with her aloneness and loneliness she needed to marry again. This was essentially a woman's only option. Most widowed people need to make sense out of the death and bring new people and new relationships into their lives, and women today have more options and more choices that can take them in many different directions. This may involve them in an ongoing conversation with the deceased, as well as themselves, as they consider their options, and experiment with new ways of thinking about their situation, and acting on it.

My concern in this book, is not only with *what* people think but also *how* they think. Some widowed are concrete thinkers who take in information and literally wait for the guidance of others, but they need to move on from there. Regardless of the way they took in information before the death, very often thinking concretely and moving one step at a time may be the strategy of choice given the pain and disruption the widowed experience after the death. Being able to think more abstractly becomes more appropriate as the widowed begin to sort out their feelings and the meaning of the death in their lives. They need to look beyond themselves to consider what they are learning and how it fits in with their own experience and to appreciate what they can contribute that expands the picture and their options. They then are no longer simply defined by the term "widow" but are able to see a life beyond that role that can include an expanded definition of the role of widowed and of person as well.

Again, this process has no ending; it is ongoing. Ideally, perhaps this outlook is how we should approach all of life's problems, but the widowed, who have no choice, are often forced into adopting this new perspective out of necessity as they find themselves examining their lives in ways they had never before considered. This is the developmental lens that I talked about early in the book. The widowed discover the variety of possibilities and choices they have that offer hope and excitement for the future. The widowed learn to act differently with new sensitivity to their own needs as well as the needs of others. In helping them to do so, we have not prevented illness but we have promoted their ability to cope competently.

I have taken the stories that these men and women shared and woven them together to show how the fabric of grief changes over time and how the widowed are affected by this process. I have tried to document how these women and men rely upon various aspects of support to move through the grieving process to a place where they have developed an expanded perspective on their new status and can make the necessary role shifts that seem to be required of them. While common threads run throughout this process for all the widowed, it may look very different for each of them, depending on who they are and where they started.

I emphasized that the widowed do not recover from their grief — they *adapt*. The relationship between adaptation and learning is an essential part of the process. As White (1974) pointed out, all adaptation involves learning, and people's learning opportunities affect their adaptive strategies. I pointed to the obvious need to respect people's learning styles and to recognize that, as a result of the transition the widowed are negotiating, they develop new learning styles. Learning styles reflect how people think, and how the widowed think involves the roles assumed by others in this process. Throughout the book, I have documented how people take in new information and how their ability to learn new ways of knowing is made easier in a mutual-help situation. Learning from a peer makes it easier to take in new information and see how to use it. In a mutual-help context, the feelings of the widowed are legitimized and their pain is acknowl-edged; no one is trying to fix it or rush them through it. They find role models to show them ways to deal with their pain. They find new ways of relating to the deceased and honoring them. They are able to reciprocate to help others.

Caserta and her colleagues (1999) warned of the need to be cautious about the use of the concept of social support. They saw support in itself as insufficient to meet the needs of the widowed. It becomes important here to define *support* in its broadest sense — that is, support that also provides people with new information and new skills. Often, both the provider and the recipient are helped.

The coping repertoires of the widowed are expanded in mutual-help groups, as is their sense of community. They are not clients, they are not consumers, but people with a common need who in coming together cre-ate opportunities to care for each other and learn from each other. Mov-ing through the grieving process always reflects the shifting nature of relationships in the lives of the widowed. Their marriages, and the com-mitted relationships that were involved, have framed and focused their lives. The death has created a very real empty space. Another widowed person can provide a link between the two worlds in which the widowed are involved — the worlds before and after the death.

For many people, effective help will come most appropriately and nat-urally from family, friends, and pre-existing social-support networks. Indeed, adequate social support is a documented prerequisite to success-ful adaptation, but it rarely can come from only one source (DeSpelder & Strickland, 2005). The Institute of Medicine of the National Academy of Science (Osterweis *et al.*, 1984) affirmed that everyone needs some help following the death of a spouse. Not surprisingly, my own judgment is that the widow-to-widow model — the opportunity to talk with other widowed people and learn from each other — is an essential part of any widowed persons' helping network. The help described in this book does not compete with or replace other sources of support, but it does provide something different and important that can only come from the widowed sharing their common experience

☐ Mutual Help Today

I will bring this book to an end by highlighting some of the long-term consequences of the work carried out in the original widow-to-widow project. I also include a brief description of how to set up programs to meet the varying needs of the widowed. The original widow-to-widow program introduced the concept of outreach, legitimized support from another widow to the community of the bereaved, and changed the landscape for providing aid to the bereaved in ways that are beyond the scope of this book to document. The helping landscape is very different now. As noted in various places throughout the book, the professional literature on the value of mutual help in the context of mutual-help organizations or in support groups continues to grow (Gottlieb, 1983; Gartner & Reisman, 1984; Powell, 1987; Lund, 1989; Caserta & Lund, 1993; Wuthnow, 1994; Lieberman, 1996; Caserta et al., 1999; Powell et al., 2000; Stewart et al., 2000, 2001). A growing number of places in our society allow the widowed to meet other widowed people and learn to adapt to this period of transition in their lives.

The literature includes many examples of projects that have explored various models for providing a mutual-help experience to the widowed. Several are described here as examples of what has been done. Caserta et al. (1999) developed the Pathfinder Program to provide a setting in which older newly widowed persons, often living alone, can systematically obtain new information to help them learn the new self-care skills necessary to meet the challenges of living a healthy life as a single person. Eleven weekly classes are offered; each class is led by healthcare professionals who have a formal agenda that provides information on a particular self-care issue. After each session, participants have time to talk with each other, share their common experiences, and take the initiative to meet on other occasions. This is an interesting psycho-educational model that builds on a person's readiness to learn when dealing with a life-cycle transition. This program collaborates with existing chapters of the Widowed Person's Service, hospice bereavement programs, funeral directors, churches, and area agencies on aging to recruit participants and either augments existing services or integrates with them.

Caserta and Lund (1996) documented the value of members' continuing contact with each other. Members experienced less loneliness and discovered interests that they could share beyond their widowhood that helped them reorganize their lives. Caserta and Lund also noted that, in the early stages of the group, women were more likely than men to reach out to people they met at the group meetings, but men's involvement increased with time. The authors reminded us that men were in the minority, which initially may have made them feel uncomfortable during the social encounters.

Stewart et al. (2001) described their experience in developing a demonstration project that offered support groups to widows who were over the age of 55. They developed their model from focus groups of widows who already were involved in mutual-help programs. They recommended a structured format, social events, and meetings in senior centers. Each group had a co-leader who was widowed herself. The group members chose the topics to be discussed, and guest lectures, case studies, audiovisual aids, and role-playing exercises expanded on these topics. When Stewart *et al.* documented the participants' general satisfaction with the group, they reported a diminished sense of loneliness and expansion of their social network, among other things.

Many support groups are convened by mental-health professionals and by clergy (Silverman, 2000a, 2003). Several models for support groups can be found in various settings in the community. No one model is associated with any one sponsoring agency. In time-limited meetings held on a regular basis for a specific number of weeks, the group of participants remains constant for that period, and they commit themselves to participate for the defined number of sessions. Usually the leader sets the agenda and makes some decisions about membership. In other cases, professionals may sponsor a variety of groups based on the length of time their members have been widowed, such as groups designed for the newly widowed or those who want to continue to meet and talk about the way their grief process is progressing. A third type of group might be referred to as the moving-on group, in which members are beginning to think about what is involved in finding new ways of dealing with their changing sense of self and the associated changes in their lives. In this group, members might occasionally meet without a leader, choosing instead to provide mutual, ongoing support for building their new lives.

Hospice programs sometimes have open-ended groups that mourners can join whenever they are ready. Other programs convene a group when they have a sufficient number ready to join. In smaller communities, groups may not be specialized (*e.g.*, for the widowed only), as a particular bereaved population may be insufficient to sustain a group.

Colin (1996) described the use of the telephone to bring people together who are isolated and unable to travel. Conference calls make it is possible for these participants to meet in real time. Some of these groups are facilitated by professionals who work for the convening agency, such as Cancer Care in New York City (Colin, 2004). Technology-based groups also provide a way to involve people who are not comfortable in face-to-face meetings or value remaining anonymous (Galinsky *et al.*, 1997).

Modern technology has expanded the options for the widowed to become involved in exchanges of experience and information. The Internet provides a tool for the widowed to find each other (Galinsky *et al.*, 1997). Madara (1997) noted that he saw no difference in the effectiveness of live *versus* online support groups; however, in his view, online support groups tend to lead to increased use of the support available because they are much easier to access. Real-time online support groups or chat rooms allow participants to respond as they wish (Colin, 2004; White & Madara, 2001). Some of these chat rooms require participants to register with the sponsoring organization before being given access to the postings. This gives those who participate some sense of security that their privacy is being protected and that really are communicating with other widowed people.

The Widowed Person's Service of the American Association of Retired Persons (AARP) has blended into what is now called the Grief and Loss program. In addition to older widowed persons, the organization wants to reach the younger widowed population as well as people who are bereaved in other ways. Local chapters can choose what to call themselves to reflect the focus of their activity. Most groups still primarily involve programs for the widowed. Approximately 250 local chapters located throughout the United States sponsor support groups and educational programs, and some reach out to the newly widowed following the original widow-to-widow model. Volunteers who do this outreach are trained by the organization using a training handbook that has evolved over the years. This and other materials are available through the organization. They also publish a series of pamphlets to provide information about emotional and practical concerns of the widowed.

The needs of the widowed with dependent children can be met in many settings; usually these involve simultaneous groups for the parents and for the children built around appropriate age-specific activities. Some are time limited, others open ended. The most popular offering is modeled after the program developed at the Dougy Center, in Portland, Oregon. The Dougy program offers biweekly meetings, about an hour and a half in length, that are for both children and their parents or caregivers. These are open-ended groups, with members staying as long as they feel the need to. More than 150 such programs exist in the United States and abroad today. Their programming is designed to facilitate a mutual exchange of support and information for children and their parents. Centers are housed in various facilities in the community. Many groups meet at churches, some have rooms in hospice facilities, and others grow into their own facilities. All of these programs depend on volunteers, be they concerned mental-health professionals, clergy, teachers, or lay people, all of whom typically have experienced a loss and who participate in an extensive training program before they begin work with either the children or the parents.

Sandler and his colleagues (2003) developed an experimental program for children who have experienced the loss of a parent. They followed the Dougy Center model to combine a mix of play and discussion; however, the program involved a fixed number of sessions, and each session was scripted to focus on the grief of these children while providing an opportunity for the participants to provide active support to each other. This was a carefully researched program using standardized measures of outcome and a control group. The children and their parents who participated in the program were found to have gained a sense of well-being and felt that they were coping effectively with any problems they experienced. These findings provided persuasive evidence in support of the value of this type of program.

In addition to its program serving the Portland, Oregon, community, the Dougy Center has developed the National Center for Grieving Children and Families, which offers training for people who want to set up programs in their own communities, both in the United States and abroad. It publishes a National Directory of Children's Grief Services, which provides information on the location of programs in various parts of the United States and Canada; a skills development training manual for volunteers; an activity manual; and handbooks concerning children who have experienced a family member being murdered or committing suicide. It also has a series of guides for school administrators and teachers. Fees from training courses and sale of books help maintain the center.

☐ How To Find Groups

Using the Internet

One of the most dramatic changes over the past decade has been the use of the Internet as a source of information about almost anything. This has changed the way people can access information as well as how they can stay in touch with each other. Geographic restrictions have become almost meaningless. Almost every organization for the widowed has its own website to provide information about the services they offer, about their organization, and how to join. For example, AARP provides comprehensive information about bereavement issues as well as online support groups and discussion boards through their website (www.griefand-loss.org). Information about how to find a site or how to join a chat room is available through the American Self Help Clearinghouse website (www.cmhc.com/selfhelp). Another way to access resources available on the Internet is to use a search engine such as Google and entering *widow* or *widower* to find available programs. Entering, for example, *self-help for widowed* will lead to a listing of organizations with a national constituency.

Finding Local Groups

Often it is possible to get local addresses from national organization websites. For example, the Grief and Loss website of AARP (www.griefand-
loss.org) lists addresses of local chapters. The Go To link at the bottom of
the page helps users identify local programs. The Dougy Center website
(www.dougy.org) provides a listing of programs that focus on the needs of
bereaved children and their widowed parents. In many communities, support groups are listed in the local newspapers and in newsletters from
senior centers. Bulletins from various faith communities list groups that
they sponsor. Many funeral homes now provide after-care themselves or
provide the families they serve with information about community
resources. Local libraries often keep listings of support groups meeting in
their area. Many hospices sponsor groups for the bereaved and sometimes
extend their services to the widowed who were not served by them before
the death.

Finding Professional Help

For some widowed people who feel the need to seek professional help, it
may not always be easy to find experienced therapists or counselors who
have experience working with the bereaved. The Association for Death
Education and Counseling website has links to certified counselors in various parts of the country. Another resource now available in almost every
community is the local hospice program. Each program has a coordinator
of bereavement services who is aware not only of what that particular
hospice offers but also what else is going on in the larger community.
These coordinators can also be helpful in identifying individual counselors who have experience with bereavement.

☐ Starting a Program

While this is not a "how-to" book, it seems appropriate to touch on what
has been learned about developing such opportunities for the widowed
since the original widow-to-widow program was designed and to give
readers some direction for initiating such programs in their communities.
The focus is not only on serving individuals but also on making the community a more caring place — making it easier for people to connect with
each other and be available with a mutuality that does not distinguish
between those being served and those who are the providers (Belenky *et*

al., 1997). Wuthnow (1994) was surprised by his finding that members of small groups were often more active in their communities and helped integrate people with families and neighborhoods. They were more likely to be aware of the widowed in their community.

Taking the Initiative

The initiative for developing new programs can come from many sources — clergy, funeral directors, human service agencies, national programs wanting to come into a local area, community centers, and, most importantly, widowed people themselves. In an ideal situation, a collaboration between these various helpers is most effective. What follows is an outline of steps that can be taken to develop a program in a given community:

- The first step is to develop a community committee interested in the needs of the bereaved. This committee should consist of those who are the natural gatekeepers for the bereaved, such as clergy and funeral directors. The widowed themselves need to be on this committee to ensure that whatever program is developed will meet their needs.
- The first task of such a committee is to choose someone to facilitate their meetings, someone who will see that decisions are implemented and that there is some continuity in what is being planned.
- The committee then has to identify what services exist in the community and who are reached by them. To identify the bereaved in any given community, a review of the death statistics is a key step. The local public health department will have information about the death rate in a community. To determine the next of kin (those who would be the target population for the projected program), it may be necessary to contact the funeral directors serving this community, clergy, or hospice staff. To avoid violating anyone's privacy, it is not necessary to obtain identifying information. What is needed are general statistics about age, who died, and who are the surviving mourners (e.g., spouse, child, sibling, partner). This will tell you something about the bereaved and what particular focus the initiative might take (i.e., whether it should focus primarily on the widowed or bereaved young families). In the case of a long illness where hospice was involved, hospice can provide this information for those they served, and they may be willing to join in this initiative.
- The committee must then match available services with the identified populations to see where gaps exist, always taking into consideration what the widowed or other bereaved populations see as needed.

- With information about the bereaved and the services already available, the committee has many decisions to make:
  - What programs seem appropriate?
    - Outreach effort
    - Support group (open-ended or time-limited)
    - Social club or other social activities
    - Other approaches for disseminating information about grief or community resources
  - Who is the program trying to reach?
    - Are there sufficient numbers to set up specialized programs for specific age groups and different kinds of losses?
    - Can the identified needs be met with one inclusive group?
  - Is there a need for sectarian sponsorship so that each faith community can develop its own program for its own constitutency? Or, is it possible to consider one sponsor that could cross ethnic, racial, and religious barriers that may exist in the community?
  - Can this be a totally volunteer program, or is some funding required?
  - Is it appropriate to consider joining a national or regional initiative?
  - What role should professionals play: advisors, leaders, facilitators?

Consider the Following in an Outreach Program

- Locate the newly bereaved. Involve the funeral directors and clergy and read obituaries.
- Establish criteria for recruiting volunteers. Such criteria have been tested in many bereavement programs. Volunteers in a program for the widowed should be widowed for at least a year, although there is no fast rule about how long a volunteer should be widowed. What is most important is that volunteers should be able to talk about their grief and reflect on their own ways of coping, can see the value of the helper being another widowed person, and should be good listeners. They should be willing to give several hours a month to the program.
- Develop an orientation for volunteers. Gather information from existing programs such as the Dougy Center, AARP's Widowed Person's Service, or hospice training for volunteers. At a minimum, new volunteers should share with each other their own experiences with widowhood — what has helped and what did not. These widowed volunteers together can explore how to expand their own coping resources as well as each other's and consider what they can do as good listeners and role models for those to whom they are reaching

out. Essentially, they need to develop a helping model that allows them to use their own experience on behalf of others. A good volunteer can respect and learn from a professional's expertise but not necessarily defer to it.

- Recruit volunteers through personal contact, existing organizations, advertising in local newspapers, or word of mouth. Some who are initially interested in volunteering discover during orientation that this is not where they want to put their energies at the time. Training sessions are often the best way to screen volunteers. The trainers can be provided by other volunteers, professionals recruited in the community, or representatives of a national program.

Role of the Professional

Human service professionals (including clergy, nurses, psychologists, and social workers) who become involved in community programs for the bereaved need to move from seeing themselves in the role of expert to that of equal partner (Silverman, 2000a; Stewart *et al.*, 2000). In many ways, these professionals become students as they learn about widowhood from the widowed with whom they are collaborating. A professional who cannot make this leap to recognize the value of knowledge gained through experience should not be involved in this kind of community work. Professionals can collaborate in many ways. A professional who has experience dealing with the bereaved can consult with a group or organization that is forming to provide information on organizational issues and on group processes. A consultant can be a facilitator to help people think through what they want to do and where they are going. These consultants can provide a bridge between an organizing committee and the larger human service system. As noted, such consultants can be most helpful when they appreciate lived experiences as a source of expertise. If issues of control and expertise are set aside, then a consultant can facilitate the process for the widowed to develop a language for describing and applying their experience. It is always important for consultants to remind those with whom they are consulting that in this case the consultants have little authority in the system and that the group need not follow their advice (Silverman, 1989).

The Professional as Leader or Facilitator

Typically, most support groups are led by mental-health professionals. Much has been written about the ways in which professionals can lead groups. One of the most difficult roles is that of facilitator, a role more suited to a mutual-help setting or to a group whose members are available to help each other. In this capacity, the professional in many ways relinquishes control to the group members. The professional's main task is to help develop an atmosphere of trust and safety, identify common themes as they come up in the discussion, see that everyone has a chance to talk and be heard, and enable members to learn from each other. When clarifying the goals of a group, it is important for everyone to recognize that the process involves more than legitimizing feelings — it involves some movement that makes change possible. A facilitator has to understand the process of grief and help the group provide the support and information that encourage people to try new things to move from here to there.

In an outreach program, the volunteers need to meet regularly with someone who can provide them with perspectives on their work, give them support, and help with any difficulties they are experiencing with various widowed people they have reached. They need an opportunity to work out the day-to-day details of an outreach program that might offer activities such as opportunities for participants to talk about their concerns, as well as educational opportunities that can expand the widowed person's knowledge about grief (not unlike what Caserta and Lund provided in the program discussed above). An outreach program can provide the newly widowed with links to other resources in their community that might help them escape their sense of isolation. They need to know that there are others like themselves and that they do not need to struggle alone with their pain. The focus here is on strengthening the community, building new communities, and recognizing the importance of one's own deeds in this work. Volunteers are not professionals who continue with this work from year to year. They need to know when to stop volunteering, but the organization requires structure to give it the necessary continuity as each generation of volunteers gets involved and moves on.

After many years of being involved in the study of widowhood, I feel that this conversation will continue as I move into the next phase of my own life cycle. We are always learning. Alcoholics Anonymous (AA) has a saying that is almost exclusively associated with them. I recently learned in a *Boston Globe* article that Reinhold Niebuhr wrote it for a sermon during World War II, and AA adopted it with his permission. As we try to make sense out of death and out of life, it seems to be very appropriate:

> Give us the grace to accept with serenity the things that cannot be changed, the courage to change the things that should be changed, and the wisdom to distinguish the one from the other.

Appendix 1: Research Findings

☐ Widow-to-Widow Program

This appendix reports on the research that was conducted during the original widow-to-widow program. This project raised many questions, as we were initiating a new area of practice with a population about which little was known. We had limited research resources, and most of our energy was devoted to seeing if this kind of outreach could work. We first needed to find out if people would accept our offer to help so we initially focused on the rate of acceptance. The demographic data were used to determine if this population had specific qualities that differentiated those who accepted from those who refused. We then turned our attention to evaluating what actually took place in the exchanges between the newly widowed and the aides. We wanted to know what meaning this service had for the widowed and how the intervention affected them.

To answer these questions, we first of all reviewed the death certificates. Our analysis was primarily grounded in what the aides reported about their work. They filled out forms that provided more demographic data about the widows, but collecting this information took a back seat to responding to what the widow needed at the moment. We taped all the staff meetings at which the aides reported on their activities of the week, and they kept diaries about their individual contacts with the widows. Staff was present when the newly widowed met informally with each other and the aides on various social occasions. We wrote down all that we could remember immediately afterwards. At the end of the project, we were able to conduct follow-up interviews with those who had accepted the offer of help and those who refused. Out of all these data, after carefully reading and rereading what was said, we were able to create various narratives about the lives of these widows. Several articles were published regarding what we had learned from specific segments of this population that we served. One paper focused on the widows whose husbands had committed suicide (Silverman, 1971b). Several papers addressed widows with dependent children (Silverman, 1971a; Silverman & Englander, 1975;

Silverman & Silverman, 1975). The group of widows whose husbands had suffered long illnesses allowed us to explore how anticipatory grief affected their experience (Silverman, 1974). What we learned from these qualitative analyses became the basis of the chapters presented in the second part of this new edition and in similar chapters in the first edition. These chapters describe the changing experiences of the widowed and how the original program influenced their lives as widows. As was evident from the first edition and the many papers that came out of the project, we were able to learn a good deal about widowhood and the bereavement process as well.

This appendix reports on who was served by the original widow-to-widow program and the Widowed Service Line, as well as the factors that affected their participation. Admittedly, the original computer printouts of the analysis of our findings have been lost with time, and gaps exist in the data that can no longer be filled. Most of what is presented here was reported on by Cecile Strugnell and Ruby Abrahams, who were research associates in the original program. Strugnell wrote about who the widow-to-widow project served, and Abrahams evaluated the Widowed Service Line; their reports appeared in the first book to come out of this project, *Helping Each Other in Widowhood* (Silverman *et al.*, 1974). I have edited these reports and added some additional data from articles published since then. *Helping Each Other in Widowhood*, now out of print, consisted of papers presented at two workshops held in the spring of 1971. The first workshop, for widows and widowers only, drew 100 widowed people from 19 states. This was the first time a community of the widowed had come together to share their experiences and discuss their ideas about helping each other. The second workshop was for clergy, funeral directors, and mental-health specialists who worked with the bereaved. The purpose of these meetings was to share what we had learned to encourage participants to develop new programs in their home communities. A representative of the American Association of Retired Persons (AARP) attended the workshop for professionals, which led to the organization's interest in sponsoring a program for the widowed that eventually developed into the Widowed Person's Service.

Who the Widow-to-Widow Program Served

Over the approximately two and a half years in which the program operated, we reached out to 430 widows, the total number of women in the target community during this period of time whose husbands were under 65 when they died. As noted, some of the original data have been

lost, so some questions about this population cannot be answered; however, the information available does provide an overview of the population served and the factors that seemed to influence who accepted and
who refused. As noted earlier, our information was taken from the death
certificates, the reports of the aides, and two sets of interviews conducted
later — one with widows who refused our offer of help and the other
with widows we had helped over a period of time. When organizing our
information for statistical analysis, we selected those widows who had
first been approached by the service at least a year before. This limited us
to the first 300 cases. People to whom we reached out after that provided
additional illustrative data.

Of those 300 widows, 37 were not available because they had moved,
the address provided did not exist, or no one at the address had ever
heard of them. Several widows listed on the death certificate had been
separated from their husbands for a long time before their deaths and
called to tell us that the offer of assistance was not appropriate. In the
African-American community, we failed to reach a number of widows
because the aide who should have seen them was sick for a time and
because periodic tensions in the community made it unsafe to visit. This
reduced the number of widows in this analysis to 233. Of this number, 140
(61%) accepted the aides' offers and 91 (39%) refused. We considered this
a very high acceptance rate considering that we were not known in the
community when we started and this kind of outreach had no precedent.

At the end of the outreach program we tried to locate the women who
did not want to accept our offer of help. A research associate went out to
the neighborhoods to verify addresses and see when she might find people at home. (This type of outreach would be impossible today due to the
restraints placed on researchers by institutional review boards to respect
people's privacy; I have no argument with this new process and would
not recommend that what we did at the time even be suggested today in
spite of its value to our understanding of this work.) The purpose of
these interviews was to learn what we could about these widows' reasons for refusing, how they had handled their problems, and whether
they had, at some later date, wished for help such as the aide might have
provided. This is not information normally available to researchers but
which provides a perspective on the broader needs in a community and
the wider range of help used by people with whom we would ordinarily
have little or no contact.

In addition, to get a clearer picture of the meaning of the aides' offers
of help to the widows who had become involved in the program, we
interviewed 35 (25%) widows who had extensive contact with the program. These were open-ended, semi-structured interviews conducted by
one of the project's research associates.

Occupation of the Deceased

We considered this community to be working class, and identifying how the deceased had earned their livings seemed to support our view. We made the following distinctions based on the occupational classifications of the U.S. Census:

Professional, managerial	17.6% (52.6% accepted)
Craftsmen, salesmen	28.2% (60.7% accepted)
Clerical, service workers	24.1% (57.7% accepted)
Operatives, laborers, and other	30.1% (66.2% accepted)

Although statistically not significant, the difference in percentage of acceptance between the highest socioeconomic group (52.6%) and the lowest one (66.2%) raises a question about why this should be so. Among the population of less skilled workers existed a group of widows whose need for help had a certain urgency about it. They lived from one check to another, and with their husband's death they had no income to pay the rent or for food. If the widow was working, she was less likely to accept; 76% of the widows who were not working accepted the aides' visits, and only 51% of those who were working became involved. Some women who had originally refused the offer of help because they were too busy with their jobs were grateful for contact with the aides later on when they felt the full impact of the loss.

Religion of Deceased

Neither race nor religion seemed to be a factor in the widows' response to the offer of help. Of the 233 we contacted, 92.2% were Caucasian, 8.8% African-American; 60% were Catholic, 10.3% Protestant, and 17.5% Jewish. The religious affiliation of 13% of the widows was unknown; given our understanding of this community at the time, we might assume these widows considered themselves Christians but their religion was not clearly stated on the death certificate. We distinguished between Christians and Jews by looking at the funeral home that served them. This was a community in flux, and during the lifetime of the project we saw a radical decline in the Jewish population, which was being replaced by African-Americans. This shift in population had an important impact on our outreach to older widows in the Jewish community who became involved in an outreach in that community after the original project ended.

Age of the Deceased

We did not always have a widow's age but we knew the husband's age from the death certificate. Based on the husband's age, a statistically significant difference was found between those widows who accepted and those who refused:

Age of Husband at Death	Percent of Population (%)	Percent Accepting (%)
Under 40	9.5	81.8
41–50	15.6	61.1
51–60	42.0	62.9
61–65	32.9	51.3

The younger widows were definitely more eager to receive help. This finding becomes more meaningful if we take into consideration the presence of dependent children in the surviving family; 81% of those with children under the age of 16 at home accepted, as compared to 58% of widows who had grown child or no children. The younger the woman was, the younger the children were and the more likely our help was to be welcome shortly after they were widowed.

Cause of Death

We looked at the causes of death. Most of the men (55.4%) had died of heart disease or strokes. Today, the rate in this age group would be lower. No significant difference was found between those widows who accepted help and the cause of death of the husband, nor was any correlation found between the length of time the husband was ill and the widow's willingness to become involved in the program. Four men were homicide victims, and all of these widows accepted help. In the group of widows who accepted the offer of help, the husbands of 39 women had suffered from a long illness. In this sample, 30 of the men were over 50, and several were over 60; one was only 25, another 38, and the remainder were in their mid-40s at the time of their death. Several of these men were bus drivers or policemen; one was an electronic technician. Several of the widows had worked as sales clerks, several were registered nurses, and one was an executive secretary; however, many of these widows had to turn to Welfare to support themselves and their families during the terminal stages of their husbands' illnesses, and some women went to work as housekeepers to supplement their incomes. From this brief profile, we can see that the impact of the death was both economic as well as emotional. While they knew their husband's death was inevitable, they were invested in making his life comfortable and taking advantage of what time they still had together. They felt that they only began to grieve after the husband was dead. Of these women, 75% accepted the aides' offers of help. They were also more likely to accept at a later date because they were too exhausted from caring for their husbands to talk about what was happening at the time of the first contact. With the resources of hospice available today, these women would receive more emotional support.

Influence of the Available Helping Network

In what way did the helping network available to the widows influence their acceptance? We have information regarding the availability of friends and family for all but 9% (3% of these were acceptances, 6% refusals). We only know three cases in which no family was available (two of these cases were refusals). The greatest potential resource was the widow's own family: mostly grown children (63.2%), siblings (48.9%), and parents (22.1%). About 40% of the cases could seek the assistance of more than one generation of relatives. This was a community in which many families had lived for several generations, and the extended family was still available. In 9.3% of the cases, the widow moved in with a relative or had a relative move in with her.

Sources of Help

The widows evaluated the help provided by their family, with the following results:

Timing of Help	Occurrence Reported by Widows (%)
Immediately after the death	82.3
Several months later	52.9
Continued, frequent visits	62.0

When we consider only those that accepted our help, 85% of the widows reported that their family visited frequently. This would indicate that those with a close family relationship were the most open to help from our service. The family relationship that seems to be the most helpful to a widow is that of grown children and grandchildren. The group of widows with grown children had the lowest acceptance rate; only 47% accepted the aides. Other sources of help mentioned by the widows using our service included:

Friends	39% found them helpful in the initial stages, and 28% reported that they continued to be helpful later on.
Doctor or clergy	21.7% were helped by either or both in the initial stages, but only 3.9% considered them still helpful later on; 14.3% mentioned clergy as being helpful in the initial stages, and 11% mentioned doctors. If either a doctor or clergyman had extended contact with the widow, this occurred primarily because of a personal friendship between them or the widow had been particularly active in the church.
Other widows	6.9% mentioned other widows as being helpful initially, but 23.7% found them helpful later on. The category of "other widows" does not include the aides but may include widows met through the program.

With a few exceptions, a natural helping network seemed to be available to the widows, which was more true among those who accepted us than those who refused; however, we do not know a good deal about how these networks helped. We do know that 16.3% of the widows mentioned that their family was a *problem*; 6.0% were in conflict with their family over financial matters, such as relatives trying to borrow money or take advantage of them, and 10.3% complained of a lack of understanding or indifference on their family's part.

The interest of family and friends often was not sustained nor was it sufficient as the widows began to recognize needs that their families could not meet, no matter how attentive they might be. This problem was frequently voiced at program-sponsored group meetings. Family and friends rallied around the widows at the time of death and shortly after, but they soon lost interest or patience. A number of widows surrounded by family and friends at the time of the death later found that they were left very much to themselves and welcomed the opportunity of contact with the aide. They also perceived this contact as fulfilling a need that their family and friends, even if they continued showing interest, could not satisfy. They noted that the aides had lived through the same experience, and they were strangers who were not involved in the home or neighborhood situation, which made it easier for the widows to unburden themselves. Sometimes other widows at work or in the neighborhood took the initiative to reach out to a new widow. This came as a surprise but was much appreciated and considered very helpful.

It is difficult to assess the role of social agencies in the lives of these widows. We did not know of all the widows who were receiving professional help, but it was rare for a widow to talk about being involved in counseling or therapy. In a few instances we knew that a family or mental-health agency was also involved but was meeting different needs of the widow or her family.

In seven families it was the children, not always the younger ones, who experienced problems (see Chapter 9). At least three of them had definite psychological problems or had received help before the death. The father's death brought their problems to crisis proportions, and in each case we helped the widow turn to an agency. Among the widows themselves three were drinking and had to be hospitalized. Four widows who received help had a past history of mental illness. One young widow whose husband had committed suicide also sought help as an outpatient for awhile. The aides were most helpful with problems caused by widowhood itself, but for problems existing before or extraneous to the bereavement (which often became worse as a result of the death) professional help had to be sought.

We got a referral from a psychiatrist who felt he was making little progress with a new widow who had come to him for help. The aide who went to see her simply said, "She is bereaved." This was a problem the aide was competent to deal with, and little by little she helped the new widow to function again and to learn how to address the problems caused by her widowhood.

An early goal of this project was to find ways of preventing emotional problems in the newly widowed, and we came to think of what we were doing as promoting competence. As we reviewed the results, we realized that the widows experienced a good deal of expected stress with which they learned to cope but in no instances did a widow develop a serious mental illness that she had not suffered before. Without more rigorous evidence we cannot be sure, but the direction of our findings seems to suggest that we did achieve our goal of limiting the risk of developing new emotional problems in this population.

Meeting the Widow

As noted earlier in the book, an offer of help to the newly widowed often had to be repeated before it was accepted. In only 22% of the cases was this letter directly followed by a visit as planned and the widow found to be home. In 28% of the cases, the widow was not home and had not canceled the appointment. If this happened, the aide would make some further effort by leaving a note, telephoning, or repeating the visit. Because the aides found that much of their time would be wasted if they did not make sure the widow was expecting them, they frequently called on the morning the visit was planned to see if the widow had received the letter, often with the excuse of asking for directions. In other cases, the widow took the initiative, calling to say she could not keep the appointment that day. This gave her the opportunity to find out more about the aide and the service and gave the aide a chance to dispel suspicion and initiate a contact. For 48% of widows this led to a telephone relationship. Some of these were initiated by widows with the clear intention of refusing but changing their minds in the course of the conversation.

For 68% of the widows who became involved in the program, their relationships with the aides extended for at least a year or more. In the remaining instances, the aides decided after awhile that they were not needed anymore or they had done all they could for the widow. The widows knew that the aides might continue to call from time to time, and the aides would occasionally drop by to be neighborly.

Many of these women told us they had always kept the telephone number on hand and that this had been a great comfort to them to know there was someone they could talk to. On several occasions, widows who thought they would never be interested in this sort of contact became overcome by a sudden need to talk to someone; they remembered their aide's card and called her, once in the middle of the night.

In some cases, a close relationship developed between the aides and the widows, leading to further visits, joint outings, and frequent telephone conversations, sometimes arising out of a particular need of the widow or out of a growing friendship between them. Although we did arrange for the widowed to meet each other, these group meeting were never a major emphasis of our program. Only 30% of those who accepted ever came to such meetings, and only 20% could be said to come with any regularity. The one-to-one relationship was most important for the majority of these women. Many widows did not care to belong to a group or were not emotionally ready to do so. They appreciated the individual relationship. Younger widows did not find the group meetings very helpful except when one was organized around their special needs as single parents. At other meetings they found themselves outnumbered by older women. In some instances, the aides successfully introduced two young widows. This informal opportunity to meet became very important to them.

On the other hand, some widows seemed shy in a one-to-one relationship and felt more at ease in the group. The meetings also provided a reason for keeping in touch and gave some widows who had initially refused us the opportunity of changing their minds or finding out about the service at a later date.

Range of Help Offered

To understand the success of the program, we looked at what kind of problems new widows presented and what kind of help the aides were able to provide. Two areas of conversation were found to provide the basis for opening contacts with a new widow: talking of her children and making sure the widow was aware of all the material benefits to which she might be entitled. Once the ice was broken, it became easier to talk of the death, her feelings about the deceased, and his death. The aides asked about the widow herself and how she saw her new situation. They often queried the widow with regard to how helpful and understanding their friends and family were being. In these initial contacts, the new widows wanted to know about their aide's experience as a widow and often asked for details about her reaction to the death. The issues the widow brought up are listed below in order of their frequency, as well as the percentage of those who raised these issues and accepted the help of the program:

Issue	Percentage of Widows Raising Issue *and* Accepting Help (%)
Need of the widow to talk, to experience companionship and friendship with the aide, to share her experience	81
Problems related to housing, mostly because of the bad neighborhood, lodging inadequacy, or a wish to move closer to relatives	34
Problems related to children	28
Need for assurance that she would successfully weather the crisis	25
Inadequate income	24
Problems in relationships with family or relatives; meeting with a lack of understanding	23
Wish to get a job or training for a job	22
Financial problems related to claims for benefits	19

The aides made a great effort to inform themselves about such things as the claims, benefits, and social services available and often were able to give assistance or advice to the widows about their material concerns. It is clear, however, that the greatest need did not arise out of material hardship. What the widows most appreciated was the opportunity to talk, let out their feelings, and discuss their emotional needs with an aide, bringing a special quality to the relationship because of the shared experience.

Reasons for Refusal

New widows refused the aides' offers to visit for many reasons. It is important to keep in mind that many widows were quite suspicious of being approached by a stranger. In some sections of this community this was a legitimate concern. In addition, many widows were particularly uneasy living without a man in the house. Several acquired a dog. One told us that she kept a heavy tool within reach when she went to sleep for use as a possible weapon. We were aware of initial hostility or suspicion in at least 21% of these women, but not all of these refused the aides' offers to visit. Some widows took the precaution of having someone in the family present at the time of the initial meeting or had arranged to be called or visited by a friend at the time of the aide's visit. Some checked with their local priest to find out if we were legitimate. We anticipated, therefore, that a number of refusals would be motivated by fear even though the widow might give another excuse at the time of the initial contact. When aides initiated contact with new widows, they encountered the following types of resistance to their offer of help:

Resistance to Help	Percentage of Widows (%)
Widow was too busy with job, family, or setting affairs in order.	28.6
Widow was receiving support from friends and family.	25.3
Widow's family (usually grown) would not accept calls.	12.1
Widow was independent and not in need of support.	12.2
Aides received no response of any kind their efforts to contact the widow.	7.7
Widow would not open the door.	7.7
Widow seemed to accept first contact but refused later because of no need.	6.5

The last group tended to have a lengthy telephone call with the aide. They showed some interest in the service but later let the aide know that they had no need for such help.

It is interesting to note that 12% of the refusals came from relatives, usually grown children, who somewhat indignantly told the aides to leave their mothers alone and that they were taking care of them. Perhaps if the widow herself had been reached, the answer might have been different. We base this supposition on the fact that several widows answered the telephone themselves and were prepared to talk to the interviewer when their children told them to hang up.

To find out more about those who continued to refuse any contact we interviewed them two years later. Of these 91 widows, 2 were remarried and not available to be interviewed, 27 had moved, and 27 formally refused to be interviewed. We were able to interview 35 widows (38% of the refusals). We asked about their reaction when they were first contacted — Would they have had a different answer if they had understood better what the service was about? How had they managed and had they at some later date wished for the kind of help the aides might have been able to provide? Of those interviewed, 28.6% suggested that they might have been receptive to our help at some later date or if we had been able to provide a more adequate explanation of what we were offering. The following table summarizes the responses received in our later interviews with those who refused our help:

Widows' Responses	Percentage of Widows (%)
Widow was independent, and this was not the sort of thing for her nor was she comfortable talking to a stranger; she keeps to herself.	42.9
Widow would still refuse the aide because of enough family support.	22.8
Widow might have accepted if contacted later.	11.4
Widow might have accepted if she had understood better what it was about.	8.6
Widow joined the program later of her own accord.	8.6
Widow remained hostile to the program.	5.7

☐ Widowed Service Line

Who the Widowed Service Line Served

A telephone service model such as the Widowed Service Line offers an opportunity for widowed people to call in for help. In contemporary society, this might be compared to those widowed people who use chat rooms on the Internet to reach out to other widowed people. In contrast to our original widow-to-widow program, we cannot know who among the widowed seek out the kind of help offered by chat rooms and who do not. On the other hand, chat rooms are often spontaneous, and people who respond often do so without any intermediary such as was available in our programs. This does not take away from their effectiveness, however.

The Widowed Service Line, an outgrowth of the original widow-to-widow program, was an attempt to reach a wider community. This section analyzes some of the characteristics and problems of those who did contact the line and describes briefly the volunteers' handling of these calls. In the first seven months of operation, 750 people called the Widowed Service Line. (Note that the recordkeeping was uneven, and the same data were not available for the entire population.) These calls were received from a wide geographic area in and around Boston. The callers heard about the line in a variety of ways, television being the most effective means of publicity. Of all callers to the line, 54% heard about it on television, 12% from local newspapers, 10% from church bulletins, 9% from the radio, 7% through a friend, and 6% from the metropolitan newspaper; 2% were referred by professionals. At the peak of the television coverage, during the first three months of operation, the line averaged 60 calls per week. After the line became better known in the community, more referrals were received from professionals such as clergy and social workers, who were unable to help with specific emotional problems of the widowed.

Callers' Ages and Duration of Widowhood

Of all callers, 90% were women, with the following age breakdown (with no significant difference in the ages of male and female callers):

Age	Percentage of Callers (%) ($n = 521$)
Under 40 years	12
41–50 years	22
51–60 years	36
61+ years	30

The ages of callers ranged from 24 to 90 years, but the most typical caller was a woman in her 50s.

Was it primarily the newly bereaved or those with longer term residual problems of widowhood who reached out to use this service?

Length of Time Being Widowed	Percentage of Widows (%) ($n = 470$)
Less than 1 year	30
1 to 2 years	16
3 to 6 years	23
7+ plus years	31

Almost half (46%) were widowed within the last 2 years and were at the stage of handling the early problems of grief, disengagement from their previous life style, and meeting the need to engage in new roles and relationships. A smaller number of the widows — those widowed 3 to 6 years (23%) — was still trying to adjust and develop a new life style. A third of the callers had not yet adapted to the loss even after 7 years of widowhood. No significant differences in the duration of widowhood were found between male and female callers.

Financial Situation of Callers

From the records, the financial situation of the callers can be summarized as follows:

Financial Situation	Percentage of Callers Reporting (%) ($n = 538$)
Well off	3
Adequate income	33
Tight finances	16
Hardship	4
No financial problem recorded	44

This table in part reflects the fact that a telephone service does not always reach the financially disadvantaged. Although the line was publicized in the local newspapers and on radio stations for low-income, inner city areas, we received few calls from these communities. Many callers were given additional information about financial benefits, but this was rarely the reason why they called the line.

Types of Problems Presented by Callers at Different Stages of Widowhood

Caller's requests were categorized as follows:

Reason for Calling	Percentage of Callers (%) ($n = 567$)
Lonely; needed a listener	20
Lonely; wanted to meet people	37
Required specific information regarding:	
Finances	6
Employment or training	4
Other (including information for handicapped people, housing and legal problems, professional care for self or children, health facilities, housekeepers, child care)	12
Requested information about the line itself (most of these were later placed in categories 1 or 2)	16
Offered services as volunteer	5

Categories 1, 2, and 4 together (in which loneliness and isolation were the main problems) accounted for 73% of all the needs expressed by callers. Of those who wanted information specifically on how to meet new people and expand their social relationships network:

- 58% were interested in social clubs for the widowed.
- 30% requested contact with another widowed person living in their own area.
- 12% asked specifically how to meet members of the opposite sex.

The three main categories of callers' needs (seeking a listener, wanting to meet people, and looking for specific practical information) were found to be significantly related to their stage of widowhood. The widowed who called within the first year of their bereavement were most likely to need an understanding listener. At this point, they are experiencing a period of turmoil as they begin to realize the full impact of their changed life situation.

Callers who have been widowed for approximately two to six years are most likely to be looking for ways to make an accommodation. They are beginning to develop new roles and relationships and look for ways to re-engage in the social system. These callers were more likely to request information about how to make new contacts and where to go to meet people and develop new friendships.

Callers who were widowed a longer time (seven years or more) still requested information about meeting people, but a higher proportion of these long-term widowed people had specific requests about financial, legal, housing, and employment problems. This may reflect another critical stage for the older widowed person, when the children have grown up and leave home. The widow or widower is then faced with living alone for the first time. At this stage, questions may arise about sharing housing accommodations that are too large or moving into a smaller dwelling unit. The older person who is approaching the age for claiming Social Security may also need help with financial problems. Indications are that the widowed persons who do not successfully build a new life style after some years of widowhood and who may have depended too heavily on family or work for meaningful self-definition may be encounter additional difficulties when the family disperses or retirement age is reached.

Types of Problems Presented by Different Age Groups

The younger caller, under age 45, is most likely to present problems other than social. Of these younger callers, 80% had children under age 16 at home, and many of the problems they discussed with volunteers concerned their children and the problems of the single parent. When they are raising young children, the widowed seem to have less need of help to make new friendships. These younger callers were more likely to ask for information on specific practical problems or they needed a listener for their emotional problems (especially the more recently bereaved). Callers 45 to 60 years of age were more likely to request help in finding ways to rebuild their lives, making new friendships, and finding new satisfying roles for themselves as widowed and single people. The callers over 60 years of age were more like the younger callers in that they more often requested information about practical problems or were in need of an understanding listener to help with their feelings and frustrations.

Type of Household as a Determinant of Need

Who is more likely to seek help from the Widowed Service Line — widowed people living alone or those living with others? Based on the information they provided, we were able to categorize the callers as follows:

Type of Household	Percentage of Callers (%) ($n = 458$)
Living alone	49
Living with children under 16	30
Living with children over 16	14
Living with other relatives or friend	7

These findings are similar to those for the widow-to-widow program. Women with younger children at home were more likely to accept help soon after the death of their spouses. The responsibilities of raising children alone plus the fact that the needs of children themselves increase immediately after the death place a heavy burden on widows struggling with their own grief. Both younger and older callers who sought help from the telephone service within the first two years of widowhood were more likely to be either living alone or with young children; therefore, regardless of age, these two groups seem to experience the most immediate pressures and tensions after the loss of the spouse, and these pressures increase the likelihood of response to a publicized service for the widowed.

Employment and Loneliness

Many widowed people find that it is helpful to get a job or return to work as soon as they have recovered from the immediate impact of the death. Were callers who were employed less likely to feel loneliness than those who were not employed? Our data suggest that was so. Although a majority of the callers to the Service Line were not employed, those who were employed full-time were the most likely to ask for help in making new friendships. This holds for all age groups and suggests that, although having a job may alleviate the distress of bereavement, relationships made in the workplace are no substitute for the intimacy being sought in new friendships outside of work:

Employment	Percentage of Callers (%) ($n = 478$)
Employed full-time	27
Employed part-time	12
Not employed	61

Because most of the callers responded as a result of television publicity, these figures may reflect the fact that people who are home all day have more exposure to the media; however, the television announcements also appeared during the evening hours, and other sources of information were available. The indications are that women who are at home all day are more oppressed by the stresses of widowhood than those who work and therefore are more likely to seek help from a service for the widowed. For some widowed, the work situation is a relief from the social isolation they may feel after the death; for others, employment does not meet this need. We have no data on the kind of work performed by those who called.

The Widower

The number of widowers served by the Widowed Service Line was relatively small. Our data reflect little age difference between callers who were widows and widowers. Differences in duration of widowhood were very slight. The widowers ranged from those in the early stages of bereavement to those unadjusted after seven years. The differences are small, but it is possible that the men were somewhat more likely than the women to seek help earlier, within the first few months after the death of the spouse. Male callers (55%) were slightly more likely than female callers (48%) to be living alone, and the proportions were identical for widows and widowers calling the line who had children at home (44%). As with the widow, the widower living alone or with young children is especially in need of help and was most likely to respond to the Widowed Service Line.

Differences again were slight in the categories of problems presented by widows and widowers. Widowers (41%) were somewhat less likely than widows (48%) to ask how to meet new friends and somewhat less likely to ask for practical information (widowers, 37%; widows, 46%). Men were less likely than women to mask their problems by making general inquiries about the line itself; they seemed to have less hesitation stating their problems directly. Widower callers usually were answered by widower volunteers, although as our experience with the line developed we found that many widowers preferred to talk to the female volunteers and often were more expressive of their emotional problems when talking to a woman. Some women also preferred to talk to widowers, especially about specific practical problems such as finances, housing, and legal matters.

The question most often presented by the widower with young children at home was how to find a housekeeper or full-time babysitter. This is a pressing problem, and for a widower with limited means it is difficult to find a solution. In one or two cases, the volunteer was able to refer a widow who had called the line asking for this kind of work, but this need still is largely unmet. To solve the problem, very often the widower considers remarriage. Discussions with clergymen and others who are involved with social groups for the widowed suggest an urgent need for "remarriage counseling" among the widowed. Few services of this kind are offered, and the pressures, especially for the widower with children, can often result in an unfortunate second marriage.

Loneliness and Isolation of the Widowed

Our data indicate that those who called the Widowed Service Line were mainly people suffering from loneliness and isolation. Volunteers asked callers about their social life:

Type of Social Life	Percentage of Callers (%) ($n = 455$)
Active	22
Isolated	61
Bereaved too recently	17
If Active, Relationships Involved	**Percentage of Callers (%) ($n = 99$)**
Friends	43
Clubs	34
Church	18
Relatives	5

Thus, among the callers who had found some new satisfactory social relationships, the majority were helped in doing so by their friends, and a considerable number had been helped by joining clubs.

Callers' responses to the question "Who has helped you most with your grief and adjustment problems?" were as follows:

Who Provided Help	Percentage of Callers (%) (*n* = 257)
Relatives	46
Friends	22
Clergy	3
Other professionals	4
Participation in organizations	4
No one	21

Relatives first and then friends seemed to have been the most helpful in the earlier stages of grief and readjustment. Professionals, especially clergy (who seem to be in a strategic position to help the widowed), apparently were able to offer little assistance. The data suggest that for most people relatives are helpful in the early stages of bereavement, but callers who established satisfactory relationships later on found them among friends or at clubs for the widowed. It is possible that widowed people who continue to live in a close family network and find satisfaction in kin relationships do not need outside help and are not likely to contact a service for the widowed. We cannot be sure of all the factors that affect who gets involved and how, but we know from the outreach program that a number of widows, with available and helpful family, did get involved.

The Volunteers

The Widowed Service Line was operated by a team of 18 volunteers (13 widows and 5 widowers). With two exceptions, these volunteers were all employed full time and had children to care for. They were almost all in their 40s and 50s, with no more than a high school education. They were recruited in various ways. Two had been helped in the widow-to-widow outreach program and moved into helping roles when this new phase of the program opened. Others heard about the program through the media and offered their services. Some heard about it from friends who had already been accepted as volunteers. Most of those who dropped out were in this last category. Commitment is more likely when the motivation to join is independent and self-initiated. In selecting volunteers the following characteristics were important:

- They had adequately adapted to their own bereavement and were making a satisfactory adjustment to their widowhood.
- They could talk about it.
- They really wanted to help others and had already done some reaching out to widowed friends of their own.
- They had enough commitment to give the necessary time for calls and regularly attending the bimonthly volunteers' meetings.

Styles of Caregiving

Observation of this group of volunteers indicated that the mutual-help concept involves a fluid, fast-moving, dynamic situation in which the needs of helpers, as well as those seeking help, are being met. The helpers enter the volunteer group at different stages in their own adjustment processes. Their needs and their life situations affected their style of caregiving; see Abrahams (1976) for a more complete discussion of these styles. Caregiving styles ranged from a style similar to the professional–client type of relationship at one extreme to a friendship type of relationship at the other extreme. In the professional–client relationship, some distance was maintained between the helper and the one being helped; the helper felt more knowledgeable and informed about the adjustment process and wished to pass on this information to the seeker of help. In the friendship relationship, the helper and the one seeking help were sharing equally their feelings and experience. Between these two extremes existed a range of helping relationships in which varying needs at different levels were being met on both sides of the helping relationship.

Some volunteers tended to focus on finding opportunities for callers to move out, get involved, develop skills, or feel needed. They were resourceful and innovative in finding appropriate outlets in the caller's own community and were successful in persuading callers to get involved in these activities. Other volunteers also suggested resources but put more emphasis on listening to the feelings and frustrations. These volunteers preferred to work more intensely with fewer callers, whereas the former type of helper often carried a heavier load. Yet another aspect of the mutual-help relationship was developed by those volunteers who sought a friendship relationship with their callers in which emotional inputs were equally exchanged during the helping process. These volunteers had frequent contacts with some of their callers, sometimes meeting them, going out with them, or inviting them to their own homes. In some cases, these volunteers were themselves helped dramatically by their involvement in the mutual-help program. It is important to recognize the importance of mutuality here, but the volunteers also had to recognize when it was important to listen and just be there as part of the help being offered (Silverman, 1978)

These different modes of helping all proved to be effective. If there had been any way to sort out the callers so that the most appropriate volunteer could be assigned to each caller, it might have been possible to maximize the volunteers' helping capacities as a whole, but no such method was found. However, given a clearer understanding of what is involved in the mutual-help process, it may be possible to devise such a sorting procedure in other programs. Further research and consideration of the different modes of helping encountered in the mutual-help process have many implications at the program level for those who are setting up and administering mutual-help groups.

Follow-Up

The volunteers felt that they could adequately deal with most of their callers in two or three telephone conversations. In telephone encounters, the unloading of feelings and delving deeper into callers' problems may be accomplished in the first or the second conversation. One or two further supportive calls were often sufficient to help the caller over a bad spell or to give the caller the necessary push to move out and start getting involved with new friends and activities. The volunteers all said that they continued making calls as long as they felt the callers needed them, and it was always left open for the caller to call back if he or she wished. Most of the volunteers were following up extensively with at least two of their callers over a longer period (3 or 4 months).

Spin-Offs From the Widowed Service Line

A major function of the telephone service model is that it provides a 24-hours-a-day, 7-days-a-week answering service. In the Widowed Service Line program, the call was returned by a widowed volunteer within 24 hours. Another widow or widower volunteer was able to help the caller because he or she has lived through the same feelings and eventually had found solutions. A second function of the telephone service program was to encourage contact between widowed people living in the same neighborhood. Sometimes the lonely caller was glad to be given the name of one or two other widowed people living close by. The widowed people might have become telephone friends or they might have met and gone out together. Alternatively, if a sufficient number of widowed callers living within a community were interested in developing a local mutual-help program, this was encouraged and supported. A number of such spin-off programs have developed from the Widowed Service Line. A third function of our telephone service was to effect an exchange of needs and offerings. For example, a number of widowed people had homes that were too large for them and they were interested in offering accommodations to other widowed persons wishing to move but not wanting to live alone. Some widows offered housekeeping or childcare services, and volunteers received requests for these services especially from widowers with young children.

Organization, Volunteer Turnover, and New Opportunities

A mutual-help program involves a dynamic, fluid process that benefits the helper as well as the seeker of help. After a few months in the program, some of the volunteers may develop their self-confidence and outreach skills to the extent that they are ready to move into new and different activities. Some of these volunteers may leave the program; others will stay with the program but ask to be moved into new roles or levels of responsibility. On the other hand, some of the callers who seek help for themselves may in turn wish to move into the helping role. With regard to the Widowed Service Line, a number of callers who were helped did eventually volunteer their services. The volunteers helped each other develop their skills further through discussions and exchanges of experiences at bimonthly volunteers' meetings. These discussions were guided by the two coordinators, who shared their own experiences with the volunteers. A professional consultant was helpful in clarifying perspectives and conceptualizing insights for these volunteers. To aid the self-growth of the volunteers, these professionals added their own skills in collaboration with, but not in control of, the non-professional caregiver. For maximum self-growth, it was clear that the volunteers needed to run their own program (Silverman, 1978, 1980, 1982a).

It is essential to keep the organization flexible enough to accommodate this ongoing, fluid process of development as it becomes appropriate for the helpers and the seekers of help to move into new roles and relationships in order to further their own self-growth. The two coordinators of the Widowed Service Line originally were aides in the widow-to-widow outreach program, during which these widows developed a high level of helping skills. On the Widowed Service Line, very disturbed, extremely depressed, or suicidal callers were referred to either of these two coordinators, who successfully handled these difficult, sometimes emergency situations. This often involved staying on the line with the caller for several hours, frequently late at night. These skillful helpers were able to help other widowed people through severe crises and moments of stress. They also moved into roles involving coordinating, supervising, training, and developing new spin-off programs — for example, training volunteers in the American Association of Widowed Persons' Widowed Person's Service.

Appendix 2:
The Widowed As Helpers

The following vignettes are examples of visits by aides in the original widow-to-widow program. These were presented at the 1971 workshops sponsored by the program and published in *Helping Each Other in Widowhood*. These excerpts provide an idea of what the widow aide offered, and they point to the significant effect people can have on each other simply by offering support and usable information. It is not always clear why this approach works, but it does.

☐ Adele Cooperband

This was an exceptional situation because the widow was not someone Mrs. Cooperband had reached out to but was referred to the program by a psychiatrist.

I was asked to help a bereaved widow who was under psychiatric treatment. I couldn't imagine what I could do when a professional person couldn't help. I have since visited her many times and have spent long hours on the telephone with her, and she has changed a great deal. She is fine today and has a warm relationship with her children. After the funeral, the widow had moved into her sister's house and the sister had sent her own daughter to sleep in the widow's house with the widow's children, so two households were disrupted. The children were understandably upset. The son seemed to be calm and tolerant of his mother; the daughter was emotional and intolerant. She had been very close to her father and felt his loss greatly, and the lack of her mother's understanding created a dreadful situation.

Let me describe my first visit. We sat in her sister's playroom, where Mrs. Smith talked and cried, and I listened. She repeated many times how good, kind, and generous her husband had been and there was no other like him and never would be. At that point, I intervened and told her not to canonize her husband in front of the children because she would make them feel they had not just lost their father but an angel, as well. The sister made a remark that she could not stand his ways, and said: "You two argued plenty." Then Mrs. Smith told me that her husband would work long hours and this did displease her. I said, "Don't berate yourself for that. It is very natural to be displeased and argue sometimes."

By that time it was 1:00 p.m., and I was getting hungry and said that I was going to leave. She asked me to stay and said she would make a sandwich for me. I declined and, instead, asked her to accompany me to a restaurant so that both of us could have lunch. In this way, she got out of the house for a while. On our way back, I asked her to show me where she lived, and when we got near the house I asked her to show me the inside. When we were inside, I asked her if she had some work that she would like to do while we were talking. She said she could put in a load of wash as she had not done any laundry since she had been in her sister's home. We went down to the basement and she put in the wash.

We stayed in her house until about 5:00 p.m., when I brought her back to her sister's house. She asked me to come again, and I told her that if she would go back to her own home, then I would visit her often. We talked several times on the phone, and she did go back home to live.

Her children liked and respected me. Every time I left the house and went to my car, the daughter followed me and sat and talked to me ("If only Mom would smile or say something kind; I haven't heard laughter since Daddy died"). I told the children to be patient with their mother. When their father was alive, the two of them shared the responsibility but now she had no one to share it with and it is very difficult to manage alone. I urged them to try to he understanding, explaining that she would change eventually. To Mrs. Smith, I would say, "Try to laugh once in awhile at the children's jokes; say something kind to them. Children who don't hear laughter or a kind word grow up with warped characters." Such a result was not something she would want to see because her children were "really good kids."

Many months later I encouraged Mrs. Smith to start driving a car and to seek part-time employment. Today, she is dating and working and is more understanding of her children and able to say how proud she is of them. The children, who were doing poorly at school, are now doing well again. She still calls me on the average of once a week to talk with me about what is going on in the family.

☐ Carrie Wynn

One of the first widows I visited was referred to me by a local minister. She was about forty-five years old and had a twelve-year-old son. The minister told me she was having a difficult time and asked me if I would go see her. When I dropped in on her, I told her I belonged to the widow-to-widow program and I knew her minister, who had told me about her. She asked me if I were a widow and how many children I had and pretty soon we were sitting at the kitchen table with a cup of coffee. She told me that her husband had been very sick with cancer for the last three years. For the last year, when he was so sick, she had to do everything to look after him. When I asked her how things were for her, she said, "I will be honest with you; it's been pretty rough. We were very, very close; he did everything for us, and he did not want me to work." Then she went on to tell me how he had been in the bedroom sick for such a long time, although he did not die there. She could not bring herself to go into the bedroom since he died (which was about three weeks earlier). So I told her, "I know what you mean about not wanting to go into the bedroom. I did not want to go into the bedroom either. But one night I had to get some things that were there, so I went in, and I just felt so funny I sat down and cried and cried. The kids heard me; they came in and asked, 'Why are you sitting there crying? You said you weren't going to go into the bedroom.' I had not meant to stay there, but all of a sudden I went to pieces." After telling her how I had felt, I added, "You will see. Something will take you back in there, too. It will just come on you all of a sudden and the next thing you know you will be walking right in there." A few days later I called her up to ask her how she was doing, and she said, "After you left, I don't know what you said to me, but in the next couple of days after you were here I went into the room." I told her that was wonderful. She also told me that she had spoken to her sister about me: "I told her I have never talked to anyone like you before. I don't know what you said to me, but it just brought something out of me." She told me about a job she was thinking of taking, and I told her it would be good for her and would get her out of the house. She is now very busy teaching and is active in community work. I still drop in on her when I am in the neighborhood. She is always glad to see me.

Another widow I have been in touch with was a neighbor from many years ago. I knew her husband, too, and had some idea of the kind of problems they had. When I called her, she was very glad to hear from me, and we both talked about our husbands. She opened up quite a bit about how she had felt about him, yet she was missing him now that he was gone. This widow was working but lost her job and took to visiting me fairly regularly on her way to the unemployment office. Most of her problems were with the youngest of her four children — a fifteen-year-old boy. The other children were married or had regular jobs. This boy had been a problem before her husband died, but now he was worse. He got into trouble with other kids for stealing cars. He was gone from home for a whole month, and she did not know where he was. She discovered that he had taken a job and had lied about his age. She had to go to the probation officer to explain the situation to him. She had to go to the school to ask them to take him back. One reason for his behavior was that he felt bad about not having been a better son and closer to his father while he was alive. This boy had gotten into a bad crowd and begged his mother to move out of the neighborhood so he could get away from it all and have another chance. I encouraged her to look for somewhere else to live and helped her put her name on the waiting lists for two different projects. The area where she lived was really rough. She came to see me quite a few times, so I guess she found it helpful to talk to me, especially as she knew I understood how she was feeling about her husband, and it was good for her to talk these things out. I have not yet heard whether she has managed to move, but I will be in touch, and I know her boy is in school.

☐ Arthur Churchill (The Widowed Service Line)

I have been a volunteer on the Widowed Service Line since it started, and it has been most interesting and rewarding. I have been widowed almost three years, and I know what it is like to raise a large family alone, as I have seven children. I am also the president of Eschaton, a club for the widowed; in fact, it was through this club that I became a volunteer. After my wife died, I knew I had to make a new life, and this is partly why I became involved. I also like people and enjoy meeting them. I do not claim to be any kind of professional in any sense. I try to relate what I have found out not only from the coordinators and volunteer meetings but also from my own experience. We try to give the information needed or get it if it is not immediately available. We let the caller know we will try to get it and call back. I've found that on the second call, people are most often more receptive. Loneliness is the most frequent reason given for calls. As president of Eschaton, I have had the pleasure of meeting many of these people, whom we invite to our meetings. I have had a few disappointing calls, and some people just call out of curiosity. I firmly believe the widowed can best help each other because we know the loneliness and grief involved. I am quite sure this is why we have done so well in this program.

Appendix 3: Resources for the Widowed

☐ National Level

ACCESS (Aircraft Casualty Emotional Support Services)

1594 York Avenue, Suite 22
New York, NY 10028
1-877-227-6435
info@accesshelp.org
http://www.accesshelp.org

The organization matches persons who have lost a loved one in an aircraft-related tragedy to volunteers who previously experienced a similar loss. The aim is to fill a void that occurs when the emergency and disaster relief organizations disband, the initial shock subsides, and the natural grieving process intensifies. Persons communicate through e-mail, phone, and special events meetings.

AARP Grief and Loss Programs

601 E Street NW
Washington, D.C. 20049
http://www.aarp.org/griefandloss

This website offers a wide range of resources and information on grief and loss issues to adults who are bereaved and to their families. Programs include one-to-one outreach support (*e.g.*, Widowed Person's Service), a grief course, support groups, interactive online support group, and informational booklets and brochures. The program works in cooperation with local organizations to develop community-based bereavement programs.

American Association of Suicidology

4201 Connecticut Avenue NW, #408
Washington, D.C. 20008
http://www.suicidology.org

This association provides referrals to local self-help groups for survivors of suicide nationwide. Directory of groups ($15). Newsletter, pamphlets, etc. available for a fee. Manual on starting self-help groups ($30).

The American Clearinghouse

St. Clare's Health Services
25 Pocono Road
Denville, NJ 07834
http://www.selfhelpgroups.org

This website has a keyword-searchable database of over 1100 member-run, self-help support groups for specific illnesses and disabilities, addiction, bereavement, parenting, caregiving, abuse, or other stressful life situations; a listing of local non-profit, self-help group clearinghouses worldwide; suggestions for starting both community and online groups; summaries of research studies; and a registry for those Americans trying to form new national or international groups that do not yet exist. To find major 9/11 support groups, enter "9/11" into the search engine at the website.

The Association for Death Education and Counseling

342 N. Main Street
W. Hartford, CT 06117
860-586-7503
http://www.adec.org

The Association for Death Education and Counseling is an international professional organization dedicated to promoting excellence in death education, care of the dying, and bereavement counseling and support. The organization sponsors on its website a Human Resource Network (HRN) that provides a list of members from throughout the United States and abroad who are willing to help someone in their geographic area find appropriate assistance.

Concerns of Police Survivors, Inc. (COPS)

P.O. Box 3199, South Highway 5
Cambenton, MO 63020
http://www.nationalcops.org

This organization provides resources for the surviving families of law enforcement officers who have died in the line of duty according to federal criteria; offers law enforcement training, departmental guidelines, peer support, and special hands-on programs for survivors; conducts summer camp for children ages 6 to 14 and their parents or guardians; sponsors parent retreats, spouse getaways, Outward Bound experiences for young adults 15 to 20, sibling retreats, adult children retreats; and publishes a quarterly newsletter.

The Dougy Center and the National Center for Grieving Children and Families

P.O. Box 86852
Portland, OR 97286
http://www.GrievingChild.org

The Dougy Center provides families in and around the Oregon area loving support in a safe place where children, teens, and families grieving a death can share their experience as they move through their grief. The National Center provides support and training locally, nationally, and internationally to individuals and organizations seeking to assist children in grief. This website provides a listing of programs throughout the United States and abroad that focus on the needs of bereaved children and their widowed parents. It also provides links to information about how to start new programs and services offered by the center to help in this process.

Heartbeat (model group)

2013 Devon Street
Colorado Springs, CO 80909
http://www.heartbeatsurvivorsaftersuicide.org

Heartbeat provides mutual support for those who have lost a loved one through suicide and offers information and referrals, telephone support, chapter development guidelines, and speakers on suicide bereavement.

MADD (Mothers Against Drunk Driving)

http://www.madd.org

The mission of MADD is to stop drunk driving, support victims of this violent crime, and prevent underage drinking. The organization publishes a newsletter and offers chapter development guidelines. Some MADD chapters have bereavement support groups.

NAMI (National Alliance for the Mentally Ill)

2101 Wilson Boulevard, Suite 302
Arlington, VA 22201
1-703-6254-7600
http://www.nami.org

NAMI is dedicated to the eradication of mental illnesses and to the improvement of the quality of life of all whose lives are affected by these decisions. NAMI is a nonprofit, grassroots, self-help support and advocacy organization of consumers, families, and friends of people with severe mental illnesses.

National Fallen Firefighters Foundation Survivors Support Network

http://www.firehero.org

This organization provides emotional support to spouses, families, and friends of firefighters who have died in the line of duty. Members are matched with survivors of similar experiences to help them cope during the difficult months following the death.

National Hospice and Palliative Care Organization

1700 Diagonal Road
Suite 625
Alexandria, VA 22314
Helpline: 1-800-658-8579
http://www.nhpco.org

Click on link to community bereavement programs.

North American Conference of Separated and Divorced Catholics

P.O. Box 360
Richland, OR 97870
http://www.nasdc.org

Religious, educational, and emotional needs with regard to separation, divorce, remarriage, and widowhood are addressed through self-help groups, conferences, and training programs. Families of all faiths are welcome. Group development guidelines are offered in addition to a newsletter. Dues are $30 (includes the newsletter).

Society of Military Widows

http://www.militarywidows.org

This organization provides support and assistance for widows and widowers of members of all U.S. uniformed services, helps the bereaved to cope with adjustment to life on their own, promotes public awareness, and provides chapter development guidelines, in addition to publishing a bimonthly journal (dues $12).

SOLES (Survivors of Law Enforcement Suicide)

http://www.tearsofacop.com

Families of police officers who have died by suicide share mutual support online. Click on SOLES, then scroll down to sign up for the "TOAC-SOLES" e-mail discussion group.

WTC United Family Group

P.O. Box 2307
Wayne, NJ 07474
1-973-216-2623
amg@wtcufg.org
http://www.wtcufg.org

This group offers support for families who lost a loved one in the World Trade Center attack and for World Trade Center survivors. It hosts special events and has peer support programs. Families and survivors can register online to participate in either of the two different forums or to participate in any online real-time "chat" meetings.

Young Widow

P.O. Box 902
Mount Kisco, NY 10549
cey56@aol.com
http://www.youngwidow.com

An online mutual-support group for widowed men and women who share experiences and strengths through an interactive message board. The site also provides a listing of local face-to-face support groups for young widowed persons and links to other related online e-mail discussion groups and websites for young widowed persons. The organization was founded by Lauren, a young widow herself, in 2001.

☐ Regional Programs

September Space

520 Eighth Avenue, 11th Floor
New York, NY 10018
Phone: 212-563-7570
Fax: 212-563-0410
http://www.septemberspace.org

Support groups for widows and widowers of 9/11. September Space is a community center founded on the volunteer spirit that swept New York City during the World Trade Center relief effort. Support groups are facilitated by experienced counselors

To Live Again (TLA)

No website; model group with over a dozen groups in existence in Pennsylvania.

References

AARP. (2003). *A report to the nation on independent living and disability.* Washington, D.C.: American Association of Retired Persons.

Abrahams, R. B. (1972). Mutual help for the widowed. *Social Work, 17,* 55–61.

Abrahams, R. B. (1976). Mutual helping: Styles of caregiving in a mutual aid program — the Widowed Service Line. In G. Caplan & M. Killilea (Eds.), *Support systems and mutual help.* New York: Grune & Stratton.

Agee, J. (1957). *A death in the family.* New York: McDowell, Obolensky.

Allen, S., & Hayslip, B. (2001). Research on gender differences in bereavement outcome: Presenting a model of experienced competence. In D. A. Lund (Ed.), *Men coping with grief* (pp. 97–115). Amityville, NY: Baywood Publishing.

Altschul, S. (Ed.) (1988). *Childhood bereavement and its aftermath,* Emotions and Behavior Monograph 8. New York: International Universities Press.

Anderson, R. (1974). Notes of a survivor. In S. B. Troup & W. A. Greene (Eds.), *The patient, death, and the family.* New York: Scribner's.

Antonovsky, A. (1979). *Health, stress, and coping.* San Francisco: Jossey-Bass.

Antonovsky, A. (1987). *Unraveling the mystery of health: How people manage stress and stay well,* Social and Behavioral Science Series. San Francisco: Jossey-Bass.

Aries, P. (1981). *The hour of our death.* New York: Alfred A. Knopf.

Arling, G. (1976). The elderly widow and her family, neighbors and friends. *Journal of Marriage and the Family, 3(4),* 757–768.

Attig, T. (1996). *How we grieve: Relearning the world.* New York: Oxford University Press.

Bandura, A. (1977). *Social learning theory.* Englewood Cliffs, NJ: Prentice-Hall.

Barrett, C. J. (1977). Effectiveness of widows' groups in facilitating change. *Journal of Consulting and Clinical Psychology, 46(1),* 20–31.

Basch, M. F. (1983). The concept of 'self': An operational definition. In B. Lee & G. G. Noam (Eds.), *Developmental approaches to the self* (pp. 7–58). New York: Plenum Press.

Belenky, M., Clinchy, B., Goldberger, N., & Tarule, J. (1996). *Women's ways of knowing.* New York: Basic Books.

Belenky, M. F., Bond, L. A., & Weinstock, J. S. (1997). *A tradition that has no name: Nurturing the development of people, families and communities.* New York: Basic Books.

Belle, D. (Ed.) (1982). *Lives in stress: Women and depression.* Oak Hills, CA: Sage Publications.

Belle, D. (1999). *The after-school lives of children: Alone and with others while parents work.* Mahwah, NJ: Lawrence Erlbaum Associates.

Boerner, K., & Silverman, P. R. (2002). Gender differences in coping patterns in widowed parents. *Omega: Journal of Death and Dying, 43(3),* 201–216.

Borkman, T. (1976). Experiential knowledge: A new concept for analysis of self help groups. *Social Service Review, 50,* 445–456.

Borkman, T. J. (1999). *Understanding self help/mutual aid: Experiential learning in the commons.* Camden, NJ: Rutgers University Press.

Bowlby, J. (1961). Processes of mourning. *International Journal of Psychoanalysis, 44,* 317.

Bowlby, J. (1969/1982). *Attachment and loss* (Vol. 1): *Attachment.* New York: Basic Books.

Bowlby, J. (1973). *Attachment and loss* (Vol. 2): *Separation.* New York: Basic Books.

Bowlby, J. (1980). *Attachment and loss* (Vol. 3): *Loss, sadness, and depression.* New York: Basic Books.

Brabant, S., Forsyth, C. J., & Melaneon, C. (1992). Grieving men: Thoughts, feelings, and behaviors following deaths of wives. *Hospice Journal — Physical, Psychosocial and Pastoral Care of the Dying, 8(4)*, 33–47.

Brener, A. (2001). *Mourning and mitzvah: A guided journal for walking the mourner's path through grief to healing* (2nd ed.). Woodstock, VT: Jewish Lights Publishing.

Broverman, I. K., Vogel, S., Broverman, D., Clarkson, F., & Rosenkrantz, P. (1970, Feb.). Sex role stereotypes and clinical judgments of mental health. *Journal of Consulting and Clinical Psychology, 3*, 1–7.

Bruner, J. (1990). *Acts of meaning*. Cambridge, MA: Harvard University Press.

Caine, L. (1974). *Widow*. New York: Morrow.

Campbell, S., & Silverman, P. R. (1996). *Widower: When men are left alone*. Amityville, NY: Baywood.

Caplan, G. (1974a) *Support systems and community mental health: Lectures on concept development*. New York: Behavioral Publications.

Caplan, G. (1974b). Foreword. In Glick, I. O., Weiss, R. S., & Parkes, C. M., *The first year of bereavement*. New York: Wiley Interscience.

Carr, D., House, J. S., Kessler, R. C., Nesse, R. M., Sonnega. J., & Wortman, C. (2001). Marital quality and psychological adjustment to widowhood among older adults: A longitudinal analysis. *Journal of Gerontology: Social Sciences, 55b(2)*, S197–S207.

Caserta, M. S., & Lund, D. A. (1992). Bereavement stress and coping among older adults: Expectations versus the actual experience. *Omega, 25(1)*, 33–45.

Caserta, M. S., & Lund, D. A. (1993). Intrapersonal resources and the effectiveness of self-help groups for bereaved older adults. *The Gerontologist, 33(5)*, 619–629.

Caserta, M. S., & Lund, D. A. (1996). Beyond bereavement support group meetings: Exploring outside social contacts. *Death Studies, 20(6)*, 537–556.

Caserta, M. S., Lund, D. A., & Rice, S. J. (1999). Pathfinders: A self-care and health education program for older widows and widowers. *The Gerontologist, 39(5)*, 615–620.

Charmaz, K. (1994). Conceptual approaches to the study of death. In R. Fulton & R. Bendickson (Eds.), *Death and identity* (3rd ed.; pp. 28–79). Philadelphia: Charles Press.

Clinchy, B. (1996). Connected and separate knowing: Toward a marriage of two minds. In N. Goldberger, J. M. Tarule, B. Clinchy, & M. Belenky (Eds.), *Knowledge, difference and power* (pp. 205–247). New York: Basic Books.

Cobb, S. (1976). Social support as a moderator of life stress. *Psychosomatic Medicine, 38*, 300–314.

Colin, Y. (1996). Telephone support groups: A non-traditional approach to reaching underserved cancer patients. *Cancer Practice, 4(3)*, 156–159.

Colin, Y. (2004) Technology-based groups and end of life in social work practice. In J. Berzoff & P. R. Silverman (Eds.), *Living with dying: A comprehensive resource for end-of-life care* (pp. 534–547). New York: Columbia University Press.

Conant, R. D. (1996). Memories of the death and life of a spouse: The role of images and sense of presence in grief. In D. Klass, P. R. Silverman, & S. L. Nickman (Eds.), *Continuing bonds: New understandings of grief* (pp. 179–196). Bristol, PA: Taylor & Francis.

Connors, S. R. (1997). *Hospice: Practice, pitfalls, promise*. New York: Taylor & Francis.

Cook. A. S., & Oltjenbruns, K. A. (1998). *Dying and grieving: Lifespan and family perspectives*. Ft. Worth, TX: Harcourt & Brace.

Cook, J. A. (1988). Dad's double binds: Rethinking father's bereavement from a men's studies perspective. *Journal of Ethnography, 17*, 285–308.

Corless, I., & Nicholas, P. (2003). Hospice and palliative care: A legacy in the making. In I. Corless, B. B. Germino, & M. A. Pittman (Eds.), *Dying, death, and bereavement: A challenge for living* (2nd ed.; pp. 181–200). New York: Springer.

Dakoff, G. A., & Taylor, S. E. (1990). Victims, perceptions of social support: What is helpful for them? *Journal of Perspectives in Social Psychology, 58(11)*, 80–90.

DeSpelder, L. A., & Strickland, A. L. (2005). *The last dance: Encountering death and dying*. Boston: McGraw-Hill.

Doka, K. (Ed.) (2002). *Disenfranchised grief: New directions, challenges, and strategies for practice*. Chicago, IL: Research Press.

Doress-Worters, P. B., & Siegal, D. L. (1994). *The new ourselves growing older: Women aging with knowledge and power*. New York: Simon & Schuster.

Eckenrode, J., & Gore, S. (1981). Stressful events and social supports: The significance of context. In B. H. Gottlieb (Ed.), *Social networks and social support* (pp. 43–81). Beverly Hills: Sage Publications.

Ehrensaft, D. (1995). Bringing in fathers: The reconstruction of mothering. In J. Shapiro, M. Diamond, & M. Greenberg (Eds.), *Becoming a father: Contemporary, social, developmental, and clinical perspectives* (pp. 43–59). New York: Springer.

Engel, G. L. (1961). Is grief a disease? *Psychosomatic Medicine, 23,* 18–22.

Erikson, E. H. (1950). *Childhood and society.* New York: Norton.

Feifel, H. (1986). Foreword. In F. Wald (Ed.), *In the quest of the spiritual component of care for the terminally ill: Proceedings of a colloquium* (pp. 15–22). New Haven, CT: Yale School of Nursing.

Feinson, M. C. (1986). Aging widows and widowers: Are there mental health differences? *International Journal of Aging and Human Development, 23(4),* 241–255.

Feldman, R. (1979). *The ambition of ghosts.* New York: Green River Press.

Field, M. J., & Behrman, R. E. (Eds.) (2002). *When children die: Improving palliative and end of life care for children and families.* Washington, D.C.: National Academy Press.

Field, M. J., & Cassel, C. K. (Eds.) (1997). *Approaching death: Improving care at the end of life.* Washington, D.C.: National Academy Press.

Field, S., & George, L. (1994). Moderating effects of prior social resources on the hospitalizations of elders who become widowed. *Journal of Aging and Health, 6(3),* 275–295.

Folkman, S. (1997). Positive psychological states and coping with severe stress. *Social Science and Medicine, 45,* 1207–1221.

Folkman, S. (2001). Revised coping theory and the process of bereavement. In M. Stroebe, W. Stroebe, R. Hansson, & H. Schut (Eds.), *New handbook of bereavement: Consequences, coping and care* (pp. 563–584). Washington, D.C.: American Psychological Association.

Folkman, S., & Moskowitz, J. T. (2000). Positive affect and the other side of coping. *American Psychologist, 55(6),* 647–645.

Frankl, V. E. (1984). *Man's search for meaning: An introduction to logotherapy.* New York: Simon & Schuster.

Freud, S. (1961). Mourning and melancholia. In J. Strachey (Ed.), *The standard edition of the complete psychological works of Sigmund Freud* (Vol. 14; pp. 243–258). New York: Basic Books.

Friedan, B. (1964). *The feminine mystique.* New York: Dell.

Friedan, B. (1976). *It changed my life.* New York: Random House.

Friedson, E. (1970). Dominant professions, bureaucracy, and client services. In W. Rosengren and M. Lefton (Eds.), *Organizations and clients.* Columbus, OH: Merrill.

Fulton, R. (1965). *Death and Identity.* New York: Wiley.

Gallagher-Thompson, D., Futterman, A., Farberow, N., Thompson, L. W., & Peterson, J. (1993). The impact of spousal bereavement on older widows and widowers. In M. Stroebe, W. Stroebe, & R. Hansson (Eds.), *Bereavement: A sourcebook of research and intervention* (pp. 227–239). New York: Cambridge University Press.

Galinsky, M. J., Schopler, J. H., & Abell, M. D. (1997). Connection group members through telephone and computer groups. *Health and Social Work, 22,* 13–18.

Gartner, A., & Reisman, F. (1977). *Help: A working guide to self-help groups.* New York: New Viewpoints, Viscom Press.

Gartner, A., & Reisman, F. (1984). *The self-help revolution.* New York: Human Sciences Press.

Giele, J. Z. (1998). Innovation in the typical life course. In J. Z. Giele & G. H. Elder (Eds.), *Methods of life course research: Qualitative and quantitative approaches.* Thousand Oaks, CA: Sage Publications.

Giele, J. Z. (1993). Women's role change and adaptation, 1920–1990. In K. D. Hulbert & D. T. Schuster (Eds.), *Women's lives through time: Education and American women in the twentieth century.* San Francisco: Jossey-Bass.

Gilligan, C. (1993). *In a different voice.* Cambridge, MA: Harvard University Press.

Glaser, B. G., & Strauss, A. (1967). *The discovery of grounded theory.* Chicago: Aldine Publishing.

Glick, I. O., Weiss, R. S., & Parkes, C. M. (1974). *The first years of bereavement.* New York: Wiley Interscience.

Goffman, E. (1963). *Stigma: Notes on the management of spoiled identities.* Englewood Cliffs, NJ: Prentice Hall.

Gorer, G. (1965). *Death, grief and mourning.* Garden City, NY: Doubleday.

Gottlieb, B. H. (Ed.) (1981). *Social networks and social support.* Beverly Hills: Sage Publications.

Gottlieb, B. H. (1983). *Social support strategies.* Beverly Hills, CA: Sage Publications.

Gottlieb, B. H. (1990, August). Quandaries in translating support concepts to interviewers, paper presented at the Annual American Psychological Association Convention, Boston, MA.

Gottlieb, B. H. (2000). Accomplishments and challenges of social support intervention. In M. Stewart (Ed.), *Chronic conditions and caregiving in Canada: Social support strategies* (pp. 294–310). Toronto: University of Toronto Press.

Gurin, G., Veroff, J., & Feld, S. (1960). *Americans view their mental health.* New York: Basic Books.

Hamburg, D. A., & Adams, J. E. (1967). A perspective on coping: Seeking and utilizing information in major transitions. *Archives of General Psychiatry, 17,* 277–284.

Hamilton, R. B. (1913). Along the road. *Century Magazine, 85(4),* 562.

Hayslip, B., Allen, S., & Roberts-McCloy, L. (2001). The role of gender in a three-year longitudinal study of bereavement: A test of the experienced competence model. In D. A. Lund (Ed.), *Men coping with grief* (pp. 121–146). Amityville, NY: Baywood Publishing.

Holmes, T., & Rahe, R. (1967). The social readjustment rating scale. *Journal of Psychosomatic Research, 11,* 213–218.

Hughes, E. C. (1971). *The sociological eye: Selected papers.* Chicago, IL: Aldine-Atherton.

Jacobs, R. H. (1991). *Be an outrageous older woman.* Manchester, CT: Knowledge, Ideas & Trends.

Jacobs, S. C. (1999). *Traumatic grief: Diagnosis, treatment, and prevention.* New York: Bruner-Mazel.

Johnson, R. J., Lund, D. A., & Dimond, M. F. (1986). Stress, self-esteem, and coping during bereavement among the elderly. *Social Psychology Quarterly, 49(3),* 273–279.

Kegan, R. (1982). *The evolving self.* Cambridge, MA: Harvard University Press.

Kissane, D. W., Bloch, S., Onghena, P., & McKenzie, D. P. (1996). The Melbourne family grief study, II: Psychosocial morbidity and grief in bereaved families. *American Journal of Psychiatry, 153(5),* 659–666.

Klass, D. (1988). *Parental grief: Solace and resolution.* New York: Springer.

Klass, D. (1996). Grief in an Eastern culture: Japanese ancestor worship. In D. Klass, P. R. Silverman, & S. L. Nickman (Eds.), *Continuing bonds: New understanding of grief* (pp. 59–70). Bristol, PA: Taylor & Francis.

Klass, D., & Walters, T. (2001). Process of grieving: how bonds are continued. In M. S. Stroebe, R. O. Hansson, W. Stroebe, & H. Schut (Eds.), *Handbook of bereavement research: Consequences, coping and care.* Washington, D.C.: American Psychological Association. 431–448.

Klass, D., Silverman, P. R., & Nickman, S. L. (1996). *Continuing bonds: New understandings of grief.* Bristol, PA: Taylor & Francis.

Kleinman, A., & Kleinman, J. (1997). The appeal of experience, the dismay of images: Cultural appropriations of suffering in our times. In A. Kleinman, V. Das, & M. Locke (Eds.), *Social suffering* (pp. 1–24). Berkeley, CA: University of California Press.

Klerman, G. L., & Weissman, M. (1986). The interpersonal approach to understanding depression. In T. Millon, & G. I. Klerman (Eds.), *Contemporary directions in psychopathology: Toward the DSM-IV* (p. 737). New York: Guilford Press.

Kramerow, E. A. (1995). The elderly who live alone in the United States: Historical perspectives on household change. *Demography, 32(3),* 335–352.

Kropotkin, P. (1902; reprinted 1972). *Mutual aid.* New York: University Press.

Kubler-Ross, E. (1969). *On death and dying.* New York: Macmillan.

Lamm, M. (2000). *The Jewish way in death and mourning.* New York: Jonathan David Publishers.

Lazarus, R. S., & Folkman, S. (1984). *Stress, appraisal, and coping.* New York: Springer.

Lenneberg, E. (1970). *Mutual aid.* In E. Lenneberg and J. L. Rowbotham (Eds.), *The illeostomy patient.* Springfield, IL: Charles C Thomas.

Lieberman, M. A., & Borman, L. D. (1979). *Self-help groups for coping with crisis: Origins, members, processes and impact.* San Francisco: Jossey-Bass.

Lieberman, M. A. & Borman, L. D. (1981). Researchers study THEOS: Report group's effort big help to members. *THEOS, 20,* 3–6.

Lieberman, M. (1996). *Doors close, doors open: Widows, grieving, and growing.* New York: Putnam.

Lifton, R. J. (1973). *Home from the war.* New York: Simon & Schuster.

Lifton, R. J. (1974). Symbolic immortality. In S. B. Troup and W. A. Greene (Eds.), *The patient, death, and the family.* New York: Scribner's.

Lindemann, E. (1944). The symptomatology and management of acute grief. *American Journal of Psychiatry, 101,* 141.

Lipman, E. (2001). *The dearly departed.* New York: Random House.

Lofland, L. H. (1985). The social shaping of emotion: The case of grief. *Symbolic Interaction, 8(2),* 171–190.

Lopata, H. Z. (1973). *Widowhood in an American city.* Cambridge, MA: Schenkman.

Lopata, H. Z. (1979). *Women as widows: Support systems.* New York: Elsevier.

Lopata, H. Z. (1994). *Circles and settings: Role changes of American women.* Albany: State University of New York Press.

Lopata, H. Z. (1996a). *Current widowhood: Myths and realities.* Thousand Oaks, CA: Sage Publications.

Lopata, H. Z. (1996b) Widowhood and husband sanctification. In D. Klass, P. R. Silverman, & S. L. Nickman (Eds.), *Continuing bonds: New understandings of grief* (pp. 149–162). Bristol, PA: Taylor & Francis.

Lund, D. A. (1989). *Older bereaved spouses: Research with clinical applications.* New York: Taylor & Francis/Hemisphere.

Lund, D. A. (2001). Introduction. In D. A. Lund (Ed.), *Men coping with grief* (pp. 1–5). Amityville, NY: Baywood Publishing.

Lund, D. A., & Caserta, M. S. (1992). Older spouses' participation in self help groups. *Omega, 25(1),* 47–61.

Lund, D. A., & Caserta, M. S. (2001). When the unexpected happens: Husbands coping with the deaths of their wives. In D. A. Lund (Ed.), *Men coping with grief* (pp. 147–167). Amityville, NY: Baywood Publishing.

Madara, G. (1997). The mutual-aid and self-help online revolution. *Social Policy, 27(3),* 20–26.

Maddison, D., & Raphael, B. (1976). Death of a spouse. In H. Grunebaum and J. Crist (Eds.), *Contemporary marriage: Structure, dynamics and therapy.* Boston: Little, Brown.

Maddison D., & Viola, A. (1968, July). The health of widows in the year following bereavement. *Journal of Psychosomatic Research, 12,* 292–306.

Maddison, D., & Walker, W. L. (1967). Factors affecting the outcome of conjugal bereavement. *British Journal of Psychiatry, 113,* 1057–1067.

Marris, P. (1958). *Widows and their families.* London: Routledge/Kegan Paul.

Marris, P. (1974). *Loss and change.* New York: Pantheon.

Martin, T. L., & Doka, K. J. (2000). *Men don't cry ... women do: Transcending gender stereotypes of grief.* New York: Bruner/Mazel.

Marwit, S. J., & Klass, D. (1996). Grief and the role of the inner representation of the deceased. In D. Klass, P. R. Silverman, & S. L. Nickman (Eds.). *Continuing bonds: New understandings of grief* (pp. 297–309). Bristol, PA: Taylor & Francis.

McDonald, C. (2002). Unpublished poem.

McKnight, J. (1995). *The careless society.* New York: Basic Books.

McMahon, M. (1995). *Engendering motherhood: Identity and self-transformation in women's lives.* New York: Guilford Press.

Mead, G. H. (1930). *Mind, self and society.* Chicago, IL: Chicago University Press.

Meyer, J. W. (1988). The social construction of the psychology of childhood: Some contemporary processes. In E. M. Hetherington, R. M. Lerner, & M. Perlmutte (Eds.), *Child development in a life span perspective* (pp. 47–65). Hillsdale, NJ: Lawrence Erlbaum Associates.

Meyers, J. (1976). Introduction. In P. R. Silverman (Ed.), *If you will lift the load, I will lift it too: A guide to the creation of a widowed to widowed service.* New York: Jewish Funeral Directors.

Miller, J. B. (1987). *The new psychology of women* (2nd ed.). Boston: Beacon Press.

Miller, J. B., & Stiver, I. P. (1997). *The healing connection: How women form relationships in therapy and in life.* Boston, MA: Beacon Press.

Miller, J. E. (1998). *Effective support groups: How to plan, facilitate and enjoy them.* Ft. Wayne, IN: Willowgreen Publishing.

Mischler, E. (1986). *Research interviewing: Context and narrative.* Cambridge, MA: Harvard University Press.

Monroe, B. & Oliviere, D. (Eds.) (2003). *Patient participation in palliative care.* London: Oxford University Press.

Moore, A. K., & Stratton, D. C. (2002). *Resilient widowers: Older men speak for themselves.* New York: Springer.

Moss, M. S., & Moss, S. Z. (1996). Remarriage of widowed persons: a triadic relationship. In D. Klass, P. R. Silverman, & S. L. Nickman (Eds.), *Continuing bonds: New understandings of grief* (pp. 163–178). Bristol, PA: Taylor & Francis.

Moss, M. S., Moss, S. Z., & Hansonn, R. O. (2001). Bereavement and old age. In M. S. Stroebe, R. O. Hansson, W. Stroebe, & H. Schut (Eds.), *Handbook of bereavement research: Consequences, coping and care* (pp. 241–260). Washington, D.C.: American Psychological Association.

Nadeau, J. W. (1998). *Families making sense of death.* Oak Hills, CA: Sage Publications.

Neimeyer, R. (1998). *Lessons of loss: A guide for coping.* New York: McGraw-Hill.

Neimeyer, R. (Ed.) (2001). *Meaning construction and experience of loss.* Washington, D.C.: American Psychological Association.

Nickman, S. L., Silverman, P. R., & Normand, C. (1998). Children's construction of their deceased parent: The surviving parent's contribution, *American Journal of Orthopsychiatry, 68(1),* 126–141.

Niebuhr, R. (1943). Cited in Sifton, E. (2003). *The serenity prayer: Faith and politics in times of peace and war.* New York: Norton.

Normand, C., Silverman, P. R., & Nickman, S. L. (1996). Bereaved children's changing relationships with the deceased. In D. Klass, P. R. Silverman, & S. L. Nickman (Eds.), *Continuing bonds: New understandings of grief* (pp. 87–111). Bristol, PA: Taylor & Francis.

Osterweis, M., Solomon, F., & Green, M. (1984). *Bereavement: Reactions, consequences and care.* Washington, D.C.: National Academy Press.

Pancoast, D. L., Parker, P., & Froland, C. (Eds.) (1983). *Rediscovering self-help: Its role in social care.* Oak Hills, CA: Sage Publications.

Parkes, C. M. (1965). Bereavement and mental illness. Part 1: A clinical study of the grief of bereaved psychiatric patients; Part 2: A classification of bereavement reactions. *British Journal of Medical Psychology, 38(1),* 1–26.

Parkes, C. M. (1993). Grief as a psychosocial transition: Process of adaptation to change. In M. Stroebe, W. Stroebe, & R. Hansson (Eds.), *Bereavement: A sourcebook of research and intervention* (pp. 91–101). London: Cambridge University Press.

Parkes, C. M. (1996). *Bereavement.* New York: Routledge.

Parkes, C. M., Laungani, P., & Young, B. (1997). *Death and bereavement across cultures.* New York: Routledge.

Parsons, T. (1994). Death in the western world. In R. Fulton & R. Bendickson (Eds.), *Death and identity* (pp. 60–79). Philadelphia, PA: Charles Press,

Pearl, A., & Reissman, F. (1965). *New careers for the poor: The nonprofessional in human service.* New York: Free Press.

Piaget, J. (1954). *The moral judgment of the child.* New York: Free Press.

Pincus, L. (1974). *Death and the family.* New York: Random House.

Pollack, W. S. (1998). *Real boys: Rescuing our sons from the myth of boyhood.* New York: Random House.

Pollack, W. S. (with Shuster, T.) (2000). *Real boys' voices.* New York: Random House.

Powell, T. J. (1987). *Self-help organizations and professional practice.* Silver Springs, MD: National Association of Social Workers.

Powell, T. J., Silk, K. R., & Albeck, J. H. (2000). Psychiatrists' referrals to self-help groups for people with mood disorders. *Psychiatric Services, 51(6),* 809–811.

Prigerson, H. G., & Jacobs, S. C. (2001). Traumatic grief as a distinct disorder: A rationale, consensus criteria, and preliminary empirical test. In M. S. Stroebe, R. O. Hansson, W. Stroebe, & H. Schut (Eds.), *Handbook of bereavement research: Consequences, coping and care* (pp. 613–637). Washington, D.C.: American Psychological Association.

Raphael, B. (1977). Preventive intervention with the recently bereaved. *Archives of General Psychiatry, 34,* 1450–1454.

Raphael, B., Minkov, C., & Dobson, M. (2001). Psychotherapeutic and pharmacological intervention for bereaved persons. In M. S. Stroebe, R. O. Hansson, W. Stroebe, & H. Schut (Eds.), *Handbook of bereavement research: Consequences, coping and care* (pp. 587–612). Washington, D.C.: American Psychological Association.

Relf, M. (2003). Risk assessment and bereavement services. In S. A. Payne, J. Seymour, J. Skilbeck, & C. Ingleton (Eds.), *Palliative care nursing: Principles and evidence for practice* (pp. 88–106). Buckingham: Open University Press.

Rosenblatt, P. C. (2001). A social constructionist perspective on cultural differences in grief. In M. S. Stroebe, R. O. Hansson, W. Stroebe, & H. Schut (Eds.), *Handbook of bereavement research: Consequences, coping and care* (pp. 285–300). Washington, D.C.: American Psychological Association.

Rosenblatt, P. C., & Elde, C. (1990). Shared reminiscence about a deceased parent: Implications for grief education and grief counseling. *Family Relations: Journal of Applied Family & Child Studies, 39(2),* 206–210.

Rosenblatt, P. C., Walsh, R. P., & Jackson, D. A. (1976). *Grief and mourning in cross-cultural perspective.* New Haven, CT: Human Relations Area Files.

Rothman, S. M. (1978). *Women's proper place.* New York: Basic Books.

Rubin, S. S. (1981). A two-track model of bereavement: Theory and research. *American Journal of Orthopsychiatry, 51(1),* 101–109.

Rubin, S. S. (1992). Adult loss and the two-track model of bereavement. *Omega, 24(3),* 183–202.

Rubin, S. S. (1996). The wounded family: Bereaved parents and the impact of adult child loss. In D. Klass, P. R. Silverman, & S. L. Nickman (Eds.), *Continuing bonds: New understandings of grief* (pp. 217–232). Bristol, PA: Taylor & Francis.

Rubin, S. S. (2004). Understanding loss and bereavement among Israel's Muslims: Acceptance of God's will, grief, and the relationship to the deceased. *Omega, 49(2),* 149–162.

Rubin, S. S., Malkinson, R., & Witztum, E. (2003). Trauma and bereavement: Conceptual and clinical issues revolving around relationships. *Death Studies, 27,* 1–23.

Rubin, Z. (1980). *Children's friendships.* Cambridge, MA: Harvard University Press.

Rutter, M. (1983). Stress, coping and development: Some issues and questions. In N. Garmazy & M. Rutter (Eds.), *Stress, coping and development in children* (p. 1041). New York: McGraw-Hill.

Sandler, I. N., Ayers, T. S., Wolchik, S. A., Tein, J. Y., Kwok, O. M., Haine, R. A., Twohey, J. L., Suter, J., Lin, K., Padgett-Jones, S., Weyer, J. L., Cole, E., Kriege, G., & Griffin, W. A. (2003). The family bereavement program: Efficacy evaluation of a theory-based prevention program for parentally bereaved children and adolescents. *Journal of Consulting and Clinical Psychology, 71,* 582–600.

Scarf, M. (1980). *Unfinished business: Pressure points in the lives of women.* New York: Doubleday.

Schut, H. A. W., Stroebe, M. S., van den Bout, J., & Terheggen, M. (2001). The efficacy of bereavement interventions: Determining who benefits. In M. S. Stroebe, R. O. Hansson, W. Stroebe, & H. Schut (Eds.), *Handbook of bereavement research: Consequences, coping, and care* (pp. 705–737). Washington, D.C.: American Psychological Association.

Schut, H. A. W., Stroebe, M. S., & van den Bout, J. (1997). Intervention for the bereaved: Gender differences in the efficacy of two counselling programmes. *British Journal of Clinical Psychology, 36(1),* 63–72.

Seremetakis, C. N. (1991). *The last word: Women, death and divination in inner mani.* Chicago, IL: University of Chicago Press.

Shapiro, E. R. (1994). *Grief as a family process: A developmental approach to clinical practice.* New York: Guilford Press.

Shernoff, M. (Ed.) (1997). *Gay widowers: Life after the death of a partner.* Binghampton, NY: Harrington Park Press.

Shuchter, S. R. (1986). *Dimensions of grief.* San Francisco: Jossey-Bass.

Silver, D. (1995, Sept.). I claim the title of widow. *Ms. Magazine,* p. 96.

Silverman, P. R. (1966). Services for the widowed during the period of bereavement. In *Social Work Practice: Selected Papers Annual Forum.* New York: Columbia University Press.

Silverman, P. R. (1967). Services to the widowed: First steps in a program of preventive intervention. *Community Mental Health Journal, 3*, 37–44.

Silverman, P. R. (1969a). Clients who drop out: A study of spoiled helping relationships, unpublished dissertation, Waltham, MA: Florence Heller School, Brandeis University.

Silverman, P. R. (1969b). The widow-to-widow program: An experiment in preventive intervention. *Mental Hygiene, 53*, 333–337.

Silverman, P. R. (1970). The widow as a caregiver in a program of preventive intervention with other widows. *Mental Hygiene, 54*, 540–547.

Silverman, P. R. (1971a). Factors involved in accepting an offer of help. *Journal of Thanatology, 3*, 161–171.

Silverman, P. R. (1971b). Intervention with the widow of a suicide. In A. Cain (Ed.), *Survivors of suicide* (pp. 186–214). Springfield, IL: Charles C Thomas. (Reprinted in *Societe de Thanatologie Journal*, 1971.)

Silverman, P. R. (1972). Widowhood and preventive intervention. *The Family Coordinator, 21(1)*, 95–102.

Silverman, P. R. (1974). Anticipatory grief from the perspective of widowhood. In B. Shonberg *et al.* (Eds.), *Anticipatory grief*. New York: Columbia University Press.

Silverman, P. R. (Ed.) (1976). *If you will lift the load, I will lift it too: A guide to the creation of a widowed to widowed service*. New York: Jewish Funeral Directors of America.

Silverman, P. R. (1978). *Mutual help: A guide for mental health workers* (NIMH/DHEW Publ. No. ADM 78-646). Washington, D.C.: U.S. Government Printing Office.

Silverman, P. R. (1980). *Mutual help groups: Organization and development*. Beverly Hills, CA: Sage Publications.

Silverman, P. R. (1981). *Helping women cope with grief*. Beverly Hills, CA: Sage Publications.

Silverman, P. R. (1982a). The mental health consultant as a linking agent. In D. Beigel & A. J. Naparstek (Eds.), *Community support systems and mental health: Practice, policy and research*. New York: Springer.

Silverman, P. R. (1982b). Transitions and models of intervention. In F. Berado (Ed.), *The annals: Special issues of transitions*. Philadelphia, PA: The American Academy of Political and Social Science.

Silverman, P. R. (1982c). People helping people: Beyond professionalism. In M. Killilae & C. Shulberg (Eds.), *Principles and practices of community mental health: A Festschrift to Dr. Gerald Caplan*. San Francisco: Jossey-Bass.

Silverman, P. R. (1985a). Counseling widows and elderly women. In A. Monk (Ed.), *Handbook for gerontological services*. New York: Columbia University Press.

Silverman, P. R. (1985b). *Widow to Widow*. New York: Springer.

Silverman, P. R. (1985c). Preventive intervention: The case for mutual help groups. In R. K. Conyne (Ed.), *The group worker's handbook: Varieties of group experience*. Springfield, IL: Charles C Thomas.

Silverman, P. R. (1986, May). The perils of borrowing: Role of the professional in mutual help groups. *Journal for Specialists in Group Work, 11*, 68–73.

Silverman, P. R. (1987a). Mutual help groups. In S. M. Rosen, D. Fanshel, & M. E. Lutz (Eds.), *Encyclopedia of Social Work* (18th ed.). Silver Springs, MD: National Association of Social Workers.

Silverman, P. R. (1987b). Widowhood as the next stage in the life cycle. In H. Z. Lopata (Ed.), *Widows: North America*. Durham, NC: Duke University Press.

Silverman, P. R. (1988a). Research as process: exploring the meaning of widowhood. In S. Reinharz & G. Rowles (Eds.), *Qualitative gerontology*. New York: Springer.

Silverman, P. R. (1988b). In search of selves: Accommodating to widowhood. In L. A. Bond (Ed.), *Families in transition: Primary prevention programs that work*. Beverly Hills, CA: Sage Publications.

Silverman, P. R. (1993). Stigmatized deaths. In I. Corless, B. Germino, & M. Pittman-Lindeman (Eds.), *Death, dying, and bereavement*. Boston, MA: Jones & Bartlett.

Silverman, P. R. (1996). Introduction. In S. Campbell, & P. R. Silveman (Eds.), *Widower: When men are left alone* (2nd ed.; pp. 1–16). Amityville, NY: Baywood.

Silverman, P. R. (2000a). *Never too young to know: Death in children's lives*. New York: Oxford University Press.

Silverman, P. R. (2000b). Widowhood revisited: The next stage in the life cycle. In *Handbook for Grief and Loss Programs*. Washington, D.C.: American Association of Retired Persons.

Silverman, P. R. (2000c). Research, clinical practice and the human experience: Putting the pieces of studies together. *Death Studies, 24(6),* 469–478.

Silverman, P. R. (2000d). *When your grandchild has a loss* (www.aarp.org/griefandloss).

Silverman, P. R. (2003). Helping the bereaved through social support and mutual help. In I. Corless, B. Germino, & M. Pittman (Eds.), *A challenge for living: Dying, death and bereavement* (2nd ed.). New York: Springer.

Silverman, P. R., & Cooperband, A. (1975). Mutual help and the elderly widow. *Journal of geriatric psychiatry, 8,* 9–27.

Silverman, P. R., & Englander, S. (1975). The widow's view of her dependent children, *Omega, 6,* 3–20.

Silverman, P. R., & Klass, D. (1996). Introduction: What's the problem? In D. Klass, P. R. Silverman, & S. L. Nickman (Eds.), *Continuing bonds: New understandings of grief* (pp. 3–27). Bristol, PA: Taylor & Francis.

Silverman, P. R., & Nickman, S. L. (1996). Children's construction of their dead parent. In D. Klass, P. R. Silverman, & S. L. Nickman (Eds.), *Continuing bonds: New understandings of grief* (pp. 73–86). Bristol, PA: Taylor & Francis.

Silverman, P. R., & Silverman, S. M. (1975). Withdrawal in bereaved children. In B. Schonberg *et al.* (Eds.), *Bereavement: Its psycho-sociological aspects.* New York: Columbia University Press.

Silverman, P. R., & Smith, D. (1984). "Helping" in mutual help groups for the physically disabled. In F. Gartner & F. Reisman (Eds.), *The self-help revolution.* New York: Human Sciences Press.

Silverman P. R., & Worden, J. W. (1993). Children's reactions to the death of a parent. In M. Stroebe, W. Stroebe, & R. Hansson (Eds.), *Bereavement: A sourcebook of research and intervention* (pp. 285–316). London: Cambridge University Press.

Silverman, P. R., MacKenzie, D., Pettipas, M., & Wilson, E. W. (Eds.) (1974). *Helping each other in widowhood.* New York: Health Sciences.

Silverman, P. R., Nickman, S. L., & Worden, J. W. (1992, Oct.). Detachment revisited: Children's construction of their deceased parent. *American Journal of Orthopsychiatry, 62(4),* 494–503.

Silverman, P. R., Baker, J., Cait, C. A., & Boerner, K. (2002). The effects of negative legacies on the adjustment of parentally bereaved children and adolescents. *Omega: Journal of Death and Dying, 46(4),* 335–352.

Silverman, S. M., & Silverman, P. R. (1979). Parent–child communication in widowed families. *American Journal of Psychotherapy, 33,* 428–441.

Staudacher, C. (1989). *Beyond grief.* Oakland, CA: New Harbinger Publications.

Stewart, M. J., & Langille, D. (2000). A framework for social support assessment and intervention in the context of chronic conditions and caregiving. In M. Stewart (Ed.), *Chronic conditions and caregiving in Canada: Social support strategies* (pp. 3–28). Toronto: University of Toronto Press.

Stewart, M. J., Banks, S., Crossman, D., & Poel, D. (2000). Relationships and partnerships between peers and professionals in mutual aide groups. In M. Stewart (Ed.), *Chronic conditions and caregiving in Canada: Social support strategies* (pp. 202–222). Toronto: University of Toronto Press.

Stewart, M. J., Craig, D., MacPherson, K., & Alexander, S. (2001). Promoting positive affect and diminishing loneliness of widowed seniors through a support intervention. *Public Health Nursing, 18(1),* 54–63.

Strauss, A. L. (1987). *Qualitative analysis for social scientists.* New York: Cambridge University Press.

Stroebe, M. S. (2001). Gender differences in adjustment to bereavement: An empirical and theoretical review. *Review of General Psychology, 5(1),* 62–83.

Stroebe, M. S., & Schut, H. (1999, April–May). The dual process model of coping with bereavement: Rationale and description. *Death Studies, 23(3),* 197–224.

Stroebe, M. S, & Schut, H. (2001a). Models of coping with bereavement: A review. In M. S. Stroebe, R. O. Hansson, W. Stroebe, & H. Schut (Eds.), *Handbook of bereavement research: Consequences, coping, and care* (pp. 375–403). Washington, D.C.: American Psychological Association.

Stroebe, M. S., & Stroebe, W. (1989) Who participates in bereavement research? A review and empirical study. *Omega: Journal of Death and Dying, 20(1),* 1–29.

Stroebe, M. S., Gergen, M., Gergen, K., & Stroebe, W. (1996). Broken hearts or broken bonds? In D. Klass, P. R. Silverman, & S. L. Nickman (Eds.)., *Continuing bonds: New understandings of grief* (pp. 31–44). Bristol, PA: Taylor & Francis.

Stroebe, M. S., van Son, M., Stroebe, W., Kleber, R., Schut, H., & van den Bout, J. (2000). On the classification and diagnosis of pathological grief. *Clinical Psychology Review, 20(1),* 57–75.

Stroebe, M. S., Hansson, R. O. Stroebe, W., & Schut, H. (2001). Future directions for bereavement research. In M. S. Stroebe, R. O. Hansson, W. Stroebe, & H. Schut (Eds.), *Handbook of bereavement research: Consequences, coping, and care* (pp. 741–766). Washington, D.C.: American Psychological Association.

Stroebe, M. S., Stroebe, W., Schut, H., Zech, E., & van den Bout, J. (2002). Does disclosure of emotions facilitate recovery from bereavement? Evidence from two prospective studies. *Journal of Consulting & Clinical Psychology, 70(1),* 169–178.

Stroebe, W., & Schut, H. (2001b). *Risk factors in bereavement outcome: A methodological and empirical review.* In M. S. Stroebe, R. O. Hansson, W. Stroebe, & H. Schut (Eds.), *Handbook of bereavement research: Consequences, coping and care* (pp. 349–371). Washington, D.C.: American Psychological Association.

Stroebe, W., & Stroebe, M. S. (1987). *Bereavement and health: The psychological and physical consequences of partner loss.* New York: Cambridge University Press.

Stroebe, W., Stroebe, M., Abakoumis, G., & Schut, H. (1996). The role of loneliness and social support in adjustment to loss: A test of attachment theory versus stress theory. *Journal of Personality and Social Psychology, 70(6),* 1241–1249.

Stroebe, W., Stroebe, M., & Abakoumis, G. (1999). Does differential social support cause sex differences in bereavement outcome? *Journal of Community and Applied Psychology, 9(1),* 1–12.

Stylianos, S. K., & Vachon, M. L. S. (1993). The role of social support in bereavement. In M. Stroebe, W. Stroebe, & R. Hansson (Eds.), *Bereavement: A sourcebook of research and intervention* (pp. 397–410). London: Cambridge University Press.

Sullivan, H. S. (1965). *The interpersonal theory of psychiatry.* New York: W.W. Norton.

Tannen, D. (1990). *You just don't understand: Women and men in conversation.* New York: Morrow.

Thompson, N. (2001). The ontology of masculinity: The roots of manhood. In D. A. Lund (Ed.), *Men coping with grief* (pp. 27–36). Amityville, NY: Baywood Publishing.

Tyhurst, J. (1958). The role of transition states, including disasters in mental illness. In *Symposium on Preventive and Social Psychiatry.* Washington, D.C.: U.S. Government Printing Office.

Umberson, D., Chen, M., House, J. S., & Hopkins, K. (1996). The effect of social relationships on psychological well-being: Are men and women really so different? *American Sociological Review, 6(5),* 837–857.

U.S. Census. (2002). *Chartbook on Trends in the Health of Americans.* Washington, D.C.: U.S. Government Printing Office.

Utz, R. L., Carr, D., Nesse, R., & Wortman, C. B. (2002). The effect of widowhood on older adults' social participation: An evaluation of activity, disengagement, and continuity theories. *The Gerontologist, 42(4),* 522–533.

Vachon, M. L. S. (1979). Identity change over the first two years of bereavement: Social relationships and social support in bereavement, unpublished doctoral dissertation. Toronto: York University.

Vachon, M. L. S., Sheldon, A. R., Lancie, W. J., Lyall, W. A. L., Rogers, J., & Freeman, S. J. (1980). A controlled study of self-help interventions for widows. *American Journal of Psychiatry, 137,* 1380–1384.

Valent, P. (2002). *Child survivors of the holocaust.* New York: Brunner-Routledge

Van den Hoonaard, D. K. (2002). Life on the margins of a Florida retirement community: The experience of snowbirds, newcomers and widowed persons. *Research on Aging, 24(1),* 50–66.

Van der Kolk, B. A., McFarlane, A. C., & Weisaeth, L. (Eds.) (1996). *Traumatic stress: The effects of overwhelming experience on mind, body, and society.* New York: Guilford Press.

van Gennep, A. (1960). *The rites of passage*. Chicago, IL: University of Chicago Press.

Videka-Sherman, L., & Lieberman, M. (1985). The effects of self-help and psychotherapy intervention on child loss: The limits of recovery. *American Journal of Orthopsychiatry, 55(1)*, 70–72.

Walter, T. (1999). *On bereavement: The culture of grief*. Philadelphia, PA: Open University Press.

Webster's Third International Dictionary (1968). Springfield, MA: Merriam.

Weeks, D. O., & Johnson, C. (Eds.) (2000). *When all the friends have gone: A guide for aftercare providers*. Amityville, NY: Baywood Publishing.

Weiss, R. S. (1969). The fund of sociability. *Transaction, 6(9)*, 36–43.

Weiss, R. S. (1990). *Staying the course: The emotional and social lives of men who do well at work*. New York: Free Press.

Weiss, R. S. (2001). Grief, bonds and relationships. In M. S. Stroebe, R. O. Hansson, W. Stroebe, & H. Schut (Eds.), *Handbook of bereavement research: Consequences, coping and care* (pp. 47–62). Washington, D.C.: American Psychological Association.

Weissman, A. (1977). *On death and denying*. New York: Behavioral Publications.

White, R. W. (1974). Strategies of adaptation: An attempt at systematic description. In G. V. Coelho *et al.* (Eds.), *Coping and adaptation*. New York: Basic Books.

White, Barbara J., & Madara, E. J. (2002). *The self-help group sourcebook: Your guide to community and online support groups* (7th ed.). Denville, NJ: St. Clare's Health Services, American Self-Help Group Clearinghouse.

White, M., & Epston, D. (1990). *Narrative means of therapeutic ends*. New York: Norton.

Wilson, E. (1974). Introduction. In P. R. Silverman, D. MacKenzie, M. Pettipas, & E. Wilson (Eds.), *Helping each other in widowhood* (p. xiv). New York: Health Sciences Publishing.

Worden, J. W. (1996). *Children and grief: When a parent dies*. New York: Guilford Press.

Worden, J. W. (2001). *Grief counseling and grief therapy: A handbook for the mental health professional*. New York: Springer.

Worden, J. W., & Silverman, P. R. (1993). Grief and depression in newly widowed parents with school age children. *Omega, 27(3)*, 251–261.

Wortman, C. B., & Silver, R. C. (1989). The myth of coping with loss. *Journal of Clinical and Consulting Psychology, 57(3)*, 349–357.

Wuthnow, R. (1994). *Sharing the journey: Support groups and America's quest for community*. New York: Free Press.

Yalom, M. (2001). *A history of the wife*. New York: Harper-Collins.

Youniss, J., & Smollar, J. (1985). *Adolescent relations with mothers, fathers, and friends*. Chicago, IL: University of Chicago Press.

Index

A

AARP, *see* American Association of Retired Persons
accommodation, 16, 22, 28, 54, 59, 67, 74, 93, 95, 134, 220, 227
adapting, 33, 60, 69, 76, 77, 78, 84, 194–196, 218, 225
adult children, 181–188, 190–191, 210
affinity, 88–89
    among Vietnam veterans, 87
aides, 9, 10–11, 14, 104, 123
    acceptance of help from, 13, 183, 207, 210, 212–214
    advice to newly widowed, 106, 109, 110, 111, 126
    as ritual specialists, 42
    examples of help provided by, 229–232
    family issues, and, 108
    identifying with, 104
    reports by, 205
Aircraft Casualty Emotional Support Services (ACCESS), 233
Alcoholics Anonymous (AA), 6, 16, 86, 138, 204
American Association of Retired Persons (AARP), 17, 198, 200, 206, 233
American Association of Suicidology, 234
American Association of Widowed Persons, 228
American Clearinghouse, The, 234
anger, 116
Association for Death Education and Counseling, 200, 234
assumptive world, loss of, 62
attachment behavior, 36

B

bedwetting, 165
bereavement; *see also* death, grief, grieving, mourning, and related topics
    as process, 16, 33, 60, 67, 194
    change of perspective, and, 65
    coping, and, 76–78
    defined, 27
    employment, and, 16
    first stage of, 97–112
    hospice, and, 17
    mental-health professionals, and, 4, 32
    mutual help, and, 84–85
    research, 33, 38
    sources of help for, 4–5
    stress, and, 62
    support groups, 85

bond, 36, 38, 39, 40, 87
    continuing, 40, 66, 147, 172
    formation of, 36

C

care, defined, 80
care, of bereaved children, 152
change, 7, 16, 17, 18, 21, 22, 27, 28,
        30, 31, 34, 43, 50, 51, 59–74,
        75, 76, 77, 78, 93, 94, 110,
        111, 122, 123, 127, 129, 141,
        170, 180–181, 204
    accommodation of, 72–73
    grief, and, 59–74, 194
    in daily life, 54, 60–61, 136–137,
        156–159, 176–177, 192,
        197, 220
    in family, 35
    in grief, 23, 40–41
    in group focus, 131
    in help, 94–95
    in meaning of word
        "widowed," 134–135
    in needs, 6, 7, 16, 94–95
    in relationship to past, 39, 132,
        143
    in relationships, 40, 66, 88, 95,
        118–119
    in roles, 22, 26, 46–49, 61, 64,
        88, 90, 177, 178
    in sense of self/self-concept,
        49, 65–66, 125, 126,
        178–179, 197
    in social mores, 146–147
    in status, 4
    inability to, 134
    influences on, 55–57
    over time, 67
    physical, 29
    political, 48
    positive, 84
    social, 31, 41, 48, 87

    types of, 177–178
    validation of, 41
Child Bereavement Study, 154, 156
children, 139
    adult, dependency on, 186–188
    adult, role of, 181–186
    adult, with problems, 190–191
    bereavement, and, 19, 35, 84,
        151–173
        needs of, 152
        understanding, 161–164
    dating, and, 144, 145
    protectiveness of, 183
    school, return to by, 166–167
Children's Health Insurance Plan
    (CHIP), 107
CHIP, *see* Children's Health
    Insurance Plan
clergy, 4, 9, 15, 80, 81, 93, 98, 133,
    154, 201, 202, 203, 211
closure, 33, 193
    9/11, and, 40
coherence, sense of, 76
communities, intentional, 85
Community Contact for the
    Widowed of Toronto, 17
companionate marriage, 46
competence
    defined, 76
    growing sense of, 141
    promotion of, 34
Concerns of Police Survivors, Inc.
    (COPS), 235
connection, with bereaved
    children, 152
conservative impulse, 72
consultants, 203, 227
context, 7, 22, 23, 27, 43, 63, 64, 65
    cultural, 32, 40
    developmental, 28–31
    mutual help, 75–91, 194–195
    relational, 34–37, 66, 94
    social, 32, 34, 40, 41, 45–52, 78

continuing bond, 40, 66, 147, 172
continuity, for bereaved children,
        152, 167–169
coping, 76–78, 166
    by the older widowed,
            176–177
    strategies, 77, 121, 194, 195
    styles, 52–53
crisis, concept of, 6–7, 10
Cruse Club, 6
crying, 115, 159–160

D
daily routine, 135–139, 156–159
dating, 143–147, 165, 190
Day of the Dead, 43
death
    age at time of, 26–27
    as end of a relationship, 38
    as universal stressor, 62
    causes of, 26, 209–210
    how to explain to children,
            152–154
    reactions to, 27, 61–63
        after long illness *vs.*
                suddenly, 68,
                99–102, 116
        children's, 162–163
    reality of, 102–103
    trauma of, 61
    unexpected *vs.* anticipated, 68,
            99–102, 116
death certificates, 205, 207
deceased
    as part of survivor's life, 38, 39
    connecting to by children, 172
    dreaming of, 118
    honoring, 94
    new relationship with, 147
    place for, 117–118
    presence of at funeral, 98
    talking to, 117, 118

denial, 39, 67–70, 77, 162
depression, 122, 175, 185, 186, 188
    men *vs.* women, 54
detachment, 37–40
    vs. transformation, 39
development, 29, 36, 73, 76–78; *see
        also* growth; identity;
        meaning making; making
        meaning, of death
    adult, 29, 77
    child, grief and, 161–164,
            170–171
    of new identity, 72
    study of, 65
disbelief, 176
disenfranchised mourners, 31
distraction, 77
divorce, 48
Dougy Center, 198–199, 200, 202,
        235
dreams, 117, 118, 168
driving, 13, 125, 142–143, 189

E
eating out, 158
eating patterns, 115
electroconvulsive therapy, 110
emotional difficulties, widowhood
        and, 2, 32, 212
employers, 5
    health insurance, and, 107
employment, *see* work
experiential knowledge, 79, 80
externalizing problem, 77

F
facilitators, 203–204
faith, 132–133, 172
family, 79, 83, 93, 97, 117, 141, 155,
        181, 188–190, 195, 210
    issues of, 14, 108–109
    seeing beyond, 118–120

fathers, role of, 50, 170
Feminine Mystic, The, 47
finances, 106–108, 158
friends, making new, 123–126
funeral directors, 5, 10, 18, 80, 93,
    154, 201, 202
funerals, children, and, 154–155
future, looking to, 129–150

G
gender differences, 45–57; *see also*
    widows *vs.* widowers
    change, and, 55–57
    coping styles, and, 52–53
    outcomes, and, 53–55
    societal context of, 45–52
grandchildren, 182, 189
grief, 132; *see also* bereavement,
    grieving, mourning, and
    related topics
    adapting to, 194
    as illness, 31–33, 37
    as life-cycle event, 33–34
    as normal life event *vs.* illness,
        31–37
    as psychiatric syndrome, 33
    as time of change, 59–74
    children, and, 36, 155–156,
        161–164; *see also*
        children, bereavement
        and
    components of, 27
    defined, 27–28
    development, and, 29
    effect of culture and society on,
        40–43
    in a relational context, 34–37
    of a man, 51
    older widowed, and, 176–177
    perspectives on, 25–43
    protecting children from,
        159–160

resolution of, 10
restoration- *vs.* loss-oriented
    behavior, 71, 77
rhythms of, 94
roller coaster of, 112
sharing with adult children,
    184
Grief and Loss program, 198, 200,
    233
grief counseling, 1, 3
    alternatives to, 4–6
grieving; *see also* bereavement,
    grief, mourning, and
    related topics
    beginning of, 109–112
    children, and, 36, 155–156,
        161–164; *see also*
        children, bereavement
        and
    correctly, 32, 110
    future, and, 129
    process of, 27, 28
    styles of, 32
growth, 22, 48, 55, 76, 78, 94, 152,
    227
guilt, 38, 102, 116

H
health insurance, 107
Heartbeat, 235
help, 189, 195; *see also* mutual help
    appropriate, 83
    as provided by widowed,
        78–79, 179–180
    children's, 169–170, 185–186
    defined, 93–95
    in mutual-help context, 75–91
    nature of, 75–78
    networks for, 79–80, 210
    objectives of, 75
    reasons for refusing, 15, 207,
        215–216

results of, 129–150
   social support, and, 82–83
   sources of, 4–6, 210–212
   timing of, 124
   transition, and, 87–91
   types offered, 214–215
historical forces, 23, 26, 41,
hospice, 17, 104, 148, 153, 200
   bereavement groups, and, 85
husband, role of, 49–50, 63

I

identity, 49, 55, 63, 64, 65, 66, 72
   crisis, 48
   new, 72–74
   revised, 90
   vs. role, 65
incorporation, 39
independence, 141–142, 180–181,
   182
in-laws, 108–109, 145
insomnia, 115, 165
Internet, as source of help, 199
intervention program, 2–3, 8–11
isolation, 120, 177

K

knowledge, professional *vs.*
   experiential, 79, 80

L

lawyers, 5
learning styles, 194
lethargy, 115
life cycle
   crises, 2
   events, lack of endings for,
      193
   stages of, 28
loneliness, 13, 14, 188, 221—224
loss-oriented behavior, 71, 77

M

MADD, *see* Mothers Against
   Drunk Driving, 18
making meaning, of death, 28–31,
   36
marriage, fulfillment of needs,
   and, 37
mask of masculinity, 50; *see also*
   men
meaning making, 28; *see also*
   making meaning, of death;
   relationships
Medicare, 107, 181
memories, 147
men; *see also* widows *vs.* widowers
   assumptive world of, 62
   behavior model for, 49–50
   consequences of spousal death
      for, 53–54
   depression, and, 54
   expression of feelings, and, 53
   maturity, and, 47
   relationships, and, 56
   separateness of, 50
   strategies of to deal with
      feelings, 52–53
mental-health centers, 3
mental-health professionals, 15, 32,
   48, 80–82, 83, 86, 110, 130,
   197, 198, 200, 203–204, 206,
   212
   grief counseling and, 1, 3, 4
Mothers Against Drunk Driving
   (MADD), 18, 236
mourners
   community of, 79–80
   denial and negation, and, 39
   disbelief, 98
   disenfranchised, 31
   stigmatization of, 62
   strategies of, 77–78
   tasks of, 38, 60

mourning; *see also* bereavement,
  grieving, and related topics
  as period of transition, 60–61
  changes in, 140
  children, and, 36
  defined, 27, 39
  movement during, 71, 204
  rituals, and, 41–43
  universal behaviors of, 41
mutual aid, *see* mutual help
mutual help, 75–91, 147–150,
  195–199
  bereaved, and, 84–85
  defined, 85–87
  failure of, 133–134
  professionalization of services,
    80–82
  vs. professional help, 84

N

Naim Conference, 5, 18
NAMI, *see* National Alliance for
  the Mentally Ill
National Alliance for the Mentally
  Ill (NAMI), 191, 236
National Center for Grieving
  Children and Families, 199,
  235
National Fallen Firefighters
  Foundation Survivors
  Support Network, 236
National Funeral Directors
  Association, 10
National Hospice and Palliative
  Care Organization, 236
needs, of humans, 36–37
negation, 39
networks, 210, 211
  help, 79–80, 83
  social, 123
New Careers for the Poor, 7–8
nightmares, 168
9/11 survivors, 33, 40, 81, 130–131

North American Conference of
  Separated and Divorced
  Catholics, 237
numbness, 67–70, 97, 176

O

outcome
  definition of, 33
  differences in, 53–55
  support, and, 84–85
outreach, 196

P

pain, intensity of, 114–117
Parents Without Partners, 5
Pathfinder Program, 196
patriarchal societies, 46
perspective, of widowed, 76, 132,
  139–140
physicians, 4, 5, 80, 81, 82, 110, 211
positive thinking, 103
Post Cana Conference, 5
presence, 89–90
  among Vietnam veterans, 87
primary prevention, 2–8
professional–client relationship,
  83, 225
professional knowledge, 79, 80
professionals, 3, 4, 6, 15, 17, 18, 31,
  34, 48, 79, 80–82, 83, 84, 85,
  86, 93, 130, 171, 196, 197,
  198, 200, 202–204; *see also*
  mental-health professionals
  advisory board of, 6, 202
protectiveness, of children, 183
public health approach, 2

R

reconstruction, 72–74
recovery, concept of, 11, 32, 33, 40,
  67
recruitment of volunteers, 202–203

redefining the self, 65–66, 140–143
relationships; *see also* making
    meaning of death
    changes in, 40, 66, 88, 95,
        118–119
    death, as end of, 38
    men, and, 56
    professional–client, 83, 225
    to past, 39, 132, 143
    same-sex, 19, 31, 98–99, 144
    with deceased, 147
relatives, 12
relief, 100–101
religion, 9, 10, 22, 43, 77, 133, 172,
    208
remarriage, 143–147, 168, 190
    men, and, 4
    counseling, 223
restoration-oriented behavior, 71,
    77
retirement communities, 147, 181
rituals, 41–43, 62
roles
    definition of, 63
    of men and women, 43, 63–65
    redefined, 65–66
    vs. identity, 65

S

same-sex relationships, 19, 31,
    98–99, 144
school, return to by children after
    losing a parent, 166–167
searching behavior, 71
self; *see also* development; making
    meaning, of death; social
    context
    defined, 65
    growth, 227
    redefining, 65–66, 140–143
    sense of, 178–179
self-generation, 90–91
    among Vietnam veterans, 88

self-help, 78
self-pity, 115
September Space, 238
sexually transmitted diseases, 146
silence, 159–160
single parents, 13, 15, 35, 54, 106,
    151–173, 198, 209; *see also*
    widowed: with dependent
    children
    parent-centered *vs.* child-
        centered, 170
    title of, 158
    worries about children, 164–167
sleeping, 115
social agencies, 3
social context, 32, 34, 40, 41, 45–52,
    78
social mores, 146
Social Security, 5, 106, 107, 181, 220
Society of Military Widows, 237
stress, 61, 62, 66, 72, 77, 84, 109, 212
stressors, universal, 62
subsidized housing, 181
suicide, 16, 111, 116, 117, 122, 205,
    212
support, 82–83, 84, 98, 105, 122,
    130, 131, 139, 181, 195
Survivors of Law Enforcement
    Suicide (SOLES), 237

T

THEOS, *see* They Help Each Other
    Spiritually
therapists, *see* mental-health
    professionals
They Help Each Other Spiritually
    (THEOS), 18, 84
To Live Again (TLA), 18, 238
traditions, 43
tranquilizers, 110
transformation, 39
transition, 6–7, 57, 59–74, 79, 87–91,
    95, 129, 194

components of, 61, 95
  negotiation, and, 74
trauma, 61

U

uncertainty, 70–72, 113–128

V

Victorian widows, 38
Vietnam veterans, 87–88
voices, 30, 35
volunteers, recruitment of,
  202–203

W

wedding rings, 143
Welfare, 107
widow, use of term, 104, 134, 194
widowed
  as helpers, 78–79, 147–150, 211,
    229–232
  changes in, 125–128, 177–178
  connecting to others, 104–106
  financial concerns of, 106–108
  finding others, 120–123
  needs of, 188–190
  new status of, 103–104,
    140–141
  new views of, 137
  number living alone, 181
  number of in United States, 4,
    175
  older population of, 175–192
  perspectives of, 76, 132,
    139–140
  resources for, 233–238
  roles of, 63–67, 164
  shift in roles in, 67
  with dependent children,
    151–173
Widowed Person's Service, 17, 179,
  190, 196, 198, 202, 206, 228

Widowed Service Line, 10, 11,
  15–16, 149, 206, 232
  callers' ages, 217–218
  caregiving styles, 225–226
  employment of callers,
    221–222
  financial situation of callers,
    218–219
  follow-up, 226
  length of time widowed,
    217–218
  loneliness, 223–224
  organization of, 227–228
  research findings, 217–228
  spin-offs from, 226–227
  types of households, 221
  types of problems
    encountered, 219–221
  volunteers for, 224–225
  who was served, 217
  widowers who called, 222–223
widowhood, defined, 134–135
widows *vs.* widowers, 45–57, 136,
  142, 177, 179, 190
widow-to-widow program,
  205–216; *see also* related
  topics
  ages of deceased, 209
  causes of death, 209–210
  help offered, 214–215
  helping networks, and, 210
  history of, 1–19
    advisory board,
      recruitment of, 9
    aides, hiring of, 10–11
    choosing a community, 9
    identifying newly
      widowed, 9–10
    length of program, 11
  implications of, 17–19
  meeting the widowed, 212–214
  occupations of deceased, 208
  population served, 206–207

refusal, reasons for, 215–216
religions of deceased, 208
research findings, 205–216
results of, 11–16
    widows accepting help, 13
    widows refusing help, 15
sources of help, 210–212
starting, 200–204
wife, role of, 46–49, 51, 55, 63–64
wisdom, types of, 79
women; *see also* widows *vs.*
    widowers
attachments, and, 49
depression, and, 54
loss of roles after spousal
    death, 63–65
multitasking, and, 157

percentage widowed, 4
periods of lives of, 46–47
roles of in marriage, 37, 45–47,
    51
roles of in society, 62, 63–65,
    178
shaping self-image of, 48
sudden death, and, 68
work, 125, 136, 189, 208, 221–222
    new widows, and, 5, 16,
        107–108, 138–139
workman's compensation, 107
world view, of a person, 30
WTC United Family Group, 237

Y

Young Widow program, 238